MATTHEW

Matthew
A LIFE APPLICATION® BIBLE STUDY

Part 1:
Complete text of Matthew with study notes
from the *Life Application Bible*

Part 2:
Thirteen lessons for individual or group study

Study questions written and edited by
REV. NEIL S. WILSON
REV. DAVID R. VEERMAN
DR. JAMES C. GALVIN
DR. BRUCE B. BARTON
DARYL J. LUCAS

Tyndale House Publishers, Inc.
Wheaton, Illinois

Life Application Bible Studies

Genesis TLB	**Matthew** NIV	**Philippians & Colossians** NIV
Joshua TLB	**Mark** TLB & NIV	**1 & 2 Thessalonians &**
Judges NIV	**Luke** NIV	**Philemon** NIV
Ruth & Esther TLB	**John** NIV	**1 & 2 Timothy & Titus** NIV
1 Samuel NIV	**Acts** TLB & NIV	**Hebrews** NIV
Ezra & Nehemiah NIV	**Romans** NIV	**James** NIV
Proverbs NIV	**1 Corinthians** NIV	**1 & 2 Peter & Jude** NIV
Daniel NIV	**2 Corinthians** NIV	**1 & 2 & 3 John** NIV
Hosea & Jonah TLB	**Galatians & Ephesians** NIV	**Revelation** NIV

Life Application Bible Studies: Matthew. Copyright © 1992 by Tyndale House Publishers, Inc., Wheaton, Illinois 60189. All rights reserved.

Life Application Notes and Bible Helps copyright © 1986 owned by assignment by Tyndale House Publishers, Inc., Wheaton, IL 60189. Maps copyright © 1986 by Tyndale House Publishers, Inc. All rights reserved.

Front cover photo copyright © 1990 by James C. Miller

Life Application is a registered trademark of Tyndale House Publishers, Inc.

The text of Matthew is from the *Holy Bible,* New International Version.® NIV®. Copyright © 1973, 1978, 1984 by International Bible Society. Used by permission of Zondervan Publishing House. All rights reserved. The "NIV" and "New International Version" trademarks are registered in the United States Patent and Trademark Office by International Bible Society.

ISBN 0-8423-2883-1

Printed in the United States of America

98
7   6

This book of Matthew is part of the *New International Version* of the Holy Bible, a completely new translation made by over a hundred scholars working directly from the best available Greek texts. It had its beginning in 1965 when, after several years of exploratory study by committees from the Christian Reformed Church and the National Association of Evangelicals, a group of scholars met at Palos Heights, Illinois, and concurred in the need for a new translation of the Bible in contemporary English. This group, though not made up of official church representatives, was transdenominational. Its conclusion was endorsed by a large number of leaders from many denominations who met in Chicago in 1966.

Responsibility for the new version was delegated by the Palos Heights group to a self-governing body of fifteen, the Committee on Bible Translation, composed for the most part of biblical scholars from colleges, universities, and seminaries. In 1967 the New York Bible Society (now the International Bible Society) generously undertook the financial sponsorship of the project—a sponsorship that made it possible to enlist the help of many distinguished scholars. The fact that participants from the United States, Great Britain, Canada, Australia, and New Zealand worked together gave the project its international scope. That they were from many denominations—including Anglican, Assemblies of God, Baptist, Brethren, Christian Reformed, Church of Christ, Evangelical Free, Lutheran, Mennonite, Methodist, Nazarene, Presbyterian, Wesleyan, and other churches—helped to safeguard the translation from sectarian bias.

How it was made helps to give the New International Version its distinctiveness. The translation of each book was assigned to a team of scholars. Next, one of the Intermediate Editorial Committees revised the initial translation, with constant reference to the Hebrew, Aramaic, or Greek. Their work then went to one of the General Editorial Committees, which checked it in detail and made another thorough revision. This revision in turn was carefully reviewed by the Committee on Bible Translation, which made further changes and then released the final version for publication. In this way the entire Bible underwent three revisions, during each of which the translation was examined for its faithfulness to the original languages and for its English style.

All this involved many thousands of hours of research and discussion regarding the meaning of the texts and the precise way of putting them into English. It may well be that no other translation has been made by a more thorough process of review and revision from committee to committee than this one.

From the beginning of the project, the Committee on Bible Translation held to certain goals for the New International Version: that it would be an accurate translation and one that would have clarity and literary quality and so prove suitable for public and private reading, teaching, preaching, memorizing, and liturgical use. The Committee also sought to preserve some measure of continuity with the long tradition of translating the Scriptures into English.

In working toward these goals, the translators were united in their commitment to the authority and infallibility of the Bible as God's Word in written form. They believe that it contains the divine answer to the deepest needs of humanity, that it sheds unique light on our path in a dark world, and that it sets forth the way to our eternal well-being.

The first concern of the translators has been the accuracy of the translation and its fidelity to the thought of the biblical writers. They have striven for more than a word-for-word translation. Because thought patterns and syntax differ from language to language, faithful communication of the meaning of the writers of the Bible demands frequent modifications in sentence structure and constant regard for the contextual meanings of words.

The Committee on Bible Translation submitted the developing version to a number of stylistic consultants. Samples of the translation were tested for clarity and ease of reading by various kinds of people—young and old, highly educated and less well educated, ministers and laymen. Concern for clear and natural English motivated the translators and consultants. In view of the international use of English, the translators sought to avoid obvious Americanisms on the one hand and obvious Anglicisms on the other. A British edition reflects the comparatively few differences of significant idiom and of spelling.

As for the traditional pronouns "thou," "thee," and "thine" in reference to the Deity, the translators judged that to use these archaisms (along with the old verb forms such as "doest," "wouldest," and "hadst") would violate accuracy in translation. Greek does not use special pronouns for the persons of the Godhead. A present-day translation is not enhanced by forms that in the time of the King James Version were used in everyday speech, whether referring to God or man.

The Greek text used in translating the New Testament was an eclectic one. No other piece of ancient literature has such an abundance of manuscript witnesses as does the New Testament. When existing manuscripts differ, the translators made their choice of readings according to accepted principles of New Testament textual criticism. Footnotes call attention to places where there was uncertainty about what the original text was. The best current printed texts of the Greek New Testament were used.

There is a sense in which the work of translation is never wholly finished. This applies to all great literature and uniquely so to the Bible. In 1973 the New Testament in the New International Version was published. Since then, suggestions for corrections and revisions have been received from various sources. The Committee on Bible Translation carefully considered the suggestions and adopted a number of them. These were incorporated in the first printing of the entire Bible in 1978. Additional revisions were made by the Committee on Bible Translation in 1983 and appear in printings after that date.

To achieve clarity the translators sometimes supplied words not in the original texts but required by the context. If there was uncertainty about such material, it is enclosed in brackets. Also for the sake of clarity or style, nouns, including some proper nouns, are sometimes substituted for pronouns, and vice versa. As an aid to the reader, italicized sectional headings are inserted in most of the books. They are not to be regarded as part of the NIV text, are not for oral reading, and are not intended to dictate the interpretation of the sections they head.

The footnotes in this version are of several kinds, most of which need no explanation. Those giving alternative translations begin with "Or" and generally introduce the alternative with the last word preceding it in the text, except when it is a single-word alternative; in poetry quoted in a footnote a slant mark indicates a line division. Footnotes introduced by "Or" do not have uniform significance. In some cases two possible translations were considered to have about equal validity. In other cases, though the translators were convinced that the translation in the text was correct, they judged that another interpretation was possible and of sufficient importance to be represented in a footnote. In the New Testament, footnotes that refer to uncertainty regarding the original text are introduced by "Some manuscripts" or similar expressions.

It should be noted that minerals, flora and fauna, architectural details, articles of clothing and jewelry, musical instruments and other articles cannot always be identified with precision. Also, measures of capacity in the biblical period are particularly uncertain.

Like all translations of the Bible, made as they are by imperfect man, this one undoubtedly falls short of its goals. Yet we are grateful to God for the extent to which he has enabled us to realize these goals and for the strength he has given us and our colleagues to complete our task. We offer this version of the Bible to him in whose name and for whose glory it has been made. We pray that it will lead many into a better understanding of the Holy Scriptures and a fuller knowledge of Jesus Christ the incarnate Word, of whom the Scriptures so faithfully testify.

The Committee on Bible Translation

June 1978
(Revised August 1983)

Names of the translators and editors may be secured
from the International Bible Society,
translation sponsors of the New International Version,
P.O. Box 62970, Colorado Springs, Colorado, 80962-2970 U.S.A.

The New International Version has one of the most accurate and best-organized cross-reference systems available.

The cross-references link words or phrases in the NIV text with counterpart Biblical references listed in a side column on every page. The raised letters containing these cross-references are set in a light italic typeface to distinguish them from the NIV text note letters, which use a bold typeface.

The lists of references are in Biblical order with one exception: If reference is made to a verse within the same chapter, that verse (indicated by "ver") is listed first.

Following is a list of abbreviations used in the cross-references:

ABBREVIATIONS FOR THE BOOKS OF THE BIBLE

Genesis . . . . Ge	Isaiah . . . . Isa	Romans . . . . Ro
Exodus . . . . Ex	Jeremiah . . . . Jer	1 Corinthians 1Co
Leviticus . . . . .Lev	Lamentations . . . . La	2 Corinthians 2Co
Numbers . . . . Nu	Ezekiel . . . . Eze	Galatians . . . . .Gal
Deuteronomy . . . . . . .Dt	Daniel . . . . .Da	Ephesians . . . . Eph
Joshua . . . . Jos	Hosea . . . . .Hos	Philippians . . . . Php
Judges . . . . .Jdg	Joel . . . . .Joel	Colossians . . . . .Col
Ruth . . . . Ru	Amos . . . . Am	1 Thessalonians 1Th
1 Samuel 1Sa	Obadiah . . . . .Ob	2 Thessalonians 2Th
2 Samuel 2Sa	Jonah . . . . Jnh	1 Timothy 1Ti
1 Kings 1Ki	Micah . . . . Mic	2 Timothy 2Ti
2 Kings 2Ki	Nahum . . . . .Na	Titus . . . . Tit
1 Chronicles 1Ch	Habakkuk . . . . .Hab	Philemon . . . . .Phm
2 Chronicles 2Ch	Zephaniah . . . . Zep	Hebrews . . . . Heb
Ezra . . . . Ezr	Haggai . . . . .Hag	James . . . . Jas
Nehemiah . . . . Ne	Zechariah . . . . Zec	1 Peter 1Pe
Esther . . . . Est	Malachi . . . . .Mal	2 Peter 2Pe
Job . . . . .Job	Matthew . . . . .Mt	1 John 1Jn
Psalms . . . . .Ps	Mark . . . . Mk	2 John 2Jn
Proverbs . . . . Pr	Luke . . . . .Lk	3 John 3Jn
Ecclesiastes . . . . .Ecc	John . . . . Jn	Jude . . . . .Jude
Song of Songs . . . . SS	Acts . . . . .Ac	Revelation . . . . Rev

Have you ever opened your Bible and asked the following:

• What does this passage really mean?
• How does it apply to my life?
• Why does some of the Bible seem irrelevant?
• What do these ancient cultures have to do with today?
• I love God; why can't I understand what he is saying to me through his Word?
• What's going on in the lives of these Bible people?

Many Christians do not read the Bible regularly. Why? Because in the pressures of daily living they cannot find a connection between the timeless principles of Scripture and the ever-present problems of day-by-day living.

God urges us to apply his Word (Isaiah 42:23; 1 Corinthians 10:11; 2 Thessalonians 3:4), but too often we stop at accumulating Bible knowledge. This is why the *Life Application Bible* was developed—to show how to put into practice what we have learned.

Applying God's Word is a vital part of one's relationship with God; it is the evidence that we are obeying him. The difficulty in applying the Bible is not with the Bible itself, but with the reader's inability to bridge the gap between the past and present, the conceptual and practical. When we don't or can't do this, spiritual dryness, shallowness, and indifference result.

The words of Scripture itself cry out to us, "Do not merely listen to the word, and so deceive yourselves. Do what it says" (James 1:22). The *Life Application Bible* helps us do just that. Developed by an interdenominational team of pastors, scholars, family counselors, and a national organization dedicated to promoting God's Word and spreading the gospel, the *Life Application Bible* took many years to complete, and all the work was reviewed by several renowned theologians under the directorship of Dr. Kenneth Kantzer.

The *Life Application Bible* does what a good resource Bible should—it helps you understand the context of a passage, gives important background and historical information, explains difficult words and phrases, and helps you see the interrelationship of Scripture. But it does much more. The *Life Application Bible* goes deeper into God's Word, helping you discover the timeless truth being communicated, see the relevance for your life, and make a personal application. While some study Bibles attempt application, over 75 percent of this Bible is application oriented. The notes answer the questions, "So what?" and "What does this passage mean to me, my family, my friends, my job, my neighborhood, my church, my country?"

Imagine reading a familiar passage of Scripture and gaining fresh insight, as if you were reading it for the first time. How much richer your life would be if you left each Bible reading with a new perspective and a small change for the better. A small change every day adds up to a changed life—and that is the very purpose of Scripture.

The best way to define application is to first determine what it is *not*. Application is *not* just accumulating knowledge. This helps us discover and understand facts and concepts, but it stops there. History is filled with philosophers who knew what the Bible said but failed to apply it to their lives, keeping them from believing and changing. Many think that understanding is the end goal of Bible study, but it is really only the beginning.

Application is *not* just illustration. Illustration only tells us how someone else handled a similar situation. While we may empathize with that person, we still have little direction for our personal situation.

Application is *not* just making a passage "relevant." Making the Bible relevant only helps us to see that the same lessons that were true in Bible times are true today; it does not show us how to apply them to the problems and pressures of our individual lives.

What, then, is application? Application begins by knowing and understanding God's Word and its timeless truths. *But we cannot stop there.* If we do, God's Word may not change our life, and it may become dull, difficult, tedious, and tiring. A good application focuses the truth of God's Word, shows the reader what to do about what is being read, and motivates the reader to respond to what God is teaching. All three are essential to application.

Application is putting into practice what we already know (see Mark 4:24 and Hebrews 5:14) and answering the question "So what?" by confronting us with the right questions and motivating us to take action (see 1 John 2:5, 6 and James 2:26). Application is deeply personal—unique for each individual. It is making a relevant truth a personal truth and involves developing a strategy and action plan to live your life in harmony with the Bible. It is the Biblical "how to" of life.

You may ask, "How can your application notes be relevant to *my* life?" Each application note has three parts: (1) an *explanation* ties the note directly to the Scripture passage and sets up the truth that is being taught, (2) the *bridge* explains the timeless truth and makes it relevant for today, (3) the *application* shows you how to take the timeless truth and apply it to your personal situation. No note, by itself, can apply Scripture directly to your life. It can only teach, direct, lead, guide, inspire, recommend, and urge. It can give you the resources and direction you need to apply the Bible; but only you can take these resources and put them into practice.

A good note, therefore, should not only give you knowledge and understanding but point you to application. Before you buy any kind of resource study Bible, you should evaluate the notes and ask the following questions: (1) Does the note contain enough information to help me understand the point of the Scripture passage? (2) Does the note assume I know too much? (3) Does the note avoid denominational bias? (4) Do the notes touch most of life's experiences? (5) Does the note help me *apply* God's Word?

NOTES

In addition to providing the reader with many application notes, the *Life Application Bible* offers several explanatory notes that help the reader understand culture, history, context, difficult-to-understand passages, background, places, theological concepts, and the relationship of various passages in Scripture to other passages.

BOOK INTRODUCTION

The Book Introduction is divided into several easy-to-find parts:

Timeline. A guide that puts the Bible book into its historical setting. It lists the key events and the dates when they occurred.

Vital Statistics. A list of straight facts about the book—those pieces of information you need to know at a glance.

Overview. A summary of the book with general lessons and applications that can be learned from the book as a whole.

Blueprint. The outline of the book. It is printed in easy-to-understand language and is designed for easy memorization. To the right of each main heading is a key lesson that is taught in that particular section.

Megathemes. A section that gives the main themes of the Bible book, explains their significance, and then tells why they are still important for us today.

Map. If included, this shows the key places found in that book and retells the story of the book from a geographical perspective.

OUTLINE

The *Life Application Bible* has a new, custom-made outline that was designed specifically from an application point of view. Several unique features should be noted:

1. To avoid confusion and to aid memory work, the book outline has only three levels for headings. Main outline heads are marked with a capital letter. Subheads are marked by a number. Minor explanatory heads have no letter or number.

2. Each main outline head marked by a letter also has a brief paragraph below it summarizing the Bible text and offering a general application.

3. Parallel passages are listed where they apply.

PERSONALITY PROFILES
Another unique feature of this Bible is the profiles of key Bible people, including their strengths and weaknesses, greatest accomplishments and mistakes, and key lessons from their lives.

MAPS
The *Life Application Bible* has a thorough and comprehensive Bible atlas built right into the book. There are two kinds of maps: A book introduction map, telling the story of the book, and thumbnail maps in the notes, plotting most geographic movements.

CHARTS AND DIAGRAMS
Many charts and diagrams are included to help the reader better visualize difficult concepts or relationships. Most charts not only present the needed information but show the significance of the information as well.

CROSS-REFERENCES
A carefully organized cross-reference system in the margins of the Bible text helps the reader find related passages quickly.

TEXTUAL NOTES
Directly related to the text of the New International Version, the textual notes provide explanations on certain wording in the translation, alternate translations, and information about readings in the ancient manuscripts.

HIGHLIGHTED NOTES
In each Bible study lesson you will be asked to read specific notes as part of your preparation. These notes have been highlighted by a bullet (•) so that you can find them easily.

MATTHEW

MATTHEW

VITAL STATISTICS

PURPOSE:
To prove that Jesus is the Messiah, the eternal King

AUTHOR:
Matthew (Levi)

TO WHOM WRITTEN:
Matthew wrote especially to the Jews

DATE WRITTEN:
Probably between A.D. 60–65

SETTING:
Matthew was a Jewish tax collector who became one of Jesus' disciples. This Gospel forms the connecting link between the Old and New Testaments because of its emphasis on the fulfillment of prophecy.

KEY VERSE:
"Do not think that I have come to abolish the Law or the Prophets; I have not come to abolish them but to fulfill them" (5:17).

KEY PEOPLE:
Jesus, Mary, Joseph, John the Baptist, the disciples, the religious leaders, Caiaphas, Pilate, Mary Magdalene

KEY PLACES:
Bethlehem, Jerusalem, Capernaum, Galilee, Judea

SPECIAL FEATURES:
Matthew is filled with Messianic language ("Son of David" is used throughout) and Old Testament references (53 quotes and 76 other references). This Gospel was not written as a chronological account; its purpose was to present the clear evidence that Jesus is the Messiah, the Savior.

AS the motorcade slowly winds through the city, thousands pack the sidewalks hoping to catch a glimpse. Marching bands with great fanfare announce the arrival, and protective agents scan the crowd and run alongside the limousine. Pomp, ceremony, protocol—modern symbols of position and evidences of importance—herald the arrival of a head of state. Whether they are leaders by birth or election, we honor and respect them.

The Jews waited for a leader who had been promised centuries before by prophets. They believed that this leader—the Messiah ("anointed one")—would rescue them from their Roman oppressors and establish a new kingdom. As their king, he would rule the world with justice. However, many Jews overlooked prophecies that also spoke of this king as a suffering servant who would be rejected and killed. It is no wonder, then, that few recognized Jesus as the Messiah. How could this humble carpenter's son from Nazareth be their king? But Jesus was and is the King of all the earth!

Matthew (Levi) was one of Jesus' 12 disciples. Once he was a despised tax collector, but his life was changed by this man from Galilee. Matthew wrote this Gospel to his fellow Jews to prove that Jesus is the Messiah and to explain God's kingdom.

Matthew begins his account by giving Jesus' genealogy. He then tells of Jesus' birth and early years, including the family's escape to Egypt from the murderous Herod and their return to Nazareth. Following Jesus' baptism by John (3:17) and his defeat of Satan in the desert, Jesus begins his public ministry by calling his first disciples and giving the Sermon on the Mount (chapters 5—7). Matthew shows Christ's authority by reporting his miracles of healing the sick and the demon-possessed, and even raising the dead.

Despite opposition from the Pharisees and others in the religious establishment (chapters 12—15), Jesus continued to teach concerning the kingdom of heaven (chapters 16—20). During this time, Jesus spoke with his disciples about his imminent death and resurrection (16:21) and revealed his true identity to Peter, James, and John (17:1-5). Near the end of his ministry, Jesus entered Jerusalem in a triumphant procession (21:1-11). But soon opposition mounted, and Jesus knew that his death was near. So he taught his disciples about the future—what they could expect before his return (chapter 24) and how to live until then (chapter 25).

In Matthew's finale (chapters 26—28), he focuses on Jesus' final days on earth—the Last Supper, his prayer in Gethsemane, the betrayal by Judas, the flight of the disciples, Peter's denial, the trials before Caiaphas and Pilate, Jesus' final words on the cross, and his burial in a borrowed tomb. But the story does not end there, for the Messiah rose from the dead—conquering death and then telling his followers to continue his work by making disciples in all nations.

As you read this Gospel, listen to Matthew's clear message: Jesus is the Christ, the King of kings and Lord of lords. Celebrate his victory over evil and death, and make Jesus the Lord of your life.

THE BLUEPRINT

A. BIRTH AND PREPARATION OF JESUS, THE KING (1:1—4:11)

The people of Israel were waiting for the Messiah, their king. Matthew begins his book by showing how Jesus Christ was a descendant of David. But Matthew goes on to show that God did not send Jesus to be an earthly king, but a heavenly king. His kingdom would be much greater than David's because it would never end. Even at Jesus' birth, many recognized him as a king. Herod, the ruler, as well as Satan, was afraid of Jesus' kingship and tried to stop him, but others worshiped him and brought royal gifts. We must be willing to recognize Jesus for who he really is and worship him as king of our lives.

B. MESSAGE AND MINISTRY OF JESUS, THE KING (4:12—25:46)
1. Jesus begins his ministry
2. Jesus gives the Sermon on the Mount
3. Jesus performs many miracles
4. Jesus teaches about the kingdom
5. Jesus encounters differing reactions to his ministry
6. Jesus faces conflict with the religious leaders
7. Jesus teaches on the Mount of Olives

Jesus gave the Sermon on the Mount, directions for living in his kingdom. He also told many parables about the difference between his kingdom and the kingdoms of earth. Forgiveness, peace, and putting others first are some of the characteristics that make one great in the future kingdom of God. And to be great in God's kingdom, we must live by God's standards right now. Jesus came to show us how to live as faithful subjects in his kingdom.

C. DEATH AND RESURRECTION OF JESUS, THE KING (26:1—28:20)

Jesus was formally presented to the nation of Israel, but rejected. How strange for the king to be accused, arrested, and crucified. But Jesus demonstrated his power even over death through his resurrection, and gained access for us into his kingdom. With all this evidence that Jesus is God's Son, we, too, should accept him as our Lord.

MEGATHEMES

THEME	EXPLANATION	IMPORTANCE
Jesus Christ, the King	Jesus is revealed as the King of kings. His miraculous birth, his life and teaching, his miracles, and his triumph over death show his true identity.	Jesus cannot be equated with any person or power. He is the supreme ruler of time and eternity, heaven and earth, humans and angels. We should give him his rightful place as king of our lives.
The Messiah	Jesus was the Messiah, the One for whom the Jews had waited to deliver them from Roman oppression. Yet, tragically, they didn't recognize him when he came because his kingship was not what they expected. The true purpose of God's anointed deliverer was to die for all people to free them from sin's oppression.	Because Jesus was sent by God, we can trust him with our lives. It is worth everything we have to acknowledge him and give ourselves to him, because he came to be our Messiah, our Savior.
Kingdom of God	Jesus came to earth to begin his kingdom. His full kingdom will be realized at his return and will be made up of anyone who has faithfully followed him.	The way to enter God's kingdom is by faith—believing in Christ to save us from sin and change our lives. We must do the work of his kingdom now to be prepared for his return.
Teachings	Jesus taught the people through sermons, illustrations, and parables. Through his teachings, he showed the true ingredients of faith and how to guard against a fruitless and hypocritical life.	Jesus' teachings show us how to prepare for life in his eternal kingdom by living properly right now. He lived what he taught, and we too must practice what we preach.

Resurrection	When Jesus rose from the dead, he rose in power as the true king. In his victory over death, he established his credentials as king and his power and authority over evil.	The resurrection shows Jesus' all-powerful life for us—not even death could stop his plan of offering eternal life. Those who believe in Jesus can hope for a resurrection like his. Our role is to tell his story to all the earth so that everyone may share in his victory.

KEY PLACES IN MATTHEW

Jesus' earthly story begins in the town of Bethlehem in the Roman province of Judea (2:1). A threat to kill the infant king led Joseph to take his family to Egypt (2:14). When they returned, God led them to settle in Nazareth in Galilee (2:22, 23). At about age 30, Jesus was baptized in the Jordan River and was tempted by Satan in the Judean desert (3:13; 4:1). Jesus set up his base of operations in Capernaum (4:12, 13) and from there ministered throughout Israel, telling parables, teaching about the kingdom, and healing the sick. He traveled to the region of the Gadarenes and healed two demon-possessed men (8:28ff); fed over 5,000 people with five loaves and two fish on the shores of Galilee near Bethsaida (14:15ff); healed the sick in Gennesaret (14:34ff); ministered to the Gentiles in Tyre and Sidon (15:21ff); visited Caesarea Philippi, where Peter declared him as the Messiah (16:13ff); and taught in Perea, across the Jordan (19:1). As he set out on his last visit to Jerusalem, he told the disciples what would happen to him there (20:17ff). He spent some time in Jericho (20:29) and then stayed in Bethany at night as he went back and forth into Jerusalem during his last week (21:17ff). In Jerusalem he would be crucified, but he would rise again.

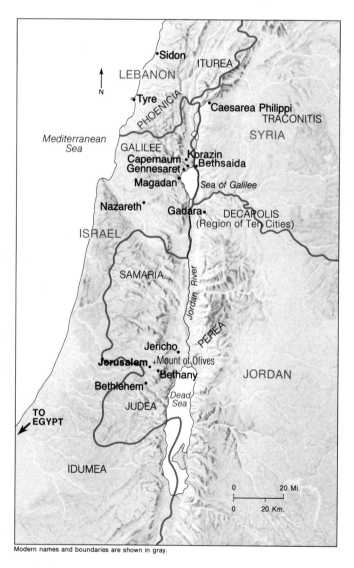

Modern names and boundaries are shown in gray.

A. BIRTH AND PREPARATION OF JESUS, THE KING (1:1 — 4:11)

Matthew opens his Gospel with a genealogy to prove that Jesus is the descendant of both King David and Abraham, just as the Old Testament had predicted. Jesus' birth didn't go unnoticed, for both shepherds and Magi came to worship him. The Jewish people were waiting for the Messiah to appear. Finally, he was born, but the Jews didn't recognize him because they were looking for a different kind of king.

The Ancestors of Jesus

(3/Luke 3:23–38)

1:1
a Isa 11:1
b Ge 22:18

1 A record of the genealogy of Jesus Christ the son of David,*a* the son of Abraham:*b*

1:2
c Ge 25:26
d Ge 29:35

1:3
e Ge 38:27-30

2 Abraham was the father of Isaac,

    Isaac the father of Jacob,*c*

    Jacob the father of Judah and his brothers,*d*

    3 Judah the father of Perez and Zerah, whose mother was Tamar,*e*

    Perez the father of Hezron,

    Hezron the father of Ram,

    4 Ram the father of Amminadab,

    Amminadab the father of Nahshon,

    Nahshon the father of Salmon,

    5 Salmon the father of Boaz, whose mother was Rahab,

    Boaz the father of Obed, whose mother was Ruth,

    Obed the father of Jesse,

1:6
f 1Sa 16:1
g 2Sa 12:24

    6 and Jesse the father of King David.*f*

David was the father of Solomon, whose mother had been Uriah's wife,*g*

    7 Solomon the father of Rehoboam,

    Rehoboam the father of Abijah,

    Abijah the father of Asa,

    8 Asa the father of Jehoshaphat,

    Jehoshaphat the father of Jehoram,

    Jehoram the father of Uzziah,

    9 Uzziah the father of Jotham,

    Jotham the father of Ahaz,

    Ahaz the father of Hezekiah,

1:10
h 2Ki 20:21

    10 Hezekiah the father of Manasseh,*h*

    Manasseh the father of Amon,

    Amon the father of Josiah,

    11 and Josiah the father of Jeconiah*a* and his brothers at the time of the exile to Babylon.*i*

1:11
i 2Ki 24:14-16;
Jer 27:20;
Da 1:1, 2

12 After the exile to Babylon:

a 11 That is, Jehoiachin; also in verse 12

● **1:1** Presenting this genealogy was one of the most interesting ways that Matthew could begin a book for a Jewish audience. Because a person's family line proved his or her standing as one of God's chosen people, Matthew began by showing that Jesus was a descendant of Abraham, the father of all Jews, and a direct descendant of David, fulfilling Old Testament prophecies about the Messiah's line. The facts of this ancestry were carefully preserved. This is the first of many proofs recorded by Matthew to show that Jesus is the true Messiah.

1:1ff More than 400 years had passed since the last Old Testament prophecies, and faithful Jews all over the world were still waiting for the Messiah (Luke 3:15). Matthew wrote this book to Jews to present Jesus as King and Messiah, the promised descendant of David who would reign forever (Isaiah 11:1–5). The Gospel of Matthew links the Old and New Testaments and contains many references that show how Jesus fulfilled Old Testament prophecy.

1:1ff Jesus entered human history when the land of Palestine was controlled by Rome and considered an insignificant outpost of the vast and mighty Roman empire. The presence of Roman soldiers in Israel gave the Jews military peace, but at the price of oppression, slavery, injustice, and immorality. Into this kind of world came the promised Messiah.

● **1:1–17** In the first 17 verses we meet 46 people whose lifetimes span 2,000 years. All were ancestors of Jesus, but they varied considerably in personality, spirituality, and experience. Some were heroes of faith — like Abraham, Isaac, Ruth, and David. Some had shady reputations — like Rahab and Tamar. Many were very ordinary — like Hezron, Ram, Nahshon, and Akim. And others were evil — like Manasseh and Abijah. God's work in history is not limited by human failures or sins, and he works through ordinary people. Just as God used all kinds of people to bring his Son into the world, he uses all kinds today to accomplish his will. And God wants to use you.

1:11 The exile occurred in 586 B.C. when Nebuchadnezzar, king of Babylonia, conquered Judah, destroyed Jerusalem, and took thousands of captives to Babylonia.

Jeconiah was the father of Shealtiel,ʲ
Shealtiel the father of Zerubbabel,
¹³Zerubbabel the father of Abiud,
Abiud the father of Eliakim,
Eliakim the father of Azor,
¹⁴Azor the father of Zadok,
Zadok the father of Akim,
Akim the father of Eliud,
¹⁵Eliud the father of Eleazar,
Eleazar the father of Matthan,
Matthan the father of Jacob,
¹⁶and Jacob the father of Joseph, the husband of Mary, of whom was born
Jesus, who is called Christ.

¹⁷Thus there were fourteen generations in all from Abraham to David, fourteen
from David to the exile to Babylon, and fourteen from the exile to the Christ.ᵇ

An Angel Appears to Joseph
(8)

¹⁸This is how the birth of Jesus Christ came about: His mother Mary was pledged
to be married to Joseph, but before they came together, she was found to be with
child through the Holy Spirit.ᵏ ¹⁹Because Joseph her husband was a righteous man
and did not want to expose her to public disgrace, he had in mind to divorceˡ her
quietly.
²⁰But after he had considered this, an angel of the Lord appeared to him in a

ᵇ 17 Or *Messiah*. "The Christ" (Greek) and "the Messiah" (Hebrew) both mean "the Anointed One."

1:12
ʲ 1Ch 3:17

1:18
ᵏ Lk 1:35
1:19
ˡ Dt 24:1

●**1:16** Because Mary was a virgin when she became pregnant, Matthew lists Joseph only as the husband of Mary, not the father of Jesus. Matthew's genealogy gives Jesus' legal (or royal) lineage through Joseph. Mary's ancestral line is recorded in Luke 3:23–38. Both Mary and Joseph were direct descendants of David.

Matthew traced the genealogy back to Abraham, while Luke traced it back to Adam. Matthew wrote to the Jews, so Jesus was shown as a descendant of their father, Abraham. Luke wrote to the Gentiles, so he emphasized Jesus as the Savior of all people.

1:17 Matthew breaks Israel's history into three sets of 14 generations, but there were probably more generations than those listed here. Genealogies often compressed history, meaning that not every generation of ancestors was specifically listed. Thus the phrase *the father of* can also be translated "the ancestor of."

●**1:18** There were three steps in a Jewish marriage. First, the two families agreed to the union. Second, a public announcement was made. At this point, the couple was "pledged." This was similar to engagement today except that their relationship could be broken only through death or divorce (even though sexual relations were not yet permitted). Third, the couple was married and began living together. Because Mary and Joseph were engaged, Mary's apparent unfaithfulness carried a severe social stigma. According to Jewish civil law, Joseph had a right to divorce her, and the Jewish authorities could have had her stoned to death (Deuteronomy 22:23, 24).

1:18 Why is the virgin birth important to the Christian faith? Jesus Christ, God's Son, had to be free from the sinful nature passed on to all other human beings by Adam. Because Jesus was born of a woman, he was a human being; but as the Son of God, Jesus was born without any trace of human sin. Jesus is both fully human and fully divine.

Because Jesus lived as a man, we know that he fully understands our experiences and struggles (Hebrews 4:15, 16). Because he is God, he has the power and authority to deliver us from sin (Colossians 2:13–15). We can tell Jesus all our thoughts, feel-

ings, and needs. He has been where we are now, and he has the ability to help.

●**1:18-25** Joseph was faced with a difficult choice after discovering that Mary was pregnant. Although he knew that taking Mary as his wife could be humiliating, Joseph chose to obey the angel's command to marry her. His action revealed four admirable qualities: (1) righteousness (1:19), (2) discretion and sensitivity (1:19), (3) responsiveness to God (1:24), and (4) self-discipline (1:25).

●**1:19** Perhaps Joseph thought he had only two options: divorce Mary quietly, or have her stoned. But God had a third option — marry her (1:20–23). In view of the circumstances, this had not occurred to Joseph. But God often shows us that there are more options available than we think. Although Joseph seemed to be doing the right thing by breaking the engagement, only God's guidance helped him make the best decision. When our decisions affect the lives of others, we must always seek God's wisdom.

1:20 The conception and birth of Jesus Christ are supernatural events beyond human logic or reasoning. Because of this, God sent angels to help certain people understand the significance of what was happening (see 2:13, 19; Luke 1:11, 26; 2:9).

Angels are spiritual beings created by God who help carry out his work on earth. They bring God's messages to people (Luke 1:26), protect God's people (Daniel 6:22), offer encouragement (Genesis 16:7ff), give guidance (Exodus 14:19), carry out punishment (2 Samuel 24:16), patrol the earth (Zechariah 1:9–14), and fight the forces of evil (2 Kings 6:16–18; Revelation 20:1, 2). There are both good and bad angels (Revelation 12:7), but because bad angels are allied with the devil, or Satan, they have considerably less power and authority than good angels. Eventually the main role of angels will be to offer continuous praise to God (Revelation 7:11, 12).

1:20-23 The angel declared to Joseph that Mary's child was conceived by the Holy Spirit and would be a son. This reveals an important truth about Jesus — he is both God and human. The infinite, unlimited God took on the limitations of humanity so he could live and die for the salvation of all who would believe in him.

dream and said, "Joseph son of David, do not be afraid to take Mary home as your wife, because what is conceived in her is from the Holy Spirit. 21 She will give birth

1:21
m Lk 1:31
n Lk 2:11;
Ac 5:31

to a son, and you are to give him the name Jesus,*c m* because he will save his people from their sins."*n*

22 All this took place to fulfill what the Lord had said through the prophet: 23 "The virgin will be with child and will give birth to a son, and they will call him Imman-

1:23
o Isa 7:14

uel"*d o* — which means, "God with us."

c 21 Jesus is the Greek form of *Joshua,* which means the Lᴏʀᴅ *saves.*   *d 23* Isaiah 7:14

The strength of what we believe is measured by how much we are willing to suffer for those beliefs. Joseph was a man with strong beliefs. He was prepared to do what was right, despite the pain he knew it would cause. But Joseph had another trait—he not only tried to do what was right, he also tried to do it in the right way.

When Mary told Joseph about her pregnancy, Joseph knew the child was not his. His respect for Mary's character and the explanation she gave him, as well as her attitude toward the expected child, must have made it hard to think his bride had done something wrong. Still, someone else was the child's father—and it was mind-boggling to accept that the "someone else" was God.

Joseph decided he had to break the engagement, but he was determined to do it in a way that would not cause public shame to Mary. He intended to act with justice and love.

At this point, God sent a messenger to Joseph to confirm Mary's story and open another way of obedience for Joseph—to take Mary as his wife. Joseph obeyed God, married Mary, and honored her virginity until the baby was born.

We do not know how long Joseph lived his role as Jesus' earthly father—he is last mentioned when Jesus was 12 years old. But Joseph trained his son in the trade of carpentry, made sure he had good spiritual training in Nazareth, and took the whole family on the yearly trip to Jerusalem for the Passover, which Jesus continued to observe during his adult years.

Joseph knew Jesus was someone special from the moment he heard the angel's words. His strong belief in that fact, and his willingness to follow God's leading, empowered him to be Jesus' chosen earthly father.

Strengths and accomplishments:
• A man of integrity
• A descendant of King David
• Jesus' legal and earthly father
• A person sensitive to God's guidance and willing to do God's will no matter what the consequence

Lessons from his life:
• God honors integrity
• Social position is of little importance when God chooses to use us
• Being obedient to the guidance we have from God leads to more guidance from him
• Feelings are not accurate measures of the rightness or wrongness of an action

Vital statistics:
• Where: Nazareth, Bethlehem
• Occupation: Carpenter
• Relatives: Wife: Mary. Children: Jesus, James, Joses, Judas, Simon, and daughters
• Contemporaries: Herod the Great, John the Baptist, Simeon, Anna

Key verses:
"Because Joseph her husband was a righteous man and did not want to expose her to public disgrace, he had in mind to divorce her quietly. But after he had considered this, an angel of the Lord appeared to him in a dream and said, 'Joseph son of David, do not be afraid to take Mary home as your wife, because what is conceived in her is from the Holy Spirit' " (Matthew 1:19, 20).

Joseph's story is told in Matthew 1:16—2:23; Luke 1:26—2:52.

1:21 *Jesus* means "the Lᴏʀᴅ saves." Jesus came to earth to save us because we can't save ourselves from sin and its consequences. No matter how good we are, we can't eliminate the sinful nature present in all of us. Only Jesus can do that. Jesus didn't come to help people save themselves; he came to be their Savior from the power and penalty of sin. Thank Christ for his death on the cross for your sin, and then ask him to take control of your life.

Your new life begins at that moment.

1:23 Jesus was to be called *Immanuel* ("God with us"), as predicted by Isaiah the prophet (Isaiah 7:14). Jesus was God in the flesh; thus God was literally among us, "with us." Through the Holy Spirit, Christ is present today in the life of every believer. Perhaps not even Isaiah understood how far-reaching the meaning of "Immanuel" would be.

24When Joseph woke up, he did what the angel of the Lord had commanded him and took Mary home as his wife. 25But he had no union with her until she gave birth to a son. And he gave him the name Jesus.

Visitors Arrive from Eastern Lands
(12)

2 After Jesus was born in Bethlehem in Judea,ᵖ during the time of King Herod, Magiᵉ from the east came to Jerusalem 2and asked, "Where is the one who has been born king of the Jews?�q We saw his starʳ in the eastᶠ and have come to worship him."

2:1
ᵖLk 2:4-7

2:2
qJer 23:5;
Jn 1:49
ʳNu 24:17

3When King Herod heard this he was disturbed, and all Jerusalem with him. 4When he had called together all the people's chief priests and teachers of the law, he asked them where the Christᵍ was to be born. 5"In Bethlehemˢ in Judea," they replied, "for this is what the prophet has written:

2:5
ˢJn 7:42

e 1 Traditionally *Wise Men* f 2 Or *star when it rose* g 4 Or *Messiah*

●**1:24** Joseph changed his plans quickly after learning that Mary had not been unfaithful to him (1:19). He obeyed God and proceeded with the marriage plans. Although others may have disapproved of his decision, Joseph went ahead with what he knew was right. Sometimes we avoid doing what is right because of what others might think. Like Joseph, we must choose to obey God rather than seek the approval of others.

2:1 Bethlehem is a small town five miles south of Jerusalem. It sits on a high ridge over 2,000 feet above sea level. It is mentioned in more detail in the Gospel of Luke. Luke also explains why Joseph and Mary were in Bethlehem when Jesus was born, rather than in Nazareth, their hometown.

2:1 The land of Israel was divided into four political districts and several lesser territories. Judea was to the south, Samaria in the middle, Galilee to the north, and Idumea to the southeast. Bethlehem of Judea (also called Judah, 2:6) had been prophesied as the Messiah's birthplace (Micah 5:2). Jerusalem was also in Judea and was the seat of government for Herod the Great, king over all four political districts. After Herod's death, the districts were divided among three separate rulers (see the note on 2:19–22). Although he was a ruthless, evil man who murdered many in his own family, Herod the Great supervised the renovation of the temple, making it much larger and more beautiful. This made him popular with many Jews. Jesus would visit Jerusalem many times because the great Jewish festivals were held there.

2:1, 2 Not much is known about these Magi (traditionally called wise men). We don't know where they came from or how many there were. Tradition says they were men of high position from Parthia, near the site of ancient Babylon. How did they know that the star represented the Messiah? (1) They could have been Jews who remained in Babylon after the exile and knew the Old Testament predictions of the Messiah's coming. (2) They may have been eastern astrologers who studied ancient manuscripts from around the world. Because of the Jewish exile centuries earlier, they would have had copies of the Old Testament in their land. (3) They may have had a special message from God directing them to the Messiah. Some scholars say these Magi were each from a different land, representing the entire world bowing before Jesus. These men from faraway lands recognized Jesus as the Messiah when most of God's chosen people in Israel did not. Matthew pictures Jesus as King over the whole world, not just Judea.

2:1, 2 The Magi traveled thousands of miles to see the king of the Jews. When they finally found him, they responded with joy, worship, and gifts. This is so different from the approach people often take today. We expect God to come looking for us, to explain himself, prove who he is, and give *us* gifts. But those who are wise still seek and worship Jesus today, not for what they can get, but for who he is.

Mediterranean Sea
N
Nazareth
Jerusalem
Bethlehem
Gaza
EGYPT
Nile River
Mount Sinai
0   50 Mi.
0   50 Km.
Red Sea

THE FLIGHT TO EGYPT
Herod planned to kill the baby Jesus, whom he perceived to be a future threat to his position. Warned of this treachery in a dream, Joseph took his family to Egypt until Herod's death, which occurred a year or two later. They then planned to return to Judea, but God led them instead to Nazareth in Galilee.

2:2 The Magi said they saw Jesus' star. Balaam referred to a coming "star . . . out of Jacob" (Numbers 24:17). Some say this star may have been a conjunction of Jupiter, Saturn, and Mars in 6 B.C., and others offer other explanations. But couldn't God, who created the heavens, have created a special star to signal the arrival of his Son? Whatever the nature of the star, these Magi traveled thousands of miles searching for a king, and they found him.

●**2:3** Herod the Great was quite disturbed when the Magi asked about a newborn king of the Jews because: (1) Herod was not the rightful heir to the throne of David; therefore many Jews hated him as a usurper. If Jesus really was an heir, trouble would arise. (2) Herod was ruthless and, because of his many enemies, he was suspicious that someone would try to overthrow him. (3) Herod didn't want the Jews, a religious people, to unite around a religious figure. (4) If these Magi were of Jewish descent and from Parthia (the most powerful region next to Rome), they would have welcomed a Jewish king who could swing the balance of power away from Rome. The land of Israel, far from Rome, would have been easy prey for a nation trying to gain more control.

●**2:4** The chief priests and teachers of the law were aware of Micah 5:2 and other prophecies about the Messiah. The Magi's news troubled Herod because he knew that the Jewish people expected the Messiah to come soon (Luke 3:15). Most Jews expected the Messiah to be a great military and political deliverer, like Alexander the Great. Herod's counselors would have told Herod this. No wonder this ruthless man took no chances and ordered all the baby boys in Bethlehem killed (2:16)!

6" 'But you, Bethlehem, in the land of Judah,
    are by no means least among the rulers of Judah;
  for out of you will come a ruler
    who will be the shepherd of my people Israel.'ʰ"

7Then Herod called the Magi secretly and found out from them the exact time the star had appeared. 8He sent them to Bethlehem and said, "Go and make a careful search for the child. As soon as you find him, report to me, so that I too may go and worship him."

9After they had heard the king, they went on their way, and the star they had seen in the eastⁱ went ahead of them until it stopped over the place where the child was. 10When they saw the star, they were overjoyed. 11On coming to the house, they saw the child with his mother Mary, and they bowed down and worshiped him.ᵗ Then they opened their treasures and presented him with giftsᵘ of gold and of incense and of myrrh. 12And having been warnedᵛ in a dream not to go back to Herod, they returned to their country by another route.

2:11
ᵗIsa 60:3
ᵘPs 72:10

2:12
ᵛHeb 11:7

The Escape to Egypt
(13)

13When they had gone, an angel of the Lord appeared to Joseph in a dream. "Get up," he said, "take the child and his mother and escape to Egypt. Stay there until I tell you, for Herod is going to search for the child to kill him."

ʰ 6 Micah 5:2   ⁱ 9 Or *seen when it rose*

GOSPEL ACCOUNTS FOUND ONLY IN MATTHEW	Passage	Subject
	1:20–24	Joseph's dream*
	2:1–12	The visit of the Magi
	2:13–15	Escape to Egypt*
	2:16–18	Slaughter of the children*
	27:3–10	The death of Judas*
	27:19	The dream of Pilate's wife
	27:52	The other resurrections
	28:11–15	The bribery of the guards
	28:19, 20	The baptism emphasis in the Great Commission*

Matthew records nine special events that are not mentioned in any of the other Gospels. In each case, the most apparent reason for Matthew's choice has to do with his purpose in communicating the gospel to Jewish people. Five cases are fulfillments of Old Testament prophecies (marked with asterisks above). The other four would have been of particular interest to the Jews of Matthew's day.

2:5, 6 Matthew often quoted Old Testament prophets. This prophecy, paraphrasing Micah 5:2, had been delivered seven centuries earlier.

2:6 Most religious leaders believed in a literal fulfillment of all Old Testament prophecy; therefore, they believed the Messiah would be born in Bethlehem. Ironically, when Jesus was born, these same religious leaders became his greatest enemies. When the Messiah for whom they had been waiting finally came, they didn't recognize him.

●**2:8** Herod did not want to worship Christ — he was lying. This was a trick to get the Magi to return to him and reveal the whereabouts of the newborn king. Herod's plan was to kill Jesus.

2:11 Jesus was probably one or two years old when the Magi found him. By this time, Mary and Joseph were married, living in a house, and intending to stay in Bethlehem for a while. For more on why Joseph and Mary stayed, see the note on Luke 2:39.

2:11 The Magi gave these expensive gifts because they were worthy presents for a future king. Bible students have seen in the gifts symbols of Christ's identity and what he would accomplish. Gold was a gift for a king; incense, a gift for deity; myrrh, a spice

for a person who was going to die. These gifts may have provided the financial resources for the trip to Egypt and back.

2:11 The Magi brought gifts and worshiped Jesus for who he was. This is the essence of true worship — honoring Christ for who he is and being willing to give him what is valuable to you. Worship God because he is the perfect, just, and almighty Creator of the universe, worthy of the best you have to give.

2:12 After finding Jesus and worshiping him, the Magi were warned by God not to return through Jerusalem as they had intended. Finding Jesus may mean that your life must take a different direction, one that is responsive and obedient to God's Word. Are you willing to be led a different way?

●**2:13** This was the second dream or vision that Joseph received from God. Joseph's first dream revealed that Mary's child would be the Messiah (1:20, 21). His second dream told him how to protect the child's life. Although Joseph was not Jesus' natural father, he was Jesus' legal father and was responsible for his safety and well-being. Divine guidance comes only to prepared hearts. Joseph remained receptive to God's guidance.

14So he got up, took the child and his mother during the night and left for Egypt, 15where he stayed until the death of Herod. And so was fulfilled what the Lord had said through the prophet: "Out of Egypt I called my son."j w

16When Herod realized that he had been outwitted by the Magi, he was furious, and he gave orders to kill all the boys in Bethlehem and its vicinity who were two years old and under, in accordance with the time he had learned from the Magi. 17Then what was said through the prophet Jeremiah was fulfilled:

> 18"A voice is heard in Ramah,
>   weeping and great mourning,
>   Rachel weeping for her children
>   and refusing to be comforted,
>   because they are no more."k x

2:15
w Hos 11:1;
Ex 4:22, 23

2:18
x Jer 31:15

The Return to Nazareth
(14)

19After Herod died, an angel of the Lord appeared in a dream to Joseph in Egypt 20and said, "Get up, take the child and his mother and go to the land of Israel, for those who were trying to take the child's life are dead."

21So he got up, took the child and his mother and went to the land of Israel. 22But when he heard that Archelaus was reigning in Judea in place of his father Herod, he was afraid to go there. Having been warned in a dream,y he withdrew to the district of Galilee,z 23and he went and lived in a town called Nazareth.a So was fulfilled what was said through the prophets: "He will be called a Nazarene."b

2:22
y ver 12, 13, 19
z Lk 2:39
2:23
a Lk 1:26
b Mk 1:24

John the Baptist Prepares the Way for Jesus
(16/Mark 1:1–8; Luke 3:1–18)

3 In those days John the Baptistc came, preaching in the Desert of Judea 2and saying, "Repent, for the kingdom of heavend is near." 3This is he who was spoken of through the prophet Isaiah:

3:1
c Lk 3:2-19
3:2
d Mt 4:17

j 15 Hosea 11:1   k 18 Jer. 31:15

2:14, 15 Going to Egypt was not unusual because there were colonies of Jews in several major Egyptian cities. These colonies had developed during the time of the great captivity (see Jeremiah 43; 44). There is an interesting parallel between this flight to Egypt and Israel's history. As an infant nation, Israel went to Egypt, just as Jesus did as a child. God led Israel out (Hosea 11:1); God brought Jesus back. Both events show God working to save his people.

• **2:16** Herod, the king of the Jews, killed all the boys under two years of age in an obsessive attempt to kill Jesus, the newborn King. He stained his hands with blood, but he did not harm Jesus. Herod was king by a human appointment; Jesus was King by a divine appointment. No one can thwart God's plans.

• **2:16** Herod was afraid that this newborn king would one day take his throne. He completely misunderstood the reason for Christ's coming. Jesus didn't want Herod's throne; he wanted to be king of Herod's life. Jesus wanted to give Herod eternal life, not take away his present life. Today people are often afraid that Christ wants to take things away when, in reality, he wants to give them real freedom, peace, and joy. Don't fear Christ — give him the throne of your life.

2:17, 18 Rachel was the wife of Jacob, one of the great men of God in the Old Testament. From Jacob's 12 sons had come the 12 tribes of Israel. Rachel was buried near Bethlehem (Genesis 35:19). For more about the significance of this verse, see the note on Jeremiah 31:15, from which this verse was quoted.

2:19–22 Herod the Great died in 4 B.C. of an incurable disease. Rome trusted him but didn't trust his sons. Herod knew that Rome wouldn't give his successor as much power, so he divided his kingdom into three parts, one for each son. Archelaus received Ju-

dea, Samaria, and Idumea; Herod Antipas received Galilee and Perea; Herod Philip II received Traconitis. Archelaus, a violent man, began his reign by slaughtering 3,000 influential people. Nine years later, he was banished. God didn't want Joseph's family to go into the region of this evil ruler.

2:23 Nazareth sat in the hilly area of southern Galilee near the crossroads of great caravan trade routes. The town itself was rather small. The Roman garrison in charge of Galilee was housed there. The people of Nazareth had constant contact with people from all over the world, so world news reached them quickly. The people of Nazareth had an attitude of independence that many of the Jews despised. This may have been why Nathanael commented, "Nazareth! Can anything good come from there?" (see John 1:46).

2:23 The Old Testament does not record this specific statement, "He will be called a Nazarene." Many scholars believe, however, that Matthew is referring to Isaiah 11:1 where the Hebrew word for "branch" is similar to the word for Nazarene. Or he may be referring to a prophecy unrecorded in the Bible. In any case, Matthew paints the picture of Jesus as the true Messiah announced by God through the prophets; and he makes the point that Jesus, the Messiah, had unexpectedly humble beginnings, just as the Old Testament had predicted (see Micah 5:2).

3:1, 2 Almost 30 years had passed since the events of chapter 2. Here John the Baptist burst onto the scene. His theme was "Repent!" Repentance means doing an about-face — a 180-degree turn — from the kind of self-centeredness that leads to wrong actions such as lying, cheating, stealing, gossiping, taking revenge, abusing, and indulging in sexual immorality. A person who repents stops rebelling and begins following God's way of living pre-

"A voice of one calling in the desert,
'Prepare the way for the Lord,
make straight paths for him.' "|e

3:3
e Isa 40:3;
Lk 1:76;
Jn 1:23 | 3 Isaiah 40:3

The Bible records history. It has proven itself an accurate and reliable record of people, events, and places. Independent historical accounts verify the Bible's descriptions and details of many famous lives. One of these was the father of the Herodian family, Herod the Great.

Herod is remembered as a builder of cities and the lavish rebuilder of the temple in Jerusalem. But he also destroyed people. He showed little greatness in either his personal actions or his character. He was ruthless in ruling his territory. His suspicions and jealousy led to the murder of several of his children and the death of his wife Mariamne.

Herod's title, king of the Jews, was granted by Rome but never accepted by the Jewish people. He was not part of the Davidic family line, and he was only partly Jewish. Although Israel benefited from Herod's lavish efforts to repair the temple in Jerusalem, he won little admiration because he also rebuilt various pagan temples. Herod's costly attempt to gain the loyalty of the people failed because it was superficial. His only loyalty was to himself.

Because his royal title was not genuine, Herod was constantly worried about losing his position. His actions when hearing from the Magi about their search for the new king are consistent with all that we know about Herod. He planned to locate and kill the child before he could become a threat. The murder of innocent children that followed is a tragic lesson in what can happen when actions are motivated by selfishness. Herod's suspicions did not spare even his own family. His life was self-destructive.

Strengths and accomplishments:
- Was given the title king of the Jews by the Romans
- Held on to his power for more than 30 years
- Was an effective, though ruthless, ruler
- Sponsored a great variety of large building projects

Weaknesses and mistakes:
- Tended to treat those around him with fear, suspicion, and jealousy
- Had several of his own children and at least one wife killed
- Ordered the killing of the infants in Bethlehem
- Although claiming to be a God-worshiper, he was still involved in many forms of pagan religion

Lessons from his life:
- Great power brings neither peace nor security
- No one can prevent God's plans from being carried out
- Superficial loyalty does not impress people or God

Vital statistics:
- Occupation: King of Judea from 37 to 4 B.C.
- Relatives: Father: Antipater. Sons: Archelaus, Antipater, Antipas, Philip, and others. Wives: Doris, Mariamne, and others
- Contemporaries: Zechariah, Elizabeth, Mary, Joseph, Mark Antony, Augustus

Notes about Herod the Great are found in Matthew 2:1–22 and Luke 1:5.

---

scribed in his Word. The first step in turning to God is to admit your sin, as John urged. Then God will receive you and help you live the way he wants. Remember that only God can get rid of sin. He doesn't expect us to clean up our lives *before* we come to him.

3:1, 2 John the Baptist's Profile is found in John 1.

3:2 The kingdom of heaven began when God himself entered human history as a man. Today Jesus Christ reigns in the hearts of believers, but the kingdom of heaven will not be fully realized until all evil in the world is judged and removed. Christ came to earth first as a suffering servant; he will come again as King and Judge to rule victoriously over all the earth.

3:3 The prophet quoted is Isaiah (40:3), one of the greatest prophets of the Old Testament and one of the most quoted in the New. Like Isaiah, John was a prophet who urged the people to

confess their sins and live for God. Both prophets taught that the message of repentance is good news to those who listen and seek the healing forgiveness of God's love, but terrible news to those who refuse to listen and thus cut off their only hope.

3:3 John the Baptist *prepared* the way for Jesus. People who do not know Jesus need to be prepared to meet him. We can prepare them by explaining their need for forgiveness, demonstrating Christ's teachings by our conduct, and telling them how Christ can give their lives meaning. We can "make straight paths for him" by correcting misconceptions that might be hindering people from approaching Christ. Someone you know may be open to a relationship with Christ. What can you do to prepare the way for this person?

4John's clothes were made of camel's hair, and he had a leather belt around his waist.ᶠ His food was locustsᵍ and wild honey. 5People went out to him from Jerusalem and all Judea and the whole region of the Jordan. 6Confessing their sins, they were baptized by him in the Jordan River.

3:4
ᶠ2Ki 1:8
ᵍLev 11:22

7But when he saw many of the Pharisees and Sadducees coming to where he was baptizing, he said to them: "You brood of vipers!ʰ Who warned you to flee from the coming wrath?ⁱ 8Produce fruit in keeping with repentance.ʲ 9And do not think you can say to yourselves, 'We have Abraham as our father.' I tell you that out of these stones God can raise up children for Abraham. 10The ax is already at the root of the trees, and every tree that does not produce good fruit will be cut down and thrown into the fire.ᵏ

3:7
ʰMt 12:34; 23:33
ⁱRo 1:18
3:8
ʲAc 26:20

11"I baptize you withᵐ water for repentance. But after me will come one who is

3:10
ᵏMt 7:19

ᵐ 11 Or in

JESUS BEGINS HIS MINISTRY

From his childhood home, Nazareth, Jesus set out to begin his earthly ministry. He was baptized by John the Baptist in the Jordan River, tempted by Satan in the desert, and then returned to Galilee. Between the temptation and his move to Capernaum (4:12, 13), he ministered in Judea, Samaria, and Galilee (see John 1–4).

Mediterranean Sea
GALILEE
N
Capernaum
Sea of Galilee
Nazareth
DECAPOLIS (Ten Cities)
Jordan River
SAMARIA
Bethany
Jerusalem
PEREA
Desert
Dead Sea
JUDEA
IDUMEA
0   20 Mi.
0   20 Km.

3:4 John was markedly different from other religious leaders of his day. While many were greedy, selfish, and preoccupied with winning the praise of the people, John was concerned only with the praise of God. Having separated himself from the evil and hypocrisy of his day, John lived differently from other people to show that his message was new. John not only preached God's law, he *lived* it. Do you practice what you preach? Could people discover what you believe by observing the way you live?

3:4–6 John must have presented a strange image! Many people came to hear this preacher who wore odd clothes and ate unusual food. Some probably came simply out of curiosity and ended up repenting of their sins as they listened to his powerful message. People may be curious about your Christian life-style and values. You can use their simple curiosity as an opener to share how Christ makes a difference in you.

3:5 Why did John attract so many people? He was the first true prophet in 400 years. He blasted both Herod and the religious leaders, daring acts that fascinated the common people. But John also had strong words for his audience — they too were sinners and needed to repent. His message was powerful and true. The people were expecting a prophet like Elijah (Malachi 4:5; Luke 1:17), and John seemed to be the one!

3:6 When you wash dirty hands, the results are immediately visible. But repentance happens inside with a cleansing that isn't seen right away. So John used a symbolic action that people could see: baptism. The Jews used baptism to initiate converts, so John's audience was familiar with the rite. Here, baptism was used as a sign of repentance and forgiveness. *Repent* means "to turn," implying a

change in behavior. It is turning from sin toward God. Have you repented of sin in your life? Can others see the difference it makes in you? A changed life with new and different behavior makes your repentance real and visible.

3:6 The Jordan River is about 70 miles long, its main section stretching between the Sea of Galilee and the Dead Sea. Jerusalem lies about 20 miles west of the Jordan. This river was Israel's eastern border, and many significant events in the nation's history took place there. It was by the Jordan River that the Israelites renewed their covenant with God before entering the promised land (Joshua 1; 2). Here John the Baptist calls them to renew their covenant with God again, this time through baptism.

3:7 The Jewish religious leaders were divided into several groups. Two of the most prominent groups were the Pharisees and the Sadducees. The Pharisees separated themselves from anything non-Jewish and carefully followed both the Old Testament laws and the oral traditions handed down through the centuries. The Sadducees believed the Pentateuch alone (Genesis — Deuteronomy) to be God's Word. They were descended mainly from priestly nobility, while the Pharisees came from all classes of people. The two groups disliked each other greatly, and both opposed Jesus. John the Baptist criticized the Pharisees for being legalistic and hypocritical, following the letter of the law while ignoring its true intent. He criticized the Sadducees for using religion to advance their political position. For more information on these two groups, see the chart in Mark 2.

3:8 John the Baptist called people to more than words or ritual; he told them to change their behavior. "Produce fruit in keeping with repentance" means that God looks beyond our words and religious activities to see if our conduct backs up what we say, and he judges our words by the actions that accompany them. Do your actions match your words?

3:9, 10 Just as a fruit tree is expected to bear fruit, God's people should produce a crop of good deeds. God has no use for people who call themselves Christians but do nothing about it. Like many people in John's day who were God's people in name only, we are of no value if we are Christians in name only. If others can't see our faith in the way we treat them, we may not be God's people at all.

3:10 God's message hasn't changed since the Old Testament — people will be judged for their unproductive lives. God calls us to be *active* in our obedience. God compared people who claim they believe God but don't live for God to unproductive trees that will be cut down. To be productive for God, we must obey his teachings, resist temptation, actively serve and help others, and share our faith. How productive are you for God?

3:11 John baptized people as a sign that they had asked God to forgive their sins and had decided to live as he wanted them to live. Baptism was an *outward* sign of commitment. To be effective, it had to be accompanied by an *inward* change of attitude leading to a changed life — the work of the Holy Spirit. John said that Jesus would baptize with the Holy Spirit and fire. This looked ahead to Pentecost (Acts 2), when the Holy Spirit would be sent by Jesus in

3:11
/ Isa 4:4

3:12
m Mt 13:30

more powerful than I, whose sandals I am not fit to carry. He will baptize you with the Holy Spirit and with fire. / 12His winnowing fork is in his hand, and he will clear his threshing floor, gathering his wheat into the barn and burning up the chaff with unquenchable fire."*m*

John Baptizes Jesus
(17/Mark 1:9–11; Luke 3:21, 22)

13Then Jesus came from Galilee to the Jordan to be baptized by John. 14But John tried to deter him, saying, "I need to be baptized by you, and do you come to me?"

15Jesus replied, "Let it be so now; it is proper for us to do this to fulfill all righteousness." Then John consented.

THE PHARISEES AND SADDUCEES	Name	Positive Characteristics	Negative Characteristics
The Pharisees and Sadducees were the two major religious groups in Israel at the time of Christ. The Pharisees were more religiously minded, while the Sadducees were more politically minded. Although the groups disliked and distrusted each other, they became allies in their common hatred for Jesus.	PHARISEES	• Were committed to obeying all of God's commands • Were admired by the common people for their apparent piety • Believed in a bodily resurrection and eternal life • Believed in angels and demons	• Behaved as though their own religious rules were just as important as God's rules for living • Their piety was often hypocritical and their efforts often forced others to try to live up to standards they themselves could not live up to • Believed that salvation came from perfect obedience to the law and was not based on forgiveness of sins • Became so obsessed with obeying their legal interpretations in every detail that they completely ignored God's message of mercy and grace • Were more concerned with appearing to be good than obeying God
	SADDUCEES	• Believed strongly in the Mosaic law and in Levitical purity • Were more practically minded than the Pharisees	• Relied on logic while placing little importance on faith • Did not believe all the Old Testament was God's Word • Did not believe in a bodily resurrection or eternal life • Did not believe in angels or demons • Were often willing to compromise their values with the Romans and others in order to maintain their status and influential positions

---

the form of tongues of fire, empowering his followers to preach the gospel. John's statement also symbolizes the work of the Holy Spirit in bringing God's judgment on those who refuse to repent. Everyone will one day be baptized — either now by God's Holy Spirit, or later by the fire of his judgment.

3:12 A winnowing fork is a pitchfork used to toss wheat in the air to separate wheat from chaff. The wheat is the part of the plant that is useful; chaff is the worthless outer shell. Because it is useless, chaff is burned; wheat, however, is gathered. "Winnowing" is often used as a picture of God's judgment. Unrepentant people will be judged and discarded because they are worthless in doing God's work; those who repent and believe will be saved and used by God.

3:13-15 John had been explaining that Jesus' baptism would be much greater than his, when suddenly Jesus came to him and asked to be baptized! John felt unqualified. He wanted Jesus to baptize him. Why did Jesus ask to be baptized? It was not for repentance for sin because Jesus never sinned. "To fulfill all righteousness" means to accomplish God's mission. Jesus saw his

baptism as advancing God's work. Jesus was baptized because (1) he was confessing sin on behalf of the nation, as Nehemiah, Ezra, Moses, and Daniel had done; (2) he was showing support for what John was doing; (3) he was inaugurating his public ministry; (4) he was identifying with the penitent people of God, not with the critical Pharisees who were only watching. Jesus, the perfect man, didn't need baptism for sin, but he accepted baptism in obedient service to the Father, and God showed his approval.

3:15 Put yourself in John's shoes. Your work is going well, people are taking notice, everything is growing. But you know that the purpose of your work is to prepare the people for Jesus (John 1:35–37). Then Jesus arrives, and his coming tests your integrity. Will you be able to turn your followers over to him? John passed the test by publicly baptizing Jesus. Soon he would say, "He must become greater; I must become less" (John 3:30). Can we, like John, put our egos and profitable work aside in order to point others to Jesus? Are we willing to lose some of our status so that everyone will benefit?

[16]As soon as Jesus was baptized, he went up out of the water. At that moment heaven was opened, and he saw the Spirit of God[n] descending like a dove and lighting on him. [17]And a voice from heaven said, "This is my Son,[o] whom I love; with him I am well pleased."[p]

Satan Tempts Jesus in the Desert
(18/Mark 1:12, 13; Luke 4:1–13)

4 Then Jesus was led by the Spirit into the desert to be tempted by the devil. [2]After fasting forty days and forty nights,[q] he was hungry. [3]The tempter[r] came to him and said, "If you are the Son of God, tell these stones to become bread."

[4]Jesus answered, "It is written: 'Man does not live on bread alone, but on every word that comes from the mouth of God.'[n]"[s]

[5]Then the devil took him to the holy city[t] and had him stand on the highest point

n 4 Deut. 8:3

3:16
n Isa 11:2
3:17
o Ps 2:7
p Mt 12:18;
Lk 9:35

4:2
q 1Ki 19:8
4:3
r 1Th 3:5
4:4
s Dt 8:3
4:5
t Ne 11:1;
Mt 27:53

3:16, 17 The doctrine of the Trinity means that God is three persons and yet one in essence. In this passage, all three persons of the Trinity are present and active. God the Father speaks; God the Son is baptized; God the Holy Spirit descends on Jesus. God is one, yet in three persons at the same time. This is one of God's incomprehensible mysteries. Other Bible references that speak of the Father, Son, and Holy Spirit are Matthew 28:19; John 15:26; 1 Corinthians 12:4–13; 2 Corinthians 13:14; Ephesians 2:18; 1 Thessalonians 1:2–5; and 1 Peter 1:2.

● **4:1** This time of testing showed that Jesus really was the Son of God, able to overcome the devil and his temptations. A person has not shown true obedience if he or she has never had an opportunity to disobey. We read in Deuteronomy 8:2 that God led Israel into the desert to humble and test them. God wanted to see whether or not his people would really obey him. We too will be tested. Because we know that testing will come, we should be alert and ready for it. Remember, your convictions are only strong if they hold up under pressure!

● **4:1** The devil, also called Satan, tempted Eve in the Garden of Eden, and here he tempted Jesus in the desert. Satan is a fallen angel. He is *real*, not symbolic, and is constantly fighting against those who follow and obey God. Satan's temptations are real, and he is always trying to get us to live his way or our way rather than God's way. Jesus will one day reign over all creation, but Satan tried to force his hand and get him to declare his kingship prematurely. If Jesus had given in, his mission on earth — to die for our sins and give us the opportunity to have eternal life — would have been lost. When temptations seem especially strong, or when you think you can rationalize giving in, consider whether Satan may be trying to block God's purposes for your life or for someone else's life.

● **4:1ff** This temptation by the devil shows us that Jesus was human, and it gave Jesus the opportunity to reaffirm God's plan for his ministry. It also gives us an example to follow when we are tempted. Jesus' temptation was an important demonstration of his sinlessness. He would face temptation and not give in.

● **4:1ff** Jesus was tempted by the devil, but he never sinned! Although we may feel dirty after being tempted, we should remember that temptation itself is not sin. We sin when we give in and disobey God. Remembering this will help us turn away from the temptation.

4:1ff Jesus wasn't tempted inside the temple or at his baptism but in the desert where he was tired, alone, and hungry, and thus most vulnerable. The devil often tempts us when we are vulnerable — when we are under physical or emotional stress (for example, lonely, tired, weighing big decisions, or faced with uncertainty). But he also likes to tempt us through our strengths, where

we are most susceptible to pride (see the note on Luke 4:3ff). We must guard at all times against his attacks.

● **4:1–10** The devil's temptations focused on three crucial areas: (1) physical needs and desires, (2) possessions and power, and (3) pride (see 1 John 2:15, 16 for a similar list). But Jesus did not give in. Hebrews 4:15 says that Jesus "has been tempted in every way, just as we are — yet was without sin." He knows firsthand what we are experiencing, and he is willing and able to help us in our struggles. When you are tempted, turn to him for strength.

● **4:3, 4** Jesus was hungry and weak after fasting for 40 days, but he chose not to use his divine power to satisfy his natural desire for food. Food, hunger, and eating are good, but the timing was wrong. Jesus was in the desert to fast, not to eat. And because Jesus had given up the unlimited, independent use of his divine power in order to experience humanity fully, he wouldn't use his power to change the stones to bread. We also may be tempted to satisfy a perfectly normal desire in a wrong way or at the wrong time. If we indulge in sex before marriage or if we steal to get food, we are trying to satisfy God-given desires in wrong ways. Remember, many of your desires are normal and good, but God wants you to satisfy them in the right way and at the right time.

● **4:3, 4** Jesus was able to resist all of the devil's temptations because he not only knew Scripture, but he also obeyed it. Ephesians 6:17 says that God's Word is a sword to use in spiritual combat. Knowing Bible verses is an important step in helping us resist the devil's attacks, but we must also obey the Bible. Note that Satan had memorized Scripture, but he failed to obey it. Knowing and obeying the Bible helps us follow God's desires rather than the devil's.

4:5 The temple was the religious center of the Jewish nation and the place where the people expected the Messiah to arrive (Malachi 3:1). Herod the Great had renovated the temple in hopes of gaining the Jews' confidence. The temple was the tallest building in the area, and this "highest point" was probably the corner wall that jutted out of the hillside, overlooking the valley below. From this spot, Jesus could see all of Jerusalem behind him and the country for miles in front of him.

4:5–7 God is not our magician in the sky ready to perform on request. In response to Satan's temptations, Jesus said not to put God to a test (Deuteronomy 6:16). You may want to ask God to do something to prove his existence or his love for you. Jesus once taught through a parable that people who don't believe what is written in the Bible won't believe even if someone were to come back from the dead to warn them (Luke 16:31)! God wants us to live by faith, not by magic. Don't try to manipulate God by asking for signs.

● **4:6** The devil used Scripture to try to convince Jesus to sin!

of the temple. 6"If you are the Son of God," he said, "throw yourself down. For it is written:

> " 'He will command his angels concerning you,
> and they will lift you up in their hands,
> so that you will not strike your foot against a stone.'**o**"*u*

4:6
u Ps 91:11, 12

7Jesus answered him, "It is also written: 'Do not put the Lord your God to the test.'**p**"*v*

4:7
v Dt 6:16

8Again, the devil took him to a very high mountain and showed him all the kingdoms of the world and their splendor. 9"All this I will give you," he said, "if you will bow down and worship me."

10Jesus said to him, "Away from me, Satan! For it is written: 'Worship the Lord your God, and serve him only.'**q**"*w*

4:10
w Dt 6:13

11Then the devil left him, and angels came and attended him.*x*

4:11
x Lk 22:43

o *6* Psalm 91:11,12   p *7* Deut. 6:16   q *10* Deut. 6:13

THE TEMPTATIONS	*Temptation*	*Real needs used as basis for temptation*	*Possible doubts that made the temptations real*	*Potential weaknesses Satan sought to exploit*	*Jesus' answer*
	Make bread	Physical need: Hunger	Would God provide food?	Hunger, impatience, need to "prove his Sonship"	Deuteronomy 8:3 "Depend on God" Focus: God's purpose
	Dare God to rescue you (based on misapplied Scripture, Psalm 91:11, 12)	Emotional need: Security	Would God protect?	Pride, insecurity, need to test God	Deuteronomy 6:16 "Don't test God" Focus: God's plan
	Worship me! (Satan)	Psychological need: Significance, power, achievement	Would God rule?	Desire for quick power, easy solutions, need to prove equality with God	Deuteronomy 6:13 "No compromise with evil" Focus: God's person

As if going through a final test of preparation, Jesus was tempted by Satan in the desert. Three specific parts of the temptation are listed by Matthew. They are familiar because we face the same kinds of temptations. As the chart shows, temptation is often the combination of a real need and a possible doubt that create an inappropriate desire. Jesus demonstrates both the importance and effectiveness of knowing and applying Scripture to combat temptation.

Sometimes friends or associates will present attractive and convincing reasons why you should try something you know is wrong. They may even find Bible verses that *seem* to support their viewpoint. Study the Bible carefully, especially the broader contexts of specific verses, so that you understand God's principles for living and what he wants for your life. Only if you really understand what the *whole* Bible says will you be able to recognize errors of interpretation when people take verses out of context and twist them to say what they want them to say.

4:8, 9 Did the devil have the power to give Jesus the kingdoms of the world? Didn't God, the Creator of the world, have control over these kingdoms? The devil may have been lying about his implied power, or he may have based his offer on his temporary control and free rein over the earth because of humanity's sinfulness. Jesus' temptation was to take the world as a political ruler right then, without carrying out his plan to save the world from sin. Satan was trying to distort Jesus' perspective by making him focus on worldly power and not on God's plans.

●**4:8–10** The devil offered the whole world to Jesus if Jesus would only bow down and worship him. Today the devil offers us the world by trying to entice us with materialism and power. We can resist temptations the same way Jesus did. If you find yourself craving something that the world offers, quote Jesus' words to the devil: "Worship the Lord your God, and serve him only."

4:11 Angels, like these who waited on Jesus, have a significant role as God's messengers. These spiritual beings were involved in Jesus' life on earth by (1) announcing Jesus' birth to Mary, (2) reassuring Joseph, (3) naming Jesus, (4) announcing Jesus' birth to the shepherds, (5) protecting Jesus by sending his family to Egypt, (6) ministering to Jesus in Gethsemane. For more on angels, see the note on 1:20.

B. MESSAGE AND MINISTRY OF JESUS, THE KING (4:12—25:46)

Matthew features Jesus' sermons. The record of Jesus' actions is woven around great passages of his teaching. This section of Matthew, then, is topical rather than chronological. Matthew records for us the Sermon on the Mount, the parables of the kingdom, Jesus' teachings on forgiveness, and parables about the end of the age.

1. Jesus begins his ministry

Jesus Preaches in Galilee
(30/Mark 1:14, 15; Luke 4:14, 15; John 4:43–45)

¹²When Jesus heard that John had been put in prison, he returned to Galilee. ¹³Leaving Nazareth, he went and lived in Capernaum, which was by the lake in the area of Zebulun and Naphtali— ¹⁴to fulfill what was said through the prophet Isaiah:

> ¹⁵"Land of Zebulun and land of Naphtali,
> the way to the sea, along the Jordan,
> Galilee of the Gentiles—
> ¹⁶the people living in darkness
> have seen a great light;
> on those living in the land of the shadow of death
> a light has dawned."[r][y]

4:16
[y]Isa 9:1, 2

¹⁷From that time on Jesus began to preach, "Repent, for the kingdom of heaven[z] is near."

4:17
[z]Mt 3:2

Four Fishermen Follow Jesus
(33/Mark 1:16–20)

¹⁸As Jesus was walking beside the Sea of Galilee, he saw two brothers, Simon called Peter and his brother Andrew. They were casting a net into the lake, for they were fishermen. ¹⁹"Come, follow me,"[a] Jesus said, "and I will make you fishers of men." ²⁰At once they left their nets and followed him.

4:19
[a]Mk 10:21, 28, 52

²¹Going on from there, he saw two other brothers, James son of Zebedee and his brother John. They were in a boat with their father Zebedee, preparing their nets. Jesus called them, ²²and immediately they left the boat and their father and followed him.

[r] *16* Isaiah 9:1,2

4:12, 13 Jesus moved from Nazareth, his hometown, to Capernaum, about 20 miles farther north. Capernaum became Jesus' home base during his ministry in Galilee. Jesus probably moved (1) to get away from intense opposition in Nazareth, (2) to have an impact on the greatest number of people (Capernaum was a busy city and Jesus' message could reach more people and spread more quickly), and (3) to utilize extra resources and support for his ministry.

Jesus' move fulfilled the prophecy of Isaiah 9:1, 2, which states that the Messiah will be a light to the land of Zebulun and Naphtali, the region of Galilee where Capernaum was located. Zebulun and Naphtali were two of the original 12 tribes of Israel.

4:14–16 By quoting from the book of Isaiah, Matthew continues to tie Jesus' ministry to the Old Testament. This was helpful for his Jewish readers, who were familiar with these Scriptures. In addition, it shows the unity of God's purposes as he works with his people throughout all ages.

4:17 The "kingdom of heaven" has the same meaning as the "kingdom of God" in Mark and Luke. Matthew uses this phrase because the Jews, out of their intense reverence and respect, did not pronounce God's name. The kingdom of heaven is still near because it has arrived in our hearts. See the note on 3:2 for more on the kingdom of heaven.

4:17 Jesus started his ministry with the very word people had heard John the Baptist say: "Repent." The message is the same to-

day as when Jesus and John gave it. Becoming a follower of Christ means turning away from our self-centeredness and "self" control and turning our lives over to Christ's direction and control.

4:18 The Sea of Galilee is really a large lake. About 30 fishing towns surrounded it during Jesus' day, and Capernaum was the largest.

4:18–20 Jesus told Peter and Andrew to leave their fishing business and become "fishers of men," to help others find God. Jesus was calling them away from their productive trades to be productive spiritually. We all need to fish for souls. If we practice Christ's teachings and share the gospel with others, we will be able to draw those around us to Christ like a fisherman who pulls fish into his boat with nets.

4:19, 20 These men already knew Jesus. He had talked to Peter and Andrew previously (John 1:35–42) and had been preaching in the area. When Jesus called them, they knew what kind of man he was and were willing to follow him. They were not in a hypnotic trance when they followed but had been thoroughly convinced that following him would change their lives forever.

4:21, 22 James and his brother, John, along with Peter and Andrew, were the first disciples that Jesus called to work with him. Jesus' call motivated these men to get up and leave their jobs— immediately. They didn't make excuses about why it wasn't a good time. They left at once and followed. Jesus calls each of us to follow him. When Jesus asks us to serve him, we must be like the disciples and do it at once.

Jesus Preaches throughout Galilee
(36/Mark 1:35–39; Luke 4:42–44)

4:23
b Mk 1:39;
Lk 4:15, 44
c Mt 9:35;
Mk 1:21
d Mk 1:14

4:24
e Lk 2:2
f Mk 1:32

4:25
g Mk 3:7, 8

²³Jesus went throughout Galilee, *b* teaching in their synagogues, *c* preaching the good news *d* of the kingdom, and healing every disease and sickness among the people. ²⁴News about him spread all over Syria, *e* and people brought to him all who were ill with various diseases, those suffering severe pain, the demon-possessed, *f* those having seizures, and the paralyzed, and he healed them. ²⁵Large crowds from Galilee, the Decapolis, *s* Jerusalem, Judea and the region across the Jordan followed him. *g*

2. Jesus gives the Sermon on the Mount

Jesus Gives the Beatitudes
(49/Luke 6:17–26)

5 Now when he saw the crowds, he went up on a mountainside and sat down. His disciples came to him, ²and he began to teach them, saying:

³"Blessed are the poor in spirit,
　　for theirs is the kingdom of heaven.
⁴Blessed are those who mourn,

5:4
h Isa 61:2, 3

　　for they will be comforted. *h*
⁵Blessed are the meek,

s 25 That is, the Ten Cities

4:23　Jesus was teaching, preaching, and healing. These were the three main aspects of his ministry. *Teaching* shows Jesus' concern for understanding; *preaching* shows his concern for commitment; and *healing* shows his concern for wholeness. His miracles of healing authenticated his teaching and preaching, proving that he truly was from God.

4:23　Jesus soon developed a powerful preaching ministry and often spoke in the synagogues. Most towns that had ten or more Jewish families had a synagogue. The building served as a religious gathering place on the Sabbath and as a school during the week. The leader of the synagogue was not a preacher as much as an administrator. His job was to find and invite rabbis to teach and preach. It was customary to invite visiting rabbis like Jesus to speak.

4:23, 24　Jesus preached the gospel — the Good News — to everyone who wanted to hear it. The gospel is that the kingdom of heaven has come, that God is with us, and that he cares for us. Christ can heal us, not just of physical sickness, but of spiritual sickness as well. There's no sin or problem too great or too small for him to handle. Jesus' words were good news because they offered freedom, hope, peace of heart, and eternal life with God.

4:25　Decapolis was a league of ten Gentile cities east of the Sea of Galilee, joined together for better trade and mutual defense. The word about Jesus was out, and Jews and Gentiles were coming long distances to hear him.

● **5:1ff**　Matthew 5 – 7 is called the Sermon on the Mount because Jesus gave it on a hillside near Capernaum. This "sermon" probably covered several days of preaching. In it, Jesus proclaimed his attitude toward the law. Position, authority, and money are not important in his kingdom — what matters is faithful obedience from the heart. The Sermon on the Mount challenged the proud and legalistic religious leaders of the day. It called them back to the messages of the Old Testament prophets who, like Jesus, taught that heartfelt obedience is more important than legalistic observance.

● **5:1, 2**　Enormous crowds were following Jesus — he was the talk of the town, and everyone wanted to see him. The disciples, who were the closest associates of this popular man, were certainly tempted to feel important, proud, and possessive. Being with Jesus gave them not only prestige, but also opportunity for receiving money and power.

The crowds were gathering once again. But before speaking to them, Jesus pulled his disciples aside and warned them about the temptations they would face as his associates. Don't expect fame and fortune, Jesus was saying, but mourning, hunger, and persecution. Nevertheless, Jesus assured his disciples, they would be rewarded — but perhaps not in this life. There may be times when following Jesus will bring us great popularity. If we don't live by Jesus' words in this sermon, we will find ourselves using God's message only to promote our personal interests.

● **5:3–5**　Jesus began his sermon with words that seem to contradict each other. But God's way of living usually contradicts the world's. If you want to live for God you must be ready to say and do what seems strange to the world. You must be willing to give when others take, to love when others hate, to help when others abuse. By giving up your own rights in order to serve others, you will one day receive everything God has in store for you.

● **5:3–12**　There are at least four ways to understand the Beatitudes. (1) They are a code of ethics for the disciples and a standard of conduct for all believers. (2) They contrast kingdom values (what is eternal) with worldly values (what is temporary). (3) They contrast the superficial "faith" of the Pharisees with the real faith Christ wants. (4) They show how the Old Testament expectations will be fulfilled in the new kingdom. These beatitudes are not multiple choice — pick what you like and leave the rest. They must be taken as a whole. They describe what we should be like as Christ's followers.

● **5:3–12**　Each beatitude tells how to be *blessed.* "Blessed" means more than happiness. It implies the fortunate or enviable state of those who are in God's kingdom. The Beatitudes don't promise laughter, pleasure, or earthly prosperity. To Jesus, "blessed" means the experience of hope and joy, independent of outward circumstances. To find hope and joy, the deepest form of happiness, follow Jesus no matter what the cost.

● **5:3–12**　With Jesus' announcement that the kingdom was near (4:17), people were naturally asking, "How do I qualify to be in God's kingdom?" Jesus said that God's kingdom is organized differently from worldly kingdoms. In the kingdom of heaven, wealth and power and authority are unimportant. Kingdom people seek different blessings and benefits, and they have different attitudes. Are your attitudes a carbon copy of the world's selfishness, pride, and lust for power, or do they reflect the humility and self-sacrifice of Jesus, your King?

for they will inherit the earth. *i*

6Blessed are those who hunger and thirst for righteousness,

for they will be filled. *j*

" 7Blessed are the merciful,

for they will be shown mercy.

8Blessed are the pure in heart,

for they will see God. *k*

9Blessed are the peacemakers,

for they will be called sons of God. *l*

10Blessed are those who are persecuted because of

righteousness, *m*

for theirs is the kingdom of heaven.

11"Blessed are you when people insult you, persecute you and falsely say all kinds of evil against you because of me. 12Rejoice and be glad, because great is your reward in heaven, for in the same way they persecuted the prophets who were before you. *n*

5:5
i Ps 37:11

5:6
j Isa 55:1, 2

5:8
k Heb 12:14

5:9
l Ro 8:14

5:10
m 1Pe 3:14

5:12
n Ac 7:52

Jesus Teaches about Salt and Light
(50)

13"You are the salt of the earth. But if the salt loses its saltiness, how can it be made salty again? It is no longer good for anything, except to be thrown out and trampled by men. *o*

14"You are the light of the world. A city on a hill cannot be hidden. 15Neither do people light a lamp and put it under a bowl. Instead they put it on its stand, and it gives light to everyone in the house. *p* 16In the same way, let your light shine before men, that they may see your good deeds and praise your Father in heaven.

5:13
o Mk 9:50;
Lk 14:34, 35

5:15
p Mk 4:21;
Lk 8:16

Jesus Teaches about the Law
(51)

17"Do not think that I have come to abolish the Law or the Prophets; I have not come to abolish them but to fulfill them. 18I tell you the truth, until heaven and

---

● **5:11, 12** Jesus said to rejoice when we're persecuted. Persecution can be good because (1) it takes our eyes off earthly rewards, (2) it strips away superficial belief, (3) it strengthens the faith of those who endure, and (4) our attitude through it serves as an example to others who follow. We can be comforted to know that God's greatest prophets were persecuted (Elijah, Jeremiah, Daniel). The fact that we are being persecuted proves that we have been faithful; faithless people would be unnoticed. In the future God will reward the faithful by receiving them into his eternal kingdom where there is no more persecution.

5:13 If a seasoning has no flavor, it has no value. If Christians make no effort to affect the world around them, they are of little value to God. If we are too much like the world, we are worthless. Christians should not blend in with everyone else. Instead, we should affect others positively, just as seasoning brings out the best flavor in food.

5:14–16 Can you hide a city that is sitting on top of a hill? Its light at night can be seen for miles. If we live for Christ, we will glow like lights, showing others what Christ is like. We hide our light by (1) being quiet when we should speak, (2) going along with the crowd, (3) denying the light, (4) letting sin dim our light, (5) not explaining our light to others, or (6) ignoring the needs of others. Be a beacon of truth — don't shut your light off from the rest of the world.

5:17 God's moral and ceremonial laws were given to help people love God with all their hearts and minds. Throughout Israel's history, however, these laws had been often misquoted and misapplied. By Jesus' time, religious leaders had turned the laws into a confusing mass of rules. When Jesus talked about a new way to understand God's law, he was actually trying to bring people back to its *original* purpose. Jesus did not speak against the law itself, but against the abuses and excesses to which it had been subjected. (See John 1:17.)

5:17–20 If Jesus did not come to abolish the law, does that mean all the Old Testament laws still apply to us today? In the Old Testament, there were three categories of law: ceremonial, civil, and moral.

(1) The *ceremonial law* related specifically to Israel's worship (see Leviticus 1:2, 3, for example). Its primary purpose was to point forward to Jesus Christ; these laws, therefore, were no longer necessary after Jesus' death and resurrection. While we are no longer bound by ceremonial laws, the principles behind them — to worship and love a holy God — still apply. Jesus was often accused by the Pharisees of violating ceremonial law.

(2) The *civil law* applied to daily living in Israel (see Deuteronomy 24:10, 11, for example). Because modern society and culture are so radically different from that time and setting, all of these guidelines cannot be followed specifically. But the principles behind the commands are timeless and should guide our conduct. Jesus demonstrated these principles by example.

(3) The *moral law* (such as the Ten Commandments) is the direct command of God, and it requires strict obedience (see Exodus 20:13, for example). The moral law reveals the nature and will of God, and it still applies today. Jesus obeyed the moral law completely.

5:18
qLk 16:17

5:19
rJas 2:10

earth disappear, not the smallest letter, not the least stroke of a pen, will by any means disappear from the Law until everything is accomplished. q 19Anyone who breaks one of the least of these commandmentsʳ and teaches others to do the same will be called least in the kingdom of heaven, but whoever practices and teaches these commands will be called great in the kingdom of heaven. 20For I tell you that unless your righteousness surpasses that of the Pharisees and the teachers of the law, you will certainly not enter the kingdom of heaven.

KEY LESSONS FROM THE SERMON ON THE MOUNT	Beatitude	Old Testament anticipation	Clashing worldly values	God's reward	How to develop this attitude
	Poor in spirit (5:3)	Isaiah 57:15	Pride and personal independence	Kingdom of heaven	James 4:7–10
	Mourning (5:4)	Isaiah 61:1, 2	Happiness at any cost	Comfort (2 Corinthians 1:4)	Psalm 51 James 4:7–10
	Meekness (5:5)	Psalm 37:5–11	Power	Inherit the earth	Matthew 11:27–30
	Righteousness (5:6)	Isaiah 11:4, 5; 42:1–4	Pursuing personal needs	Filled (satisfied)	John 16:5–11 Philippians 3:7–11
	Mercy (5:7)	Psalm 41:1	Strength without feeling	Be shown mercy	Ephesians 5:1, 2
	Pure in heart (5:8)	Psalm 24:3, 4; 51:10	Deception is acceptable	See God	1 John 3:1–3
	Peacemaker (5:9)	Isaiah 57:18, 19; 60:17	Personal peace is pursued without concern for the world's chaos	Be called sons of God	Romans 12:9–21 Hebrews 12:10, 11
	Persecuted (5:10)	Isaiah 52:13; 53:12	Weak commitments	Inherit the kingdom of heaven	2 Timothy 3:12

In his longest recorded sermon, Jesus began by describing the traits he was looking for in his followers. He called those who lived out those traits blessed because God had something special in store for them. Each beatitude is an almost direct contradiction of society's typical way of life. In the last beatitude, Jesus even points out that a serious effort to develop these traits is bound to create opposition. The best example of each trait is found in Jesus himself. If our goal is to become like him, the Beatitudes will challenge the way we live each day.

5:19 Some of those in the crowd were experts at telling others what to do, but they missed the central point of God's laws themselves. Jesus made it clear, however, that obeying God's law is more important than explaining it. It's much easier to study God's laws and tell others to obey them than to put them into practice. How are you doing at obeying God *yourself?*

5:20 The Pharisees were exacting and scrupulous in their attempts to follow their laws. So how could Jesus reasonably call us to a greater righteousness than theirs? The Pharisees' weakness was that they were content to obey the laws outwardly without allowing God to change their hearts (or attitudes). Jesus was saying, therefore, that the *quality* of our goodness should be greater than that of the Pharisees. They looked pious, but they were far from the

kingdom of God. God judges our hearts as well as our deeds, for it is in the heart that our real allegiance lies. Be just as concerned about your attitudes that people don't see as about your actions that are seen by all.

5:20 Jesus was saying that his listeners needed a different kind of righteousness altogether (love and obedience), not just a more intense version of the Pharisees' righteousness (legal compliance). Our righteousness must (1) come from what God does in us, not what we can do by ourselves, (2) be God-centered, not self-centered, (3) be based on reverence for God, not approval from people, and (4) go beyond keeping the law to living by the principles behind the law.

Jesus Teaches about Anger
(52)

21"You have heard that it was said to the people long ago, 'Do not murder,^t^s and anyone who murders will be subject to judgment.' 22But I tell you that anyone who is angry with his brother^u will be subject to judgment.^t Again, anyone who says to his brother, 'Raca,^v' is answerable to the Sanhedrin. But anyone who says, 'You fool!' will be in danger of the fire of hell.

5:21
^sEx 20:13

5:22
^t1Jn 3:15

23"Therefore, if you are offering your gift at the altar and there remember that your brother has something against you, 24leave your gift there in front of the altar. First go and be reconciled to your brother; then come and offer your gift.

25"Settle matters quickly with your adversary who is taking you to court. Do it while you are still with him on the way, or he may hand you over to the judge, and the judge may hand you over to the officer, and you may be thrown into prison. 26I tell you the truth, you will not get out until you have paid the last penny.^w

Jesus Teaches about Lust
(53)

27"You have heard that it was said, 'Do not commit adultery.'^x^u 28But I tell you that anyone who looks at a woman lustfully has already committed adultery with her in his heart.^v 29If your right eye causes you to sin,^w gouge it out and throw it away. It is better for you to lose one part of your body than for your whole body to be thrown into hell. 30And if your right hand causes you to sin, cut it off and throw it away. It is better for you to lose one part of your body than for your whole body to go into hell.

5:27
^uEx 20:14;
Dt 5:18

5:28
^vPr 6:25

5:29
^wMk 9:42-47

^t21 Exodus 20:13 ^u22 Some manuscripts *brother without cause* ^v22 An Aramaic term of contempt
^w26 Greek *kodrantes* ^x27 Exodus 20:14

5:21, 22 When Jesus said, "But I tell you," he was not doing away with the law or adding his own beliefs. Rather, he was giving a fuller understanding of why God made that law in the first place. For example, Moses said, "You shall not murder" (Exodus 20:13); Jesus taught that we should not even become angry enough to murder, for then we have already committed murder in our heart. The Pharisees read this law and, not having literally murdered anyone, felt righteous. Yet they were angry enough with Jesus that they would soon plot his death, though they would not do the dirty work themselves. We miss the intent of God's Word when we read his rules for living without trying to understand why he made them. When do you keep God's rules but close your eyes to his intent?

5:21, 22 Killing is a terrible sin, but *anger* is a great sin too because it also violates God's command to love. Anger in this case refers to a seething, brooding bitterness against someone. It is a dangerous emotion that always threatens to leap out of control, leading to violence, emotional hurt, increased mental stress, and spiritual damage. Anger keeps us from developing a spirit pleasing to God. Have you ever been proud that you didn't strike out and say what was really on your mind? Self-control is good, but Christ wants us to practice thought-control as well. Jesus said that we will be held accountable even for our attitudes.

5:23, 24 Broken relationships can hinder our relationship with God. If we have a problem or grievance with a friend, we should resolve the problem as soon as possible. We are hypocrites if we claim to love God while we hate others. Our attitudes toward others reflect our relationship with God (1 John 4:20).

5:25, 26 In Jesus' day, someone who couldn't pay a debt was thrown into prison until the debt was paid. Unless someone came to pay the debt for the prisoner, he or she would probably die there. It is practical advice to resolve our differences with our enemies before their anger causes more trouble (Proverbs 25:8-10). You may not get into a disagreement that takes you to court, but

even small conflicts mend more easily if you try to make peace right away. In a broader sense, these verses advise us to get things right with our brothers and sisters before we have to stand before God.

5:27, 28 The Old Testament law said that it is wrong for a person to have sex with someone other than his or her spouse (Exodus 20:14). But Jesus said that the *desire* to have sex with someone other than your spouse is mental adultery and thus sin. Jesus emphasized that if the *act* is wrong, then so is the *intention*. To be faithful to your spouse with your body but not your mind is to break the trust so vital to a strong marriage. Jesus is not condemning natural interest in the opposite sex or even healthy sexual desire, but the deliberate and repeated filling of one's mind with fantasies that would be evil if acted out.

5:27, 28 Some think that if lustful thoughts are sin, why shouldn't a person go ahead and do the lustful actions too? Acting out sinful desires is harmful in several ways: (1) it causes people to excuse sin rather than to stop sinning; (2) it destroys marriages; (3) it is deliberate rebellion against God's Word; (4) it always hurts someone else in addition to the sinner. Sinful action is more dangerous than sinful desire, and that is why desires should not be acted out. Nevertheless, sinful desire is just as damaging to righteousness. Left unchecked, wrong desires will result in wrong actions and turn people away from God.

5:29, 30 When Jesus said to get rid of your hand or your eye, he was speaking figuratively. He didn't mean literally to gouge out your eye, because even a blind person can lust. But if that were the only choice, it would be better to go into heaven with one eye or hand than to go to hell with two. We sometimes tolerate sins in our lives that, left unchecked, could eventually destroy us. It is better to experience the pain of removal (getting rid of a bad habit or something we treasure, for instance) than to allow the sin to bring judgment and condemnation. Examine your life for anything that causes you to sin, and take every necessary action to remove it.

Jesus Teaches about Divorce
(54)

5:31
xDt 24:1-4

5:32
yLk 16:18

31"It has been said, 'Anyone who divorces his wife must give her a certificate of divorce.'y x 32But I tell you that anyone who divorces his wife, except for marital unfaithfulness, causes her to become an adulteress, and anyone who marries the divorced woman commits adultery.y

Jesus Teaches about Vows
(55)

5:33
zLev 19:12
aNu 30:2;
Mt 23:16-22

5:34
bJas 5:12
cIsa 66:1

5:35
dPs 48:2

33"Again, you have heard that it was said to the people long ago, 'Do not break your oath,z but keep the oaths you have made to the Lord.'a 34But I tell you, Do not swear at all:b either by heaven, for it is God's throne;c 35or by the earth, for it is his footstool; or by Jerusalem, for it is the city of the Great King.d 36And do not swear by your head, for you cannot make even one hair white or black. 37Simply let your 'Yes' be 'Yes,' and your 'No,' 'No'; anything beyond this comes from the evil one.

y 31 Deut. 24:1

	Reference	Example	It's not enough to:	We must also:
SIX WAYS TO THINK LIKE CHRIST	5:21, 22	Murder	Avoid killing	Avoid anger and hatred
	5:23–26	Offerings	Offer regular gifts	Have right relationships with God and others
	5:27–30	Adultery	Avoid adultery	Keep our hearts from lusting and be faithful
	5:31, 32	Divorce	Be legally married	Live out our marriage commitments
	5:33–37	Oaths	Make an oath	Avoid casual and irresponsible commitments to God
	5:38–47	Revenge	Seek justice for ourselves	Show mercy and love to others

We are, more often than not, guilty of avoiding the extreme sins while regularly committing the types of sins with which Jesus was most concerned. In these six examples, our real struggle with sin is exposed. Jesus pointed out what kind of lives would be required of his followers. Are you living as Jesus taught?

5:31, 32 Divorce is as hurtful and destructive today as in Jesus' day. God intends marriage to be a lifetime commitment (Genesis 2:24). When entering into marriage, people should never consider divorce an option for solving problems or a way out of a relationship that seems dead. In these verses, Jesus is also attacking those who purposefully abuse the marriage contract, using divorce to satisfy their lustful desire to marry someone else. Are your actions today helping your marriage grow stronger, or are you tearing it apart?

5:32 Jesus said that divorce is not permissible except for unfaithfulness. This does not mean that divorce should automatically occur when a spouse commits adultery. The word translated "unfaithfulness" implies a sexually immoral life-style, not a confessed and repented act of adultery. Those who discover that their partner has been unfaithful should first make every effort to forgive, reconcile, and restore their relationship. We are always to look for reasons to restore the marriage relationship rather than for excuses to leave it.

5:33ff Here, Jesus was emphasizing the importance of telling the truth. People were breaking promises and using sacred language casually and carelessly. Keeping oaths and promises is important; it builds trust and makes committed human relationships possible. The Bible condemns making vows or taking oaths casually, giving your word while knowing that you won't keep it, or swearing falsely in God's name (Exodus 20:7; Leviticus 19:12; Numbers 30:1, 2; Deuteronomy 19:16–20). Oaths are needed in certain situations only because we live in a sinful society that breeds distrust.

5:33-37 Oaths, or vows, were common, but Jesus told his followers not to use them — their word alone should be enough (see James 5:12). Are you known as a person of your word? Truthfulness seems so rare that we feel we must end our statements with "I promise." If we tell the truth all the time, we will have less pressure to back up our words with an oath or promise.

Jesus Teaches about Retaliation
(56)

38"You have heard that it was said, 'Eye for eye, and tooth for tooth.'z e 39But   **5:38**
I tell you, Do not resist an evil person. If someone strikes you on the right cheek,   e Ex 21:24;
turn to him the other also. f 40And if someone wants to sue you and take your tunic,   Lev 24:20;
let him have your cloak as well. 41If someone forces you to go one mile, go with   **5:39**
him two miles. 42Give to the one who asks you, and do not turn away from the one   f Lk 6:29
who wants to borrow from you. g

                                                                                         5:42
                                                                                         g Lk 6:30

Jesus Teaches about Loving Enemies
(57/Luke 6:27–36)

43"You have heard that it was said, 'Love your neighbora h and hate your en-   **5:43**
emy.'i 44But I tell you: Love your enemiesb and pray for those who persecute   h Lev 19:18
you,j 45that you may be sons of your Father in heaven. He causes his sun to rise   i Dt 23:6
on the evil and the good, and sends rain on the righteous and the unrighteous. 46If   **5:44**
you love those who love you, what reward will you get? Are not even the tax col-   j Lk 6:27, 28;
lectors doing that? 47And if you greet only your brothers, what are you doing more   Ac 7:60
than others? Do not even pagans do that? 48Be perfect, therefore, as your heavenly
Father is perfect. k

                                                                                         5:48
                                                                                         k Lev 19:2

Jesus Teaches about Giving to the Needy
(58)

6 "Be careful not to do your 'acts of righteousness' before men, to be seen by
them. If you do, you will have no reward from your Father in heaven.

2"So when you give to the needy, do not announce it with trumpets, as the hypocrites do in the synagogues and on the streets, to be honored by men. I tell you the
truth, they have received their reward in full. 3But when you give to the needy, do

z 38 Exodus 21:24; Lev. 24:20; Deut. 19:21 a 43 Lev. 19:18 b 44 Some late manuscripts *enemies, bless those
who curse you, do good to those who hate you*

5:38 God's purpose behind this law was an expression of mercy.
The law was given to judges and said, in effect, "Make the punishment fit the crime." It was not a guide for personal revenge (Exodus 21:23–25; Leviticus 24:19, 20; Deuteronomy 19:21). These
laws were given to *limit* vengeance and help the court administer
punishment that was neither too strict nor too lenient. Some people, however, were using this phrase to justify their vendettas
against others. People still try to excuse their acts of revenge by
saying, "I was just doing to him what he did to me."

5:38–42 When we are wronged, often our first reaction is to get
even. Instead Jesus said we should do *good* to those who wrong
us! Our desire should not be to keep score, but to love and forgive.
This is not natural—it is supernatural. Only God can give us the
strength to love as he does. Instead of planning vengeance, pray
for those who hurt you.

5:39–44 To many Jews of Jesus' day, these statements were of-
fensive. Any Messiah who would turn the other cheek was not the
military leader they wanted to lead a revolt against Rome. Since
they were under Roman oppression, they wanted retaliation
against their enemies, whom they hated. But Jesus suggested a
new, radical response to injustice: instead of demanding rights,
give them up freely! According to Jesus, it is more important to
give justice and mercy than to receive it.

5:43, 44 By telling us not to retaliate, Jesus keeps us from taking
the law into our own hands. By loving and praying for our enemies,
we can overcome evil with good.

The Pharisees interpreted Leviticus 19:18 as teaching that they
should love only those who love in return, and Psalm 139:19–22
and 140:9–11 as meaning that they should hate their enemies. But
Jesus says we are to love our enemies. If you love your enemies
and treat them well, you will truly show that Jesus is Lord of your
life. This is possible only for those who give themselves fully to
God, because only he can deliver people from natural selfishness.

We must trust the Holy Spirit to help us *show* love to those for
whom we may not *feel* love.

5:48 How can we be perfect? (1) *In character.* In this life we cannot be flawless, but we can aspire to be as much like Christ as
possible. (2) *In holiness.* Like the Pharisees, we are to separate
ourselves from the world's sinful values. But unlike the Pharisees,
we are to be devoted to God's desires rather than our own, and
carry his love and mercy into the world. (3) *In maturity.* We can't
achieve Christlike character and holy living all at once, but we
must grow toward maturity and wholeness. Just as we expect different behavior from a baby, a child, a teenager, and an adult, so
God expects different behavior from us, depending on our stage of
spiritual development. (4) *In love.* We can seek to love others as
completely as God loves us.

We can be perfect if our behavior is appropriate for our maturity
level—perfect, yet with much room to grow. Our tendency to sin
must never deter us from striving to be more like Christ. Christ calls
all of his disciples to excel, to rise above mediocrity, and to mature
in every area, becoming like him. Those who strive to become perfect will one day be perfect, even as Christ is perfect (1 John
3:2, 3).

●**6:2** The term *hypocrites*, as used here, describes people who do
good acts for appearances only—not out of compassion or other
good motives. Their actions may be good, but their motives are
hollow. These empty acts are their only reward, but God will reward those who are sincere in their faith.

●**6:3** When Jesus says not to let your left hand know what your
right hand is doing, he is teaching that our motives for giving to
God and to others must be pure. It is easy to give with mixed motives, to do something for someone if it will benefit us in return. But
believers should avoid all scheming and give for the pleasure of
giving and as a response to God's love. Why do *you* give?

●**6:3, 4** It's easier to do what's right when we gain recognition and

not let your left hand know what your right hand is doing, 4so that your giving may be in secret. Then your Father, who sees what is done in secret, will reward you.

Jesus Teaches about Prayer
(59)

5"And when you pray, do not be like the hypocrites, for they love to pray standing*l* in the synagogues and on the street corners to be seen by men. I tell you the truth, they have received their reward in full. 6But when you pray, go into your room, close the door and pray to your Father,*m* who is unseen. Then your Father, who sees what is done in secret, will reward you. 7And when you pray, do not keep on babbling like pagans, for they think they will be heard because of their many words.*n* 8Do not be like them, for your Father knows what you need before you ask him.

9"This, then, is how you should pray:

" 'Our Father in heaven,
hallowed be your name,
10your kingdom come,
your will be done*o*
on earth as it is in heaven.

6:5
l Mk 11:25

6:6
m 2Ki 4:33

6:7
n 1Ki 18:26-29

6:10
o Mt 26:39

JESUS AND THE OLD TESTAMENT LAW	Reference	Examples of Old Testament mercy in justice:
	Leviticus 19:18	"Do not seek revenge or bear a grudge against one of your people, but love your neighbor as yourself. I am the LORD."
	Proverbs 24:28, 29	"Do not testify against your neighbor without cause, or use your lips to deceive. Do not say, 'I'll do to him as he has done to me; I'll pay that man back for what he did.' "
	Proverbs 25:21, 22	"If your enemy is hungry, give him food to eat; if he is thirsty, give him water to drink. In doing this, you will heap burning coals on his head, and the LORD will reward you."
	Lamentations 3:27-31	"It is good for a man to . . . offer his cheek to one who would strike him, and let him be filled with disgrace. For men are not cast off by the Lord forever."

What seems to be a case of Jesus contradicting the laws of the Old Testament deserves a careful look. It is too easy to overlook how much mercy was written into the Old Testament laws. Above are several examples. What God designed as a system of justice with mercy had been distorted over the years into a license for revenge. It was this misapplication of the law that Jesus attacked.

---

praise. To be sure our motives are not selfish, we should do our good deeds quietly or in secret, with no thought of reward. Jesus says we should check our motives in three areas: generosity (6:4), prayer (6:6), and fasting (6:18). Those acts should not be self-centered, but God-centered, done not to make us look good but to make God look good. The reward God promises is not material, and it is never given to those who seek it. Doing something only for ourselves is not a loving sacrifice. With your next good deed, ask, "Would I still do this if no one would ever know I did it?"

● **6:5, 6** Some people, especially the religious leaders, wanted to be seen as "holy," and public prayer was one way to get attention. Jesus saw through their self-righteous acts, however, and taught that the essence of prayer is not public style but private communication with God. There is a place for public prayer, but to pray only where others will notice you indicates that your real audience is not God.

6:7, 8 Repeating the same words over and over like a magic incantation is no way to ensure that God will hear your prayer. It's not wrong to come to God many times with the same requests — Jesus encourages *persistent* prayer. But he condemns the shallow repetition of words that are not offered with a sincere heart. We can never pray too much if our prayers are honest and sincere. Before you start to pray, make sure you mean what you say.

6:9 This is often called the Lord's Prayer because Jesus gave it to the disciples. It can be a pattern for our prayers. We should praise God, pray for his work in the world, pray for our daily needs, and pray for help in our daily struggles.

6:9 The phrase "Our Father in heaven" indicates that God is not only majestic and holy, but also personal and loving. The first line of this model prayer is a statement of praise and a commitment to hallow, or honor, God's holy name. We can honor God's name by being careful to use it respectfully. If we use God's name lightly, we aren't remembering God's holiness.

6:10 The phrase "Your kingdom come" is a reference to God's spiritual reign, not Israel's freedom from Rome. God's kingdom was announced in the covenant with Abraham (8:11; Luke 13:28), is present in Christ's reign in believers' hearts (Luke 17:21), and will be complete when all evil is destroyed and God establishes the new heaven and earth (Revelation 21:1).

6:10 When we pray "Your will be done," we are not resigning ourselves to fate, but praying that God's perfect purpose will be accomplished in this world as well as in the next.

11Give us today our daily bread. p

12Forgive us our debts,

    as we also have forgiven our debtors. q

13And lead us not into temptation,

    but deliver us from the evil one. c '

14For if you forgive men when they sin against you, your heavenly Father will also forgive you. r 15But if you do not forgive men their sins, your Father will not forgive your sins. s

Jesus Teaches about Fasting
(60)

16"When you fast, do not look somber t as the hypocrites do, for they disfigure their faces to show men they are fasting. I tell you the truth, they have received their reward in full. 17But when you fast, put oil on your head and wash your face, 18so that it will not be obvious to men that you are fasting, but only to your Father, who is unseen; and your Father, who sees what is done in secret, will reward you. u

Jesus Teaches about Money
(61)

19"Do not store up for yourselves treasures on earth, v where moth and rust destroy, and where thieves break in and steal. 20But store up for yourselves treasures in heaven, w where moth and rust do not destroy, and where thieves do not break in and steal. 21For where your treasure is, there your heart will be also.

22"The eye is the lamp of the body. If your eyes are good, your whole body will be full of light. 23But if your eyes are bad, your whole body will be full of darkness. If then the light within you is darkness, how great is that darkness!

24"No one can serve two masters. Either he will hate the one and love the other,

c 13 Or from evil; some late manuscripts one, / for yours is the kingdom and the power and the glory forever. Amen.

6:11
p Pr 30:8

6:12
q Mt 18:21-35

6:14
r Mk 11:25, 26; Col 3:13

6:15
s Mt 18:35

6:16
t Isa 58:5

6:18
u ver 4, 6

6:19
v Heb 13:5

6:20
w Mt 19:21; Lk 12:33; 1 Ti 6:19

6:11 When we pray "Give us today our daily bread," we are acknowledging that God is our sustainer and provider. It is a misconception to think that we provide for our needs ourselves. We must trust God *daily* to provide what he knows we need.

6:13 God doesn't lead us into temptations, but sometimes he allows us to be tested by them. As disciples, we should pray to be delivered from these trying times and for deliverance from Satan ("the evil one") and his deceit. All Christians struggle with temptation. Sometimes it is so subtle that we don't even realize what is happening to us. God has promised that he won't allow us to be tempted beyond what we can bear (1 Corinthians 10:13). Ask God to help you recognize temptation and to give you strength to overcome it and choose God's way instead. For more on temptation, see the notes on 4:1.

6:14, 15 Jesus gives a startling warning about forgiveness: if we refuse to forgive others, God will also refuse to forgive us. Why? Because when we don't forgive others, we are denying our common ground as sinners in need of God's forgiveness. God's forgiveness of sin is not the direct result of our forgiving others, but it is based on our realizing what forgiveness means (see Ephesians 4:32). It is easy to ask God for forgiveness, but difficult to grant it to others. Whenever we ask God to forgive us for sin, we should ask ourselves, "Have I forgiven the people who have wronged me?"

●**6:16** Fasting — going without food in order to spend time in prayer — is noble *and* difficult. It gives us time to pray, teaches self-discipline, reminds us that we can live with a lot less, and helps us appreciate God's gifts. Jesus was not condemning fasting, but hypocrisy — fasting in order to gain public approval. Fasting was mandatory for the Jewish people once a year, on the Day of Atonement (Leviticus 23:32). The Pharisees voluntarily fasted twice a week to impress the people with their "holiness." Jesus commended acts of self-sacrifice done quietly and sincerely. He

wanted people to adopt spiritual disciplines for the right reasons, not from a selfish desire for praise.

●**6:17** Olive oil was used as a common cosmetic like a lotion. Jesus was saying, "Go about your normal daily routine when you fast. Don't make a show of it."

●**6:20** Storing up treasures in heaven is not limited to tithing but is accomplished by all acts of obedience to God. There is a sense in which giving our money to God's work is like investing in heaven. But our intention should be to seek the fulfillment of God's purposes in all we do, not merely what we do with our money.

●**6:22, 23** Spiritual vision is our capacity to see clearly what God wants us to do and to see the world from his point of view. But this spiritual insight can be easily clouded. Self-serving desires, interests, and goals block that vision. Serving God is the best way to restore it. A "good" eye is one that is fixed on God.

6:24 Jesus says we can have only one master. We live in a materialistic society where many people serve money. They spend all their lives collecting and storing it, only to die and leave it behind. Their desire for money and what it can buy far outweighs their commitment to God and spiritual matters. Whatever you store up, you will spend much of your time and energy thinking about. Don't fall into the materialistic trap, because "the love of money is a root of all kinds of evil" (1 Timothy 6:10). Can you honestly say that God, and not money, is your master? One test is to ask which one occupies more of your thoughts, time, and efforts.

6:24 Jesus contrasted heavenly values with earthly values when he explained that our first loyalty should be to those things that do not fade, cannot be stolen or used up, and never wear out. We should not be fascinated with our possessions, lest *they* possess *us*. This means we may have to do some cutting back if our possessions are becoming too important to us. Jesus is calling for a decision that allows us to live contentedly with whatever we have

or he will be devoted to the one and despise the other. You cannot serve both God and Money. *x*

6:24
*x*Lk 16:13

Jesus Teaches about Worry
(62)

6:25
*y*Lk 12:11, 22

25"Therefore I tell you, do not worry*y* about your life, what you will eat or drink; or about your body, what you will wear. Is not life more important than food, and the body more important than clothes? 26Look at the birds of the air; they do not sow or reap or store away in barns, and yet your heavenly Father feeds them. *z* Are you not much more valuable than they? 27Who of you by worrying can add a single hour to his life**d**? *a*

6:26
*z*Ps 147:9

6:27
*a*Ps 39:5

28"And why do you worry about clothes? See how the lilies of the field grow. They do not labor or spin. 29Yet I tell you that not even Solomon in all his splendor*b* was dressed like one of these. 30If that is how God clothes the grass of the field, which is here today and tomorrow is thrown into the fire, will he not much more clothe you, O you of little faith?*c* 31So do not worry, saying, 'What shall we eat?' or 'What shall we drink?' or 'What shall we wear?' 32For the pagans run after all these things, and your heavenly Father knows that you need them. 33But seek first his kingdom and his righteousness, and all these things will be given to you as well. *d* 34Therefore do not worry about tomorrow, for tomorrow will worry about itself. Each day has enough trouble of its own.

6:29
*b*1Ki 10:4-7

6:30
*c*Mt 8:26

6:33
*d*Mt 19:29

Jesus Teaches about Criticizing Others
(63/Luke 6:37–42)

7:1
*e*1Co 4:5

7 "Do not judge, or you too will be judged. *e* 2For in the same way you judge others, you will be judged, and with the measure you use, it will be measured to you. *f*

7:2
*f*Mk 4:24

d 27 Or *single cubit to his height*

SEVEN REASONS NOT TO WORRY		
	6:25	The same God who created life in you can be trusted with the details of your life.
	6:26	Worrying about the future hampers your efforts for today.
	6:27	Worrying is more harmful than helpful.
	6:28–30	God does not ignore those who depend on him.
	6:31, 32	Worry shows a lack of faith in and understanding of God.
	6:33	There are real challenges God wants us to pursue, and worrying keeps us from them.
	6:34	Living one day at a time keeps us from being consumed with worry.

---

because we have chosen what is eternal and lasting.

6:25 Because of the ill effects of worry, Jesus tells us not to worry about those needs that God promises to supply. Worry may (1) damage your health, (2) cause the object of your worry to consume your thoughts, (3) disrupt your productivity, (4) negatively affect the way you treat others, and (5) reduce your ability to trust in God. How many ill effects of worry are you experiencing? Here is the difference between worry and genuine concern — worry immobilizes, but concern moves you to action.

● **6:33** To "seek first his kingdom and his righteousness" means to turn to God first for help, to fill your thoughts with his desires, to take his character for your pattern, and to serve and obey him in everything. What is really important to you? People, objects, goals, and other desires all compete for priority. Any of these can quickly bump God out of first place if you don't actively choose to give him first place in *every* area of your life.

6:34 Planning for tomorrow is time well spent; worrying about tomorrow is time wasted. Sometimes it's difficult to tell the difference. Careful planning is thinking ahead about goals, steps, and schedules, and trusting in God's guidance. When done well, planning

can help alleviate worry. Worriers, by contrast, are consumed by fear and find it difficult to trust God. They let their plans interfere with their relationship with God. Don't let worries about tomorrow affect your relationship with God today.

7:1, 2 Jesus tells us to examine our own motives and conduct instead of judging others. The traits that bother us in others are often the habits we dislike in ourselves. Our untamed bad habits and behavior patterns are the very ones that we most want to change in others. Do you find it easy to magnify others' faults while excusing your own? If you are ready to criticize someone, check to see if you deserve the same criticism. Judge yourself first, and then lovingly forgive and help your neighbor.

7:1–5 Jesus' statement, "Do not judge," is against the kind of hypocritical, judgmental attitude that tears others down in order to build oneself up. It is not a blanket statement against all critical thinking, but a call to be *discerning* rather than negative. Jesus said to expose false teachers (7:15–23), and Paul taught that we should exercise church discipline (1 Corinthians 5:1, 2) and trust God to be the final Judge (1 Corinthians 4:3–5).

3"Why do you look at the speck of sawdust in your brother's eye and pay no attention to the plank in your own eye? 4How can you say to your brother, 'Let me take the speck out of your eye,' when all the time there is a plank in your own eye? 5You hypocrite, first take the plank out of your own eye, and then you will see clearly to remove the speck from your brother's eye.

6"Do not give dogs what is sacred; do not throw your pearls to pigs. If you do, they may trample them under their feet, and then turn and tear you to pieces.

Jesus Teaches about Asking, Seeking, Knocking
(64)

7"Ask and it will be given to you;*g* seek and you will find; knock and the door will be opened to you. 8For everyone who asks receives; he who seeks finds;*h* and to him who knocks, the door will be opened.

9"Which of you, if his son asks for bread, will give him a stone? 10Or if he asks for a fish, will give him a snake? 11If you, then, though you are evil, know how to give good gifts to your children, how much more will your Father in heaven give good gifts to those who ask him! 12So in everything, do to others what you would have them do to you,*i* for this sums up the Law and the Prophets.*j*

7:7
*g*Jn 15:7, 16;
16:23,24;
1Jn 3:22; 5:14, 15

7:8
*h*Jer 29:12, 13

7:12
*i*Lk 6:31
*j*Ro 13:8-10;
Gal 5:14

Jesus Teaches about the Way to Heaven
(65)

13"Enter through the narrow gate.*k* For wide is the gate and broad is the road that leads to destruction, and many enter through it. 14But small is the gate and narrow the road that leads to life, and only a few find it.

7:13
*k*Lk 13:24

Jesus Teaches about Fruit in People's Lives
(66/Luke 6:43–45)

15"Watch out for false prophets.*l* They come to you in sheep's clothing, but inwardly they are ferocious wolves.*m* 16By their fruit you will recognize them.*n* Do people pick grapes from thornbushes, or figs from thistles? 17Likewise every good tree bears good fruit, but a bad tree bears bad fruit. 18A good tree cannot bear

7:15
*l*2Pe 2:1;
1Jn 4:1
*m*Ac 20:29

7:16
*n*Lk 6:44

7:6 Pigs were unclean animals according to God's law (Deuteronomy 14:8). Anyone who touched an unclean animal became "ceremonially unclean" and could not go to the temple to worship until the uncleanness was removed. Jesus says that we should not entrust holy teachings to unholy or unclean people. It is futile to try to teach holy concepts to people who don't want to listen and will only tear apart what we say. We should not stop giving God's Word to unbelievers, but we should be wise and discerning in what we teach to whom, so that we will not be wasting our time.

7:7, 8 Jesus tells us to persist in pursuing God. People often give up after a few halfhearted efforts and conclude that God cannot be found. But knowing God takes faith, focus, and follow-through, and Jesus assures us that we will be rewarded. Don't give up in your efforts to seek God. Continue to ask him for more knowledge, patience, wisdom, love, and understanding. He will give them to you.

7:9, 10 The child in Jesus' example asked his father for bread and fish — good and necessary items. If the child had asked for a poisonous snake, would the wise father have granted his request? Sometimes God knows we are praying for "snakes" and does not give us what we ask for, even though we persist in our prayers. As we learn to know God better as a loving Father, we learn to ask for what is good for us, and then he grants it.

7:11 Christ is showing us the heart of God the Father. God is not selfish, begrudging, or stingy, and we don't have to beg or grovel as we come with our requests. He is a loving Father who understands, cares, and comforts. If humans can be kind, imagine how kind God, the Creator of kindness, can be.

7:11 Jesus used the expression "If you, then, though you are evil" to contrast sinful and fallible human beings with the holy and perfect God.

7:12 This is commonly known as the Golden Rule. In many religions it is stated negatively: "Don't do to others what you don't want done to you." By stating it positively, Jesus made it more significant. It is not very hard to refrain from harming others; it is much more difficult to take the initiative in doing something good for them. The Golden Rule as Jesus formulated it is the foundation of active goodness and mercy — the kind of love God shows to us every day. Think of a good and merciful action you can take today.

7:13, 14 The gate that leads to eternal life (John 10:7–9) is called "narrow." This does not mean that it is difficult to become a Christian, but that there is only *one* way to live eternally with God and only a few that decide to walk that road. Believing in Jesus is the only way to heaven, because he alone died for our sins and made us right before God. Living his way may not be popular, but it is true and right. Thank God there is one way!

7:15 False prophets were common in Old Testament times. They prophesied only what the king and the people wanted to hear, claiming it was God's message. False teachers are just as common today. Jesus says to beware of those whose words sound religious but who are motivated by money, fame, or power. You can tell who they are because in their teaching they minimize Christ and glorify themselves.

7:20 We should evaluate teachers' words by examining their lives. Just as trees are consistent in the kind of fruit they produce,

bad fruit, and a bad tree cannot bear good fruit. 19Every tree that does not bear good fruit is cut down and thrown into the fire. 20Thus, by their fruit you will recognize them.

Jesus Teaches about Those Who Build Houses on Rock and Sand
(67/Luke 6:46–49)

7:21
o Mt 25:11
p Jas 1:22

21"Not everyone who says to me, 'Lord, Lord,'*o* will enter the kingdom of heaven, but only he who does the will of my Father who is in heaven.*p* 22Many will say to me on that day, 'Lord, Lord, did we not prophesy in your name, and in your name drive out demons and perform many miracles?' 23Then I will tell them plainly, 'I never knew you. Away from me, you evildoers!'*q*

7:23
q Ps 6:8;
Lk 13:25-27

24"Therefore everyone who hears these words of mine and puts them into practice is like a wise man who built his house on the rock. 25The rain came down, the streams rose, and the winds blew and beat against that house; yet it did not fall, because it had its foundation on the rock. 26But everyone who hears these words of mine and does not put them into practice is like a foolish man who built his house on sand. 27The rain came down, the streams rose, and the winds blew and beat against that house, and it fell with a great crash."

7:28
r Mt 13:53
s Mk 1:22; 6:2;
Lk 4:32

28When Jesus had finished saying these things,*r* the crowds were amazed at his teaching,*s* 29because he taught as one who had authority, and not as their teachers of the law.

3. Jesus performs many miracles
Jesus Heals a Man with Leprosy
(38/Mark 1:40–45; Luke 5:12–16)

8 When he came down from the mountainside, large crowds followed him. 2A man with leprosy*e* came and knelt before him and said, "Lord, if you are willing, you can make me clean."

e 2 The Greek word was used for various diseases affecting the skin—not necessarily leprosy.

---

good teachers consistently exhibit good behavior and high moral character as they attempt to live out the truths of Scripture. This does not mean we should have witch hunts, throwing out church school teachers, pastors, and others who are less than perfect. Every one of us is subject to sin, and we must show the same mercy to others that we need for ourselves. When Jesus talks about bad trees, he means teachers who deliberately teach false doctrine. We must examine the teachers' motives, the direction they are taking, and the results they are seeking.

●**7:21** Some self-professed athletes can "talk" a great game, but that tells you nothing about their athletic skills. And not everyone who talks about heaven belongs to God's kingdom. Jesus is more concerned about our *walk* than our *talk*. He wants us to *do* right, not just *say* the right words. Your house (which represents your life, 7:24) will withstand the storms of life only if you do what is right instead of just talking about it. What you do cannot be separated from what you believe.

●**7:21-23** Jesus exposed those people who sounded religious but had no personal relationship with him. On "that day" (the day of judgment), only our relationship with Christ—our acceptance of him as Savior and our obedience to him—will matter. Many people think that if they are "good" people and say religious things, they will be rewarded with eternal life. In reality, faith in Christ is what will count at the judgment.

●**7:22** "That day" is the final day of reckoning when God will settle all accounts, judging sin and rewarding faith.

●**7:24** To build "on the rock" means to be a hearing, responding disciple, not a phony, superficial one. Practicing obedience becomes the solid foundation to weather the storms of life. See

James 1:22-27 for more on putting into practice what we hear.

●**7:26** Like a house of cards, the fool's life crumbles. Most people do not deliberately seek to build on a false or inferior foundation; instead, they just don't think about their life's purpose. Many people are headed for destruction, not out of stubbornness but out of thoughtlessness. Part of our responsibility as believers is to help others stop and think about where their lives are headed and to point out the consequences of ignoring Christ's message.

●**7:29** The teachers of the law (religious scholars) often cited traditions and quoted authorities to support their arguments and interpretations. But Jesus spoke with a new authority—his own. He didn't need to quote anyone because he was the original Word (John 1:1).

8:2, 3 Leprosy, like AIDS today, was a terrifying disease because there was no known cure. In Jesus' day, the Greek word for *leprosy* was used for a variety of similar diseases, and some forms were contagious. If a person contracted the contagious type, a priest declared him a leper and banished him from his home and city. The leper was sent to live in a community with other lepers until he either got better or died. Yet when the leper begged Jesus to heal him, Jesus reached out and touched him, even though his skin was covered with the dread disease.

Sin is also an incurable disease—and we all have it. Only Christ's healing touch can miraculously take away our sins and restore us to real living. But first, just like the leper, we must realize our inability to cure ourselves and ask for Christ's saving help.

³Jesus reached out his hand and touched the man. "I am willing," he said. "Be clean!" Immediately he was cured[f] of his leprosy. ⁴Then Jesus said to him, "See that you don't tell anyone.[t] But go, show yourself to the priest and offer the gift Moses commanded,[u] as a testimony to them."

8:4
[t]Mk 5:43
[u]Lev 14:2-32

A Roman Centurion Demonstrates Faith
(68/Luke 7:1–10)

⁵When Jesus had entered Capernaum, a centurion came to him, asking for help. ⁶"Lord," he said, "my servant lies at home paralyzed and in terrible suffering."

⁷Jesus said to him, "I will go and heal him."

⁸The centurion replied, "Lord, I do not deserve to have you come under my roof. But just say the word, and my servant will be healed. ⁹For I myself am a man under authority, with soldiers under me. I tell this one, 'Go,' and he goes; and that one, 'Come,' and he comes. I say to my servant, 'Do this,' and he does it."

¹⁰When Jesus heard this, he was astonished and said to those following him, "I tell you the truth, I have not found anyone in Israel with such great faith. ¹¹I say to you that many will come from the east and the west,[v] and will take their places at the feast with Abraham, Isaac and Jacob in the kingdom of heaven.[w] ¹²But the subjects of the kingdom will be thrown outside, into the darkness, where there will be weeping and gnashing of teeth."[x]

8:11
[v]Isa 49:12; 59:19;
Mal 1:11
[w]Lk 13:29

8:12
[x]Mt 13:42, 50;
22:13; 24:51; 25:30;
Lk 13:28

¹³Then Jesus said to the centurion, "Go! It will be done just as you believed it would." And his servant was healed at that very hour.

Jesus Heals Peter's Mother-in-Law and Many Others
(35/Mark 1:29–34; Luke 4:38–41)

¹⁴When Jesus came into Peter's house, he saw Peter's mother-in-law lying in bed with a fever. ¹⁵He touched her hand and the fever left her, and she got up and began to wait on him.

[f]3 Greek made clean

**JESUS'
MIRACULOUS
POWER
DISPLAYED**
Jesus finished the sermon he had given on a hillside near Galilee and returned to Capernaum. As he and his disciples crossed the Sea of Galilee, Jesus calmed a fierce storm. Then, in the Gentile Gadarene region, Jesus commanded demons to come out of two men.

8:8-12 A centurion was a career military officer in the Roman army with control over 100 soldiers. Roman soldiers, of all people, were hated by the Jews for their oppression, control, and ridicule. Yet this man's genuine faith amazed Jesus! This hated Gentile's faith put to shame the stagnant piety of many of the Jewish religious leaders.

8:10-12 Jesus told the crowd that many religious Jews who should be in the kingdom would be excluded because of their lack of faith. Entrenched in their religious traditions, they could not accept Christ and his new message. We must be careful not to become so set in our religious habits that we expect God to work only in specified ways. Don't limit God by your mind-set and lack of faith.

8:11, 12 "The east and the west" stands for the four corners of the earth. All the faithful people of God will be gathered to feast with the Messiah (Isaiah 6; 55). The Jews should have known that when the Messiah came, his blessings would be for Gentiles too (see Isaiah 66:12, 19). But this message came as a shock because they were too wrapped up in their own affairs and destiny. In claiming God's promises, we must not apply them so personally that we forget to see what God wants to do to reach all the people he loves.

8:11, 12 Matthew emphasizes this universal theme—Jesus' message is for everyone. The Old Testament prophets knew this (see Isaiah 56:3, 6–8; 66:12, 19; Malachi 1:11), but many New Testament Jewish leaders chose to ignore it. Each individual has to choose to accept or reject the gospel, and no one can become part of God's kingdom on the basis of heritage or connections. Having a Christian family is a wonderful blessing, but it won't guarantee you eternal life. You must believe in and follow Christ.

8:14 Peter was one of Jesus' 12 disciples. His Profile is found in chapter 27.

8:4 The law required a healed leper to be examined by the priest (Leviticus 14). Jesus wanted this man to give his story firsthand to the priest to prove that his leprosy was completely gone so that he could be restored to his community.

8:5, 6 The centurion could have let many obstacles stand between him and Jesus — pride, doubt, money, language, distance, time, self-sufficiency, power, race. But he didn't. If he did not let these barriers block his approach to Jesus, we don't need to either. What keeps you from Christ?

¹⁶When evening came, many who were demon-possessed were brought to him, and he drove out the spirits with a word and healed all the sick. ¹⁷This was to fulfill what was spoken through the prophet Isaiah:

"He took up our infirmities
and carried our diseases."^g^y

8:17
^yIsa 53:4

Jesus Teaches about the Cost of Following Him
(122/Luke 9:51–62)

¹⁸When Jesus saw the crowd around him, he gave orders to cross to the other side of the lake.^z ¹⁹Then a teacher of the law came to him and said, "Teacher, I will follow you wherever you go."

8:18
^zMk 4:35

²⁰Jesus replied, "Foxes have holes and birds of the air have nests, but the Son of Man has no place to lay his head."

²¹Another disciple said to him, "Lord, first let me go and bury my father."

²²But Jesus told him, "Follow me, and let the dead bury their own dead."

Jesus Calms the Storm
(87/Mark 4:35–41; Luke 8:22–25)

²³Then he got into the boat and his disciples followed him. ²⁴Without warning, a furious storm came up on the lake, so that the waves swept over the boat. But Jesus was sleeping. ²⁵The disciples went and woke him, saying, "Lord, save us! We're going to drown!"

²⁶He replied, "You of little faith, why are you so afraid?" Then he got up and rebuked the winds and the waves, and it was completely calm.^a

8:26
^aPs 65:7; 89:9; 107:29

²⁷The men were amazed and asked, "What kind of man is this? Even the winds and the waves obey him!"

g *17* Isaiah 53:4

8:14, 15 Peter's mother-in-law gives us a beautiful example to follow. Her response to Jesus' touch was to wait on Jesus and his disciples — immediately. Has God ever helped you through a dangerous or difficult situation? If so, you should ask, "How can I express my gratitude to him?" Because God has promised us all the rewards of his kingdom, we should look for ways to serve him and his followers now.

8:16, 17 Matthew continues to show Jesus' kingly nature. Through a single touch, Jesus healed (8:3, 15); when he spoke a single word, evil spirits fled his presence (8:16). Jesus has authority over all evil powers and all earthly disease. He also has power and authority to conquer sin. Sickness and evil are consequences of living in a fallen world. But in the future, when God removes all sin, there will be no more sickness and death. Jesus' healing miracles were a taste of what the whole world will one day experience in God's kingdom.

● **8:19, 20** Following Jesus is not always easy or comfortable. Often it means great cost and sacrifice, with no earthly rewards or security. Jesus didn't have a place to call home. You may find that following Christ costs you popularity, friendships, leisure time, or treasured habits. But while the cost of following Christ is high, the value of being Christ's disciple is even higher. Discipleship is an investment that lasts for eternity and yields incredible rewards.

● **8:21, 22** It is possible that this disciple was not asking permission to go to his father's funeral, but rather to put off following Jesus until his elderly father died. Perhaps he was the firstborn son and wanted to be sure to claim his inheritance. Perhaps he didn't want to face his father's wrath if he left the family business to follow an itinerant preacher. Whether his concern was financial security, family approval, or something else, he did not want to commit himself to Jesus just yet. Jesus, however, would not accept his excuse.

● **8:21, 22** Jesus was always direct with those who wanted to follow him. He made sure they counted the cost and set aside any conditions they might have for following him. As God's Son, Jesus did not hesitate to demand complete loyalty. Even family loyalty was not to take priority over the demands of obedience. His direct challenge forces us to ask ourselves about our own priorities in following him. The decision to follow Jesus should not be put off, even though other loyalties compete for our attention. Nothing should be placed above a total commitment to living for him.

8:23 This would have been a fishing boat because many of Jesus' disciples were fishermen. Josephus, an ancient historian, wrote that there were usually more than 300 fishing boats on the Sea of Galilee at one time. This boat was large enough to hold Jesus and his 12 disciples and was powered both by oars and sails. During a storm, however, the sails were taken down to keep them from ripping and to make the boat easier to control.

8:24 The Sea of Galilee is an unusual body of water. It is relatively small (13 miles long, 7 miles wide), but it is 150 feet deep, and the shoreline is 680 feet below sea level. Sudden storms can appear over the surrounding mountains with little warning, stirring the water into violent 20-foot waves. The disciples had not foolishly set out in a storm. They had been caught without warning, and their danger was great.

8:25 Although the disciples had witnessed many miracles, they panicked in this storm. As experienced sailors, they knew its danger; what they did not know was that Christ could control the forces of nature. There is often a stormy area of our human nature where we feel God can't or won't work. When we truly understand who God is, however, we will realize that he controls both the storms of nature and the storms of the troubled heart. Jesus' power that calmed this storm can also help us deal with the problems we face. Jesus is willing to help if we only ask him. We should never discount his power even in terrible trials.

Jesus Sends the Demons into a Herd of Pigs
(88/Mark 5:1–20; Luke 8:26–39)

28When he arrived at the other side in the region of the Gadarenes,ʰ two demon-possessed men coming from the tombs met him. They were so violent that no one could pass that way. 29"What do you want with us,ᵇ Son of God?" they shouted. "Have you come here to torture us before the appointed time?"

30Some distance from them a large herd of pigs was feeding. 31The demons begged Jesus, "If you drive us out, send us into the herd of pigs."

32He said to them, "Go!" So they came out and went into the pigs, and the whole herd rushed down the steep bank into the lake and died in the water. 33Those tending the pigs ran off, went into the town and reported all this, including what had happened to the demon-possessed men. 34Then the whole town went out to meet Jesus. And when they saw him, they pleaded with him to leave their region.ᶜ

Jesus Heals a Paralyzed Man
(39/Mark 2:1–12; Luke 5:17–26)

9 Jesus stepped into a boat, crossed over and came to his own town.ᵈ 2Some men brought to him a paralytic, lying on a mat. When Jesus saw their faith, he said to the paralytic, "Take heart, son; your sins are forgiven."

3At this, some of the teachers of the law said to themselves, "This fellow is blaspheming!"

4Knowing their thoughts,ᵉ Jesus said, "Why do you entertain evil thoughts in your hearts? 5Which is easier: to say, 'Your sins are forgiven,' or to say, 'Get up

8:29
ᵇ Jdg 11:12;
2Sa 16:10;
Mk 1:24;
Jn 2:4

8:34
ᶜ Lk 5:8;
Ac 16:39

9:1
ᵈ Mt 4:13

9:4
ᵉ Mt 12:25;
Lk 6:8; 9:47; 11:17

ʰ *28* Some manuscripts *Gergesenes*; others *Gerasenes*

8:28 The region of the Gadarenes is located southeast of the Sea of Galilee, near the town of Gadara, one of the most important cities of the region (see map). Gadara was a member of the Decapolis (see the note on Mark 5:20). These ten cities with independent governments were largely inhabited by Gentiles, which explains the herd of pigs (8:30). The Jews did not raise pigs because pigs were considered unclean and thus unfit to eat.

8:28 Demon-possessed people are under the control of one or more demons. Demons are fallen angels who joined Satan in his rebellion against God and are now evil spirits under Satan's control. They help Satan tempt people to sin and have great destructive powers. But whenever they are confronted by Jesus, they lose their power. These demons recognized Jesus as God's Son (8:29), but they didn't think they had to obey him. Just believing is not enough (see James 2:19 for a discussion of belief and devils). Faith is more than belief. By faith, you accept what Jesus has done for you, receive him as the only one who can save you from sin, and live out your faith by obeying his commands.

8:28 Matthew says there were two demon-possessed men, while Mark and Luke refer only to one. Apparently Mark and Luke mention only the man who did the talking.

8:28 According to Jewish ceremonial laws, the men Jesus encountered were unclean in three ways: they were Gentiles (non-Jews), they were demon-possessed, and they lived in a graveyard. Jesus helped them anyway. We should not turn our backs on people who are "unclean" or repulsive to us, or who violate our moral standards and religious beliefs. Instead, we must realize that every human individual is a unique creation of God, needing to be touched by his love.

8:29 The Bible tells us that at the end of the world the devil and his angels will be thrown into the lake of burning sulfur (Revelation 20:10). When the demons asked if Jesus had come to torment them "before the appointed time," they showed they knew their ultimate fate.

8:32 When the demons entered the pigs, they drove the animals into the sea. The demons' action proves their destructive intent — if they could not destroy the men, they would destroy the pigs. Jesus'

action, by contrast, shows the value he places on each human life.

8:34 Why did the people ask Jesus to leave? Unlike their own pagan gods, Jesus could not be contained, controlled, or appeased. They feared Jesus' supernatural power, a power that they had never before witnessed. And they were upset about losing a herd of pigs more than they were glad about the deliverance of the demon-possessed men. Are you more concerned about property and programs than people? Human beings are created in God's image and have eternal value. How foolish and yet how easy it is to value possessions, investments, and even animals above human life. Would you rather have Jesus leave you than finish his work in you?

9:1 "His own town" was Capernaum, a good choice for Jesus' base of operations. It was a wealthy city due to fishing and trade. Situated on the Sea of Galilee in a densely populated area, Capernaum housed the Roman garrison that kept peace in the region. The city was a cultural melting pot, greatly influenced by Greek and Roman manners, dress, architecture, and politics.

9:2 Among the first words Jesus said to the paralyzed man were "Your sins are forgiven." Then he healed the man. We must be careful not to concentrate on God's power to heal physical sickness more than on his power to forgive spiritual sickness in the form of sin. Jesus saw that even more than physical health, this man needed spiritual health. Spiritual health comes only from Jesus' healing touch.

9:2 Both the man's body and his spirit were paralyzed — he could not walk, and he did not know Jesus. But the man's spiritual state was Jesus' first concern. If God does not heal us or someone we love, we need to remember that physical healing is not Christ's only concern. We will all be completely healed in Christ's coming kingdom; but first we have to come to know Jesus.

9:3 Blaspheming is claiming to be God and applying his characteristics to yourself. The religious leaders rightly saw that Jesus was claiming to be God. What they did not understand was that he *is* God and thus has the authority to heal and to forgive sins.

9:5, 6 It's easy to tell someone his sins are forgiven; it's a lot more difficult to reverse a case of paralysis! Jesus backed up his words by healing the man's legs. Jesus' action showed that his

and walk'? 6But so that you may know that the Son of Man has authority on earth to forgive sins. . . ." Then he said to the paralytic, "Get up, take your mat and go home." 7And the man got up and went home. 8When the crowd saw this, they were filled with awe; and they praised God, *f* who had given such authority to men.

9:8
*f*Mt 5:16;
Ac 4:21

Jesus Eats with Sinners at Matthew's House
(40/Mark 2:13–17; Luke 5:27–32)

9As Jesus went on from there, he saw a man named Matthew sitting at the tax collector's booth. "Follow me," he told him, and Matthew got up and followed him.

More than any other disciple, Matthew had a clear idea of how much it would cost to follow Jesus, yet he did not hesitate a moment. When he left his tax-collecting booth, he guaranteed himself unemployment. For several of the other disciples, there was always fishing to return to, but for Matthew, there was no turning back.

Two changes happened to Matthew when he decided to follow Jesus. First, Jesus gave him a new life. He not only belonged to a new group; he belonged to the Son of God. He was not just accepting a different way of life; he was now an accepted person. For a despised tax collector, that change must have been wonderful! Second, Jesus gave Matthew a new purpose for his skills. When he followed Jesus, the only tool from his past job that he carried with him was his pen. From the beginning, God had made him a record-keeper. Jesus' call eventually allowed him to put his skills to their finest work. Matthew was a keen observer, and he undoubtedly recorded what he saw going on around him. The Gospel that bears his name came as a result.

Matthew's experience points out that each of us, from the beginning, is one of God's works in progress. Much of what God has for us he gives long before we are able to consciously respond to him. He trusts us with skills and abilities ahead of schedule. He has made us each capable of being his servant. When we trust him with what he has given us, we begin a life of real adventure. Matthew couldn't have known that God would use the very skills he had sharpened as a tax collector to record the greatest story ever lived. And God has no less meaningful a purpose for each one of us. Have you recognized Jesus saying to you, "Follow me"? What has been your response?

Strengths and accomplishments:
- Was one of Jesus' 12 disciples
- Responded immediately to Jesus' call
- Invited many friends to his home to meet Jesus
- Compiled the Gospel of Matthew
- Clarified for his Jewish audience Jesus' fulfillment of Old Testament prophecies

Lessons from his life:
- Jesus consistently accepted people from every level of society
- Matthew was given a new life, and his God-given skills of record-keeping and attention to detail were given new purpose
- Having been accepted by Jesus, Matthew immediately tried to bring others into contact with Jesus

Vital statistics:
- Where: Capernaum
- Occupations: Tax collector, disciple of Jesus
- Relative: Father: Alphaeus
- Contemporaries: Jesus, Pilate, Herod, other disciples

Key verse:
"As he walked along, he saw Levi son of Alphaeus sitting at the tax collector's booth. 'Follow me,' Jesus told him, and Levi got up and followed him" (Mark 2:14).

Matthew's story is told in the Gospels. He is also mentioned in Acts 1:13.

words were true; he had the power to forgive as well as to heal. Talk is cheap, but our words lack meaning if our actions do not back them up. We can say we love God or others, but if we are not taking practical steps to demonstrate that love, our words are empty and meaningless. How well do your actions back up what you say?

9:9 Matthew was a Jew who was appointed by the Romans to be the area's tax collector. He collected taxes from the citizens as well as from merchants passing through town. Tax collectors were expected to take a commission on the taxes they collected, but most of them overcharged and kept the profits. Thus, tax collectors were hated by the Jews because of their reputation for cheating and because of their support of Rome.

9:9 When Jesus called Matthew to be one of his disciples, Matthew got up and followed, leaving a lucrative career. When God calls you to follow or obey him, do you do it with as much abandon as Matthew? Sometimes the decision to follow Christ requires difficult or painful choices. Like Matthew, we must decide to leave behind those things that would keep us from following Christ.

10While Jesus was having dinner at Matthew's house, many tax collectors and "sinners" came and ate with him and his disciples. 11When the Pharisees saw this, they asked his disciples, "Why does your teacher eat with tax collectors and 'sinners'?"*g*

12On hearing this, Jesus said, "It is not the healthy who need a doctor, but the sick. 13But go and learn what this means: 'I desire mercy, not sacrifice.'*h* For I have not come to call the righteous, but sinners."*i*

Religious Leaders Ask Jesus about Fasting
(41/Mark 2:18–22; Luke 5:33–39)

14Then John's disciples came and asked him, "How is it that we and the Pharisees fast,*j* but your disciples do not fast?"

15Jesus answered, "How can the guests of the bridegroom mourn while he is with them?*k* The time will come when the bridegroom will be taken from them; then they will fast.*l*

16"No one sews a patch of unshrunk cloth on an old garment, for the patch will pull away from the garment, making the tear worse. 17Neither do men pour new wine into old wineskins. If they do, the skins will burst, the wine will run out and the wineskins will be ruined. No, they pour new wine into new wineskins, and both are preserved."

Jesus Heals a Bleeding Woman and Restores a Girl to Life
(89/Mark 5:21–43; Luke 8:40–56)

18While he was saying this, a ruler came and knelt before him and said, "My daughter has just died. But come and put your hand on her, and she will live." 19Jesus got up and went with him, and so did his disciples.

20Just then a woman who had been subject to bleeding for twelve years came up behind him and touched the edge of his cloak.*m* 21She said to herself, "If I only touch his cloak, I will be healed."

i 13 Hosea 6:6

9:11
g Mt 11:19

9:13
h Hos 6:6;
Mt 12:7
i 1Ti 1:15

9:14
j Lk 18:12

9:15
k Jn 3:29
l Ac 13:2, 3

9:20
m Mt 14:36

9:10-13 When he visited Matthew, Jesus hurt his own reputation. Matthew was cheating the people, but Jesus found and changed him. We should not be afraid to reach out to people who are living in sin — God's message can change anyone.

9:11, 12 The Pharisees constantly tried to trap Jesus, and they thought his association with these "lowlifes" was the perfect opportunity. They were more concerned with their own appearance of holiness than with helping people, with criticism than encouragement, with outward respectability than practical help. But God is concerned for all people, including the sinful and hurting ones. The Christian life is not a popularity contest! Following Jesus' example, we should share the gospel with the poor, immoral, lonely, and outcast, not just the rich, moral, popular, and powerful.

9:13 Those who are sure that they are righteous can't be saved because the first step in following Jesus is acknowledging our need and admitting that we don't have all the answers. For more on "I desire mercy, not sacrifice," see the chart in Hosea 7.

9:14 John's disciples fasted (went without food) as a sign of mourning for sin and to prepare for the Messiah's coming. Jesus' disciples did not need to fast because he is the Messiah and was with them! Jesus did not condemn fasting — he himself fasted (4:2). He emphasized that fasting must be done for the right reasons.

9:14 John the Baptist's message was harsh, and it focused on law. When people look at God's law and compare themselves to it, they realize how far they fall short and how badly they need to repent. Jesus' message focused on life, the result of turning from sin and turning to him. John's disciples had the right start, but they needed to take the next step and trust in Jesus. Where is your focus — on law or on Christ?

9:15 The arrival of the kingdom of heaven was like a wedding feast with Jesus as the bridegroom. His disciples, therefore, were filled with joy. It would not be right to mourn or fast when the bridegroom was present.

9:17 In Bible times, wine was not kept in glass bottles but in goatskins sewn around the edges to form watertight bags. New wine expanded as it fermented, stretching its wineskin. After the wine had aged, the stretched skin would burst if more new wine was poured into it. New wine, therefore, was always put into new wineskins.

9:17 Jesus did not come to patch up the old religious system of Judaism with its rules and traditions. If he had, his message would have damaged it. His purpose was to bring in something new, though it had been prophesied for centuries. This new message, the gospel, said that Jesus Christ, God's Son, came to earth to offer all people forgiveness of sins and reconciliation with God. The gospel did not fit into the old rigid legalistic system of religion. It needed a fresh start. The message will always remain "new" because it must be accepted and applied in every generation. When we follow Christ, we must be prepared for new ways to live, new ways to look at people, and new ways to serve.

9:18 Mark and Luke say this man's name was Jairus (Mark 5:22; Luke 8:41). As ruler of the synagogue, Jairus was responsible for administration — looking after the building, supervising worship, running the school on weekdays, and finding rabbis to teach on the Sabbath. For more information on synagogues, read the first note on Mark 1:21.

9:20-22 This woman had suffered for 12 years with bleeding (perhaps a menstrual disorder). In our times of desperation, we don't have to worry about the correct way to reach out to God. Like this woman, we can simply reach out in faith. He will respond.

9:22
nLk 7:50; 17:19;
18:42
oMt 15:28

9:23
p2Ch 35:25

9:24
qAc 20:10
rJn 11:11-14

9:27
sMt 15:22;
Mk 10:47

9:30
tMt 8:4

9:31
uMk 7:36

9:32
vMt 12:22-24

9:34
wMt 12:24

22Jesus turned and saw her. "Take heart, daughter," he said, "your faith has healed you."n And the woman was healed from that moment. o

23When Jesus entered the ruler's house and saw the flute players and the noisy crowd,p 24he said, "Go away. The girl is not deadq but asleep."r But they laughed at him. 25After the crowd had been put outside, he went in and took the girl by the hand, and she got up. 26News of this spread through all that region.

Jesus Heals the Blind and Mute
(90)

27As Jesus went on from there, two blind men followed him, calling out, "Have mercy on us, Son of David!"s

28When he had gone indoors, the blind men came to him, and he asked them, "Do you believe that I am able to do this?"

"Yes, Lord," they replied.

29Then he touched their eyes and said, "According to your faith will it be done to you"; 30and their sight was restored. Jesus warned them sternly, "See that no one knows about this."t 31But they went out and spread the news about him all over that region. u

32While they were going out, a man who was demon-possessed and could not talkv was brought to Jesus. 33And when the demon was driven out, the man who had been mute spoke. The crowd was amazed and said, "Nothing like this has ever been seen in Israel."

34But the Pharisees said, "It is by the prince of demons that he drives out demons."w

Jesus Urges the Disciples to Pray for Workers
(92)

35Jesus went through all the towns and villages, teaching in their synagogues, preaching the good news of the kingdom and healing every disease and sickness.

9:22 God changed a situation that had been a problem for years. Like the leper and the demon-possessed men (see the notes on 8:2, 3 and the second note on 8:28), this diseased woman was considered unclean. For 12 years, she too had been one of the "untouchables" and had not been able to lead a normal life. But Jesus changed that and restored her. Sometimes we are tempted to give up on people or situations that have not changed for many years. God can change what seems unchangeable, giving new purpose and hope.

9:23–26 The synagogue ruler didn't come to Jesus until his daughter was dead — it was too late for anyone else to help. But Jesus simply went to the girl and raised her! In our lives, Christ can make a difference when it seems too late for anyone else to help. He can bring healing to broken relationships, release from addicting habits, and forgiveness and healing to emotional scars. If your situation looks hopeless, remember that Christ can do the impossible.

9:27 "Son of David" was a popular way of addressing Jesus as the Messiah because it was known that the Messiah would be a descendant of David (Isaiah 9:7). This is the first time the title is used in Matthew. Jesus' ability to give sight to the blind was prophesied in Isaiah 29:18; 35:5; 42:7.

9:27–30 Jesus didn't respond immediately to the blind men's pleas. He waited to see if they had faith. Not everyone who says he wants help really believes God can help him. Jesus may have waited and questioned these men to emphasize and increase their faith. When you think that God is too slow in answering your prayers, consider that he might be testing you as he did the blind men. Do you believe that God can help you? Do you *really* want his help?

9:28 These blind men were persistent. They went right into the house where Jesus was staying. They knew Jesus could heal

them, and they would let nothing stop them from finding him. That's real faith in action. If you believe Jesus is the answer to your every need, don't let anything or anyone stop you from reaching him.

9:30 Jesus told the people to keep quiet about his healings because he did not want to be known only as a miracle worker. He healed because he had compassion on people, but he also wanted to bring *spiritual* healing to a sin-sick world.

9:32 While Jesus was on earth, demonic forces seemed especially active. Although we cannot always be sure why or how demon-possession occurs, it causes both physical and mental problems. In this case, the demon made the man unable to talk. For more on demons and demon-possession, read the notes on 8:28 and Mark 1:23.

9:34 In chapter 9, the Pharisees accuse Jesus of four different sins: blasphemy, befriending outcasts, impiety, and serving Satan. Matthew shows how Jesus was maligned by those who should have received him most gladly. Why did the Pharisees do this? (1) Jesus bypassed their religious authority. (2) He weakened their control over the people. (3) He challenged their cherished beliefs. (4) He exposed their insincere motives.

9:34 While the Pharisees questioned, debated, and dissected Jesus, people were being healed and lives changed right in front of them. Their skepticism was based not on insufficient evidence but on jealousy of Jesus' popularity.

9:35 The good news of the kingdom was that the promised and long-awaited Messiah had finally come. His healing miracles were a sign that his teaching was true.

9:35–38 Jesus needs workers who know how to deal with people's problems. We can comfort others and show them the way to live because we have been helped with our problems by God and his laborers (2 Corinthians 1:3–7).

36When he saw the crowds, he had compassion on them, because they were ha-
rassed and helpless, like sheep without a shepherd. 37Then he said to his disciples,
"The harvest is plentiful but the workers are few.ˣ 38Ask the Lord of the harvest,
therefore, to send out workers into his harvest field."

9:37
ˣLk 10:2

Jesus Sends Out the Twelve Disciples
(93/Mark 6:7–13; Luke 9:1–6)

10 He called his twelve disciples to him and gave them authority to drive out
evilʲ spiritsʸ and to heal every disease and sickness.

2These are the names of the twelve apostles: first, Simon (who is called Peter)
and his brother Andrew; James son of Zebedee, and his brother John; 3Philip and
Bartholomew; Thomas and Matthew the tax collector; James son of Alphaeus, and
Thaddaeus; 4Simon the Zealot and Judas Iscariot, who betrayed him.ᶻ

5These twelve Jesus sent out with the following instructions: "Do not go among
the Gentiles or enter any town of the Samaritans.ᵃ 6Go rather to the lost sheep of
Israel.ᵇ 7As you go, preach this message: 'The kingdom of heavenᶜ is near.'
8Heal the sick, raise the dead, cleanse those who have leprosy,ᵏ drive out demons.
Freely you have received, freely give. 9Do not take along any gold or silver or
copper in your belts; 10take no bag for the journey, or extra tunic, or sandals or a
staff; for the worker is worth his keep.ᵈ

11"Whatever town or village you enter, search for some worthy person there and
stay at his house until you leave. 12As you enter the home, give it your greeting.
13If the home is deserving, let your peace rest on it; if it is not, let your peace return
to you. 14If anyone will not welcome you or listen to your words, shake the dust off

10:1
ʸMk 3:13-15

10:4
ᶻJn 13:2, 26, 27

10:5
ᵃLk 9:52

10:6
ᵇMt 15:24

10:7
ᶜMt 3:2

10:10
ᵈ1Ti 5:18

ʲ1 Greek *unclean*   ᵏ8 The Greek word was used for various diseases affecting the skin—not necessarily leprosy.

9:36   Ezekiel also compared Israel to sheep without a shepherd
(Ezekiel 34:5, 6). Jesus came to be the Shepherd, the One who
could show people how to avoid life's pitfalls (see John 10:14).

9:37, 38   Jesus looked at the crowds following him and referred
to them as a field ripe for harvest. Many people are ready to give
their lives to Christ if someone would show them how. Jesus commands us to pray that people will respond to this need for workers.
Often, when we pray for something, God answers our prayers by
using *us*. Be prepared for God to use you to show another person
the way to him.

10:1   Jesus *called* his 12 disciples. He didn't draft them, force
them, or ask them to volunteer; he chose them to serve him in a
special way. Christ calls us today. He doesn't twist our arms and
make us do something we don't want to do. We can choose to join
him or remain behind. When Christ calls you to follow him, how do
you respond?

10:2–4   The list of Jesus' 12 disciples doesn't give us many
details—probably because there weren't many impressive details
to tell. Jesus called people from all walks of life—fishermen, political activists, tax collectors. He called common people and uncom-
mon leaders; rich and poor; educated and uneducated. Today,
many people think only certain people are fit to follow Christ, but
this was not the attitude of the Master himself. God can use anyone, no matter how insignificant he or she appears. When you feel
small and useless, remember that God uses ordinary people to do
his extraordinary work.

10:3   Bartholomew is probably another name for Nathanael,
whom we meet in John 1:45–51. Thaddaeus is also known as Judas son of James. The disciples are also listed in Mark 3:16–19;
Luke 6:14–16; and Acts 1:13.

10:4   Simon the Zealot may have been a member of the Zealots, a
radical political party working for the violent overthrow of Roman
rule in Israel.

10:5, 6   Why didn't Jesus send the disciples to the Gentiles or the
Samaritans? A Gentile is anyone who is not a Jew. The Samaritans
were a race that resulted from intermarriage between Jews and
Gentiles after the Old Testament captivities (see 2 Kings 17:24).

Jesus asked his disciples to go only to the Jews because he came
first to the Jews (Romans 1:16). God chose them to tell the rest of
the world about him. Jewish disciples and apostles preached the
gospel of the risen Christ all around the Roman empire, and soon
Gentiles were pouring into the church. The Bible clearly teaches
that God's message of salvation is for *all* people, regardless of
race, sex, or national origin (Genesis 12:3; Isaiah 25:6; 56:3–7;
Malachi 1:11; Acts 10:34, 35; Romans 3:29, 30; Galatians 3:28).

10:7   The Jews were waiting for the Messiah to usher in his kingdom. They hoped for a political and military kingdom that would
free them from Roman rule and bring back the days of glory under
David and Solomon. But Jesus was talking about a spiritual kingdom. The gospel today is that the kingdom is still *near*. Jesus, the
Messiah, has already begun his kingdom on earth in the hearts of
his followers. One day the kingdom will be fully realized. Then evil
will be destroyed and all people will live in peace with one another.

10:8   Jesus gave the disciples a principle to guide their actions
as they ministered to others: "Freely you have received, freely
give." Because God has showered us with his blessings, we
should give generously to others of our time, love, and possessions.

10:10   Jesus said that those who minister are to be cared for. The
disciples could expect food and shelter in return for the spiritual
service they provided. Who ministers to you? Make sure you take
care of the pastors, missionaries, and teachers who serve God by
serving you (see 1 Corinthians 9:9, 10; 1 Timothy 5:17).

10:10   Mark's account (6:8) says to take a staff (walking stick),
and Matthew and Luke (9:3) say not to. Jesus may have meant that
they were not to take an *extra* pair of sandals, staff, and bag. In
any case, the principle was that they were to go out ready for duty
and travel, unencumbered by excess material goods.

10:14   Why did Jesus tell his disciples to shake the dust off their
feet if a city or home didn't welcome them? When leaving Gentile
cities, pious Jews often shook the dust from their feet to show their
separation from Gentile practices. If the disciples shook the dust of
a *Jewish* town from their feet, it would show their separation from
Jews who rejected their Messiah. This gesture was to show the

10:14
eAc 13:51

10:15
fMt 11:22, 24

10:16
gLk 10:3

10:17
hMk 13:9

10:21
iMic 7:6

10:24
jJn 13:16

your feet e when you leave that home or town. 15I tell you the truth, it will be more bearable for Sodom and Gomorrah on the day of judgment than for that town. f 16I am sending you out like sheep among wolves. g Therefore be as shrewd as snakes and as innocent as doves.

Jesus Prepares the Disciples for Persecution
(94)

17"Be on your guard against men; they will hand you over to the local councils and flog you in their synagogues. h 18On my account you will be brought before governors and kings as witnesses to them and to the Gentiles. 19But when they arrest you, do not worry about what to say or how to say it. At that time you will be given what to say, 20for it will not be you speaking, but the Spirit of your Father speaking through you.

21"Brother will betray brother to death, and a father his child; children will rebel against their parents i and have them put to death. 22All men will hate you because of me, but he who stands firm to the end will be saved. 23When you are persecuted in one place, flee to another. I tell you the truth, you will not finish going through the cities of Israel before the Son of Man comes.

24"A student is not above his teacher, nor a servant above his master. j 25It is enough for the student to be like his teacher, and the servant like his master. If the

COUNTING THE COST OF FOLLOWING CHRIST Jesus helped his disciples prepare for the rejection many of them would experience by being Christians. Being God's person will usually create reactions from others who are resisting him.	Who may oppose us?	Natural response	Possible pressures		Needed truth
	GOVERNMENT 10:18–19		Threats 10:26	→	The truth will be revealed (10:26)
			Physical harm 10:28	→	Our soul cannot be harmed (10:28)
	RELIGIOUS PEOPLE 10:17	Fear and worry	Public ridicule 10:22	→	God himself will acknowledge us if we acknowledge him (10:32)
	FAMILY 10:21		Rejection by loved ones 10:34–37	→	God's love can sustain us (10:31)

people that they were making a wrong choice — that the opportunity to choose Christ might not present itself again. Are you receptive to teaching from God? If you ignore the Spirit's prompting, you may not get another chance.

10:15 The cities of Sodom and Gomorrah were destroyed by fire from heaven because of their wickedness (Genesis 19:24, 25). Those who reject the gospel when they hear it will be worse off than the wicked people of these destroyed cities, who never heard the gospel at all.

10:16 The opposition of the Pharisees would be like ravaging wolves. The disciples' only hope would be to look to their Shepherd for protection. We may face similar hostility. Like the disciples, we are not to be sheeplike in our attitude but sensible and prudent. We are not to be gullible pawns but neither are we to be deceitful connivers. We must find a balance between wisdom and vulnerability to accomplish God's work.

●**10:17, 18** Later the disciples experienced these hardships (Acts 5:40; 12:1–3), not only from without (governments, courts), but also from within (friends, family; 10:21). Living for God often brings on persecution, but with it comes the opportunity to tell the good news of salvation. In times of persecution, we can be confident because Jesus has "overcome the world" (John 16:33). And those who stand firm to the end will be saved (10:22).

●**10:19, 20** Jesus told the disciples that when arrested for preach-

ing the gospel, they should not worry about what to say in their defense — God's Spirit would speak through them. This promise was fulfilled in Acts 4:8–14 and elsewhere. Some mistakenly think this means we don't have to prepare to present the gospel because God will take care of everything. Scripture teaches, however, that we are to make carefully prepared, thoughtful statements (Colossians 4:6). Jesus is not telling us to stop preparing but to stop worrying.

●**10:22** Standing firm to the end is not a way to be saved but the evidence that a person is really committed to Jesus. Persistence is not a means to earn salvation; it is the by-product of a truly devoted life.

●**10:23** Christ warned the disciples against premature martyrdom. They were to leave before the persecution got too great. We have plenty of work to do and many people to reach. Our work won't be finished until Christ returns. And only after he returns will the whole world realize his true identity (see 24:14; Romans 14:9–12).

●**10:25** Beelzebub was also known as the lord of flies and the prince of demons. The Pharisees accused Jesus of using Beelzebub's power to drive out demons (see 12:24). Good is sometimes labeled evil. If Jesus, who is perfect, was called evil, his followers should expect that similar accusations will be directed at them. But those who stand firm will be vindicated (10:22).

head of the house has been called Beelzebub,[lk] how much more the members of his household!

26"So do not be afraid of them. There is nothing concealed that will not be disclosed, or hidden that will not be made known.[l] 27What I tell you in the dark, speak in the daylight; what is whispered in your ear, proclaim from the roofs. 28Do not be afraid of those who kill the body but cannot kill the soul. Rather, be afraid of the One[m] who can destroy both soul and body in hell. 29Are not two sparrows sold for a penny[m]? Yet not one of them will fall to the ground apart from the will of your Father. 30And even the very hairs of your head are all numbered.[n] 31So don't be afraid; you are worth more than many sparrows.

32"Whoever acknowledges me before men,[o] I will also acknowledge him before my Father in heaven. 33But whoever disowns me before men, I will disown him before my Father in heaven.

34"Do not suppose that I have come to bring peace to the earth. I did not come to bring peace, but a sword. 35For I have come to turn

> " 'a man against his father,
>   a daughter against her mother,
>   a daughter-in-law against her mother-in-law —
> 36   a man's enemies will be the members of his own
>   household.'[np]

37"Anyone who loves his father or mother more than me is not worthy of me; anyone who loves his son or daughter more than me is not worthy of me;[q] 38and anyone who does not take his cross and follow me is not worthy of me. 39Whoever finds his life will lose it, and whoever loses his life for my sake will find it.[r]

40"He who receives you receives me,[s] and he who receives me receives the one who sent me.[t] 41Anyone who receives a prophet because he is a prophet will receive a prophet's reward, and anyone who receives a righteous man because he is a righteous man will receive a righteous man's reward. 42And if anyone gives even a cup of cold water to one of these little ones because he is my disciple, I tell you the truth, he will certainly not lose his reward."[u]

l 25 Greek *Beezeboul* or *Beelzeboul*   m 29 Greek *an assarion*   n 36 Micah 7:6

10:25
k Mk 3:22

10:26
l Mk 4:22;
Lk 8:17

10:28
m Heb 10:31

10:30
n Lk 21:18;
Ac 27:34

10:32
o Ro 10:9

10:36
p Mic 7:6

10:37
q Lk 14:26

10:39
r Jn 12:25

10:40
s Gal 4:14
t Lk 9:48;
Jn 12:44

10:42
u Mt 25:40;
Heb 6:10

● **10:29-31** Jesus said that God is aware of everything that happens even to sparrows, and you are far more valuable to him than they are. You are so valuable that God sent his only Son to die for you (John 3:16). Because God places such value on you, you need never fear personal threats or difficult trials. These can't shake God's love or dislodge his Spirit from within you.

But this doesn't mean that God will take away all your troubles (see 10:16). The real test of value is how well something holds up under the wear, tear, and abuse of everyday life. Those who stand up for Christ in spite of their troubles truly have lasting value and will receive great rewards (see 5:11, 12).

● **10:34** Jesus did not come to bring the kind of peace that glosses over deep differences just for the sake of superficial harmony. Conflict and disagreement will arise between those who choose to follow Christ and those who don't. Yet we can look forward to the day when all conflict will be resolved. For more on Jesus as peacemaker, see Isaiah 9:6; Matthew 5:9; John 14:27.

● **10:34-39** Christian commitment may separate friends and loved ones. In saying this, Jesus was not encouraging disobedience to parents or conflict at home. Rather, he was showing that his presence demands a decision. Because some will follow Christ and some won't, conflict will inevitably arise. As we take our cross and follow him, our different values, morals, goals, and purposes will set us apart from others. Don't neglect your family, but remember that your commitment to God is even more important than they are. God should be your first priority.

● **10:37** Christ calls us to a higher mission than to find comfort and tranquility in this life. Love of family is a law of God, but even this love can be self-serving and used as an excuse not to serve God or do his work.

● **10:38** To take our cross and follow Jesus means to be willing to publicly identify with him, to experience almost certain opposition, and to be committed to face even suffering and death for his sake.

● **10:39** This verse is a positive and negative statement of the same truth: clinging to this life may cause us to forfeit the best from Christ in this world *and* in the next. The more we love this life's rewards (leisure, power, popularity, financial security), the more we will discover how empty they really are. The best way to enjoy life, therefore, is to loosen our greedy grasp on earthly rewards so that we can be free to follow Christ. In doing so, we will inherit eternal life and begin at once to experience the benefits of following Christ.

10:42 How much we love God can be measured by how well we treat others. Jesus' example of giving a cup of cold water to a thirsty child is a good model of unselfish service. A child usually can't or won't return a favor. God notices every good deed we do or don't do as if he were the one receiving it. Is there something unselfish you can do for someone else today? Although no one else may see you, God will notice.

4. Jesus teaches about the kingdom
Jesus Eases John's Doubt
(70/Luke 7:18–35)

11 After Jesus had finished instructing his twelve disciples, he went on from there to teach and preach in the towns of Galilee. o

2When John heard in prison v what Christ was doing, he sent his disciples 3to ask him, "Are you the one who was to come, or should we expect someone else?"

4Jesus replied, "Go back and report to John what you hear and see: 5The blind receive sight, the lame walk, those who have leprosy p are cured, the deaf hear, the dead are raised, and the good news is preached to the poor. w 6Blessed is the man who does not fall away on account of me."

7As John's x disciples were leaving, Jesus began to speak to the crowd about John: "What did you go out into the desert to see? A reed swayed by the wind? 8If not, what did you go out to see? A man dressed in fine clothes? No, those who wear fine clothes are in kings' palaces. 9Then what did you go out to see? A prophet? y Yes, I tell you, and more than a prophet. 10This is the one about whom it is written:

" 'I will send my messenger ahead of you,
who will prepare your way before you.' q z

11I tell you the truth: Among those born of women there has not risen anyone greater than John the Baptist; yet he who is least in the kingdom of heaven is greater than he. 12From the days of John the Baptist until now, the kingdom of heaven has been forcefully advancing, and forceful men lay hold of it. 13For all the Prophets and the Law prophesied until John. 14And if you are willing to accept it, he is the Elijah who was to come. a 15He who has ears, let him hear. b

16"To what can I compare this generation? They are like children sitting in the marketplaces and calling out to others:

17" 'We played the flute for you,
and you did not dance;
we sang a dirge,
and you did not mourn.'

18For John came neither eating nor drinking, and they say, 'He has a demon.' 19The Son of Man came eating and drinking, and they say, 'Here is a glutton and a drunkard, a friend of tax collectors and "sinners." ' c But wisdom is proved right by her actions."

o *1* Greek *in their towns* p *5* The Greek word was used for various diseases affecting the skin—not necessarily leprosy. q *10* Mal. 3:1

11:2
v Mt 14:3

11:5
w Isa 35:4-6; 61:1;
Lk 4:18, 19

11:7
x Mt 3:1

11:9
y Lk 1:76

11:10
z Mal 3:1;
Mk 1:2

11:14
a Mal 4:5;
Lk 1:17

11:15
b Mt 13:9, 43

11:19
c Mt 9:11

11:2, 3 John had been put in prison by Herod. Herod had married his own sister-in-law, and John publicly rebuked Herod's flagrant sin (14:3–5). John's Profile is found in John 1. Herod's Profile is found in Mark 6.

11:4–6 As John sat in prison, he began to have some doubts about whether Jesus really was the Messiah. If John's purpose was to prepare people for the coming Messiah (3:3), and if Jesus really was that Messiah, then why was John in prison when he could have been preaching to the crowds, preparing their hearts?

Jesus answered John's doubts by pointing to Jesus' acts of healing the blind, lame, and deaf, curing the lepers, raising the dead, and preaching the good news to the poor. With so much evidence, Jesus' identity was obvious. If you sometimes doubt your salvation, the forgiveness of your sins, or God's work in your life, look at the evidence in Scripture and the changes in your life. When you doubt, don't turn away from Christ; turn *to* him.

11:11 No man ever fulfilled his God-given purpose better than John. Yet in God's coming kingdom all members will have a greater spiritual heritage than John because they will have seen

and known Christ and his finished work on the cross.

11:12 There are three common views about the meaning of this verse. (1) Jesus may have been referring to a vast movement toward God, the momentum that began with John's preaching. (2) He may have been reflecting the Jewish activists' expectation that God's kingdom would come through a violent overthrow of Rome. (3) Or he may have meant that entering God's kingdom takes courage, unwavering faith, determination, and endurance because of the growing opposition leveled at Jesus' followers.

11:14 John was not a resurrected Elijah, but he took on Elijah's prophetic role—boldly confronting sin and pointing people to God (Malachi 3:1). See Elijah's Profile in 1 Kings 18.

11:16–19 Jesus condemned the attitude of his generation. No matter what he said or did, they took the opposite view. They were cynical and skeptical because he challenged their comfortable, secure, and self-centered lives. Too often we justify our inconsistencies because listening to God may require us to change the way we live.

Jesus Promises Rest for the Soul
(71)

20Then Jesus began to denounce the cities in which most of his miracles had been performed, because they did not repent. 21"Woe to you, Korazin! Woe to you, Bethsaida! If the miracles that were performed in you had been performed in Tyre and Sidon, they would have repented long ago in sackcloth and ashes. *d* 22But I tell you, it will be more bearable for Tyre and Sidon on the day of judgment than for you. *e* 23And you, Capernaum, will you be lifted up to the skies? No, you will go down to the depths. *rf* If the miracles that were performed in you had been performed in Sodom, it would have remained to this day. 24But I tell you that it will be more bearable for Sodom on the day of judgment than for you." *g*

25At that time Jesus said, "I praise you, Father, Lord of heaven and earth, because you have hidden these things from the wise and learned, and revealed them to little children. 26Yes, Father, for this was your good pleasure.

27"All things have been committed to me *h* by my Father. *i* No one knows the Son except the Father, and no one knows the Father except the Son and those to whom the Son chooses to reveal him.

28"Come to me, *j* all you who are weary and burdened, and I will give you rest. 29Take my yoke upon you and learn from me, *k* for I am gentle and humble in heart, and you will find rest for your souls. *l* 30For my yoke is easy and my burden is light."

The Disciples Pick Wheat on the Sabbath
(45/Mark 2:23–28; Luke 6:1–5)

12 At that time Jesus went through the grainfields on the Sabbath. His disciples were hungry and began to pick some heads of grain *m* and eat them. 2When the Pharisees saw this, they said to him, "Look! Your disciples are doing what is unlawful on the Sabbath." *n*

3He answered, "Haven't you read what David did when he and his companions were hungry? *o* 4He entered the house of God, and he and his companions ate the consecrated bread — which was not lawful for them to do, but only for the priests. 5Or haven't you read in the Law that on the Sabbath the priests in the temple dese-

r 23 Greek *Hades*

11:21
d Jnh 3:5-9

11:22
e ver 24;
Mt 10:15

11:23
f Isa 14:13-15

11:24
g Mt 10:15

11:27
h Mt 28:18
i Jn 3:35

11:28
j Jn 7:37

11:29
k Jn 13:15;
Php 2:5;
1Pe 2:21;
1Jn 2:6
l Jer 6:16

12:1
m Dt 23:25

12:2
n ver 10;
Lk 13:14; 14:3;
Jn 5:10; 9:16

12:3
o 1Sa 21:6

11:21-24 Tyre, Sidon, and Sodom were ancient cities with a long-standing reputation for wickedness (Genesis 18; 19; Ezekiel 27; 28). Each was destroyed by God for its evil. The people of Bethsaida, Korazin, and Capernaum saw Jesus firsthand, and yet they stubbornly refused to repent of their sins and believe in him. Jesus said that if some of the wickedest cities in the world had seen him, they would have repented. Because Bethsaida, Korazin, and Capernaum saw Jesus and didn't believe, they would suffer even greater punishment than that of the wicked cities who didn't see Jesus. Similarly, nations and cities with churches on every corner and Bibles in every home will have no excuse on judgment day if they do not repent and believe.

11:25 Jesus mentioned two kinds of people in his prayer: the "wise" — arrogant in their own knowledge — and the "little children" — humbly open to receive the truth of God's Word. Are you wise in your own eyes, or do you seek the truth in childlike faith, realizing that only God holds all the answers?

11:27 In the Old Testament, "know" means more than knowledge. It implies an intimate relationship. The communion between God the Father and God the Son is the core of their relationship. For anyone else to know God, God must reveal himself to that person, by the Son's choice. How fortunate we are that Jesus has clearly revealed to us God, his truth, and how we can know him.

11:28-30 A yoke is a heavy wooden harness that fits over the shoulders of an ox or oxen. It is attached to a piece of equipment the oxen are to pull. A person may be carrying heavy burdens of (1) sin, (2) excessive demands of religious leaders (23:4; Acts

15:10), (3) oppression and persecution, or (4) weariness in the search for God.

Jesus frees people from all these burdens. The rest that Jesus promises is love, healing, and peace with God, not the end of all labor. A relationship with God changes meaningless, wearisome toil into spiritual productivity and purpose.

12:1, 2 The Pharisees had established 39 categories of actions forbidden on the Sabbath, based on interpretations of God's law and on Jewish custom. Harvesting was one of those forbidden actions. By picking wheat and rubbing it in their hands, the disciples were technically harvesting, according to the religious leaders. Jesus and the disciples were picking grain because they were hungry, not because they wanted to harvest the grain for a profit. They were not working on the Sabbath. The Pharisees, however, could not (and did not want to) see beyond their law's technicalities. They had no room for compassion, and they were determined to accuse Jesus of wrongdoing.

12:4 This story is recorded in 1 Samuel 21:1–6. The bread of the Presence was replaced every week, and the old loaves were eaten by the priests. The loaves given to David were the old loaves that had just been replaced with fresh ones. Although the priests were the only ones allowed to eat this bread, God did not punish David because his need for food was more important than the priestly regulations. Jesus was saying, "If you condemn me, you must also condemn David," something the religious leaders could never do without causing a great uproar among the people. Jesus was not condoning disobedience to God's laws. Instead he was emphasizing discernment and compassion in enforcing the laws.

12:5
pNu 28:9, 10

12:7
qHos 6:6

crate the day p and yet are innocent? 6I tell you that one s greater than the temple is here. 7If you had known what these words mean, 'I desire mercy, not sacrifice,'t q you would not have condemned the innocent. 8For the Son of Man is Lord of the Sabbath."

Jesus Heals a Man's Hand on the Sabbath
(46/Mark 3:1–6; Luke 6:6–11)

9Going on from that place, he went into their synagogue, 10and a man with a shriveled hand was there. Looking for a reason to accuse Jesus, they asked him, "Is it lawful to heal on the Sabbath?"

11He said to them, "If any of you has a sheep and it falls into a pit on the Sabbath, will you not take hold of it and lift it out? 12How much more valuable is a man than a sheep! Therefore it is lawful to do good on the Sabbath."

13Then he said to the man, "Stretch out your hand." So he stretched it out and it was completely restored, just as sound as the other. 14But the Pharisees went out and plotted how they might kill Jesus. r

12:14
rMk 3:6;
Jn 11:53

Large Crowds Follow Jesus
(47/Mark 3:7–12)

15Aware of this, Jesus withdrew from that place. Many followed him, and he healed all their sick, 16warning them not to tell who he was. 17This was to fulfill what was spoken through the prophet Isaiah:

18"Here is my servant whom I have chosen,
        the one I love, in whom I delight; s

12:18
sMt 3:17

s 6 Or something; also in verses 41 and 42   t 7 Hosea 6:6

12:5 The Ten Commandments prohibit work on the Sabbath (Exodus 20:8–11). That was the *letter* of the law. But because the *purpose* of the Sabbath is to rest and to worship God, the priests were allowed to work by performing sacrifices and conducting worship services. This "Sabbath work" was serving and worshiping God. Jesus always emphasized the intent of the law, the meaning behind the letter. The Pharisees had lost the spirit of the law and were rigidly demanding that the letter (and their interpretation of it) be obeyed.

12:6 The Pharisees were so concerned about religious rituals that they missed the whole purpose of the temple — to bring people to God. And because Jesus Christ is even greater than the temple, how much better can he bring people to God. God is far more important than the created instruments of worship. If we become more concerned with the means of worship than with the One we worship, we will miss God even as we think we are worshiping him.

12:7 Jesus repeated to the Pharisees words the Jewish people had heard time and again throughout their history (1 Samuel 15:22, 23; Psalm 40:6–8; Isaiah 1:11–17; Jeremiah 7:21–23; Hosea 6:6). Our heart attitude toward God comes first. Only then can we properly obey and observe religious regulations and rituals.

12:8 When Jesus said he was Lord of the Sabbath, he claimed to be greater than the law and above the law. To the Pharisees, this was heresy. They did not realize that Jesus, the divine Son of God, had created the Sabbath. The Creator is always greater than the creation; thus Jesus had the authority to overrule their traditions and regulations.

12:9 For more information on synagogues, read the notes on Mark 1:21 and 5:22.

12:10 As they pointed to the man with the shriveled hand, the Pharisees tried to trick Jesus by asking him if it was legal to heal on the Sabbath. Their Sabbath rules said that people could be helped on the Sabbath only if their lives were in danger. Jesus healed on the Sabbath several times, and none of those healings were in response to emergencies. If Jesus had waited until another day, he would have been submitting to the Pharisees' authority,

showing that their petty rules were equal to God's law. If he healed the man on the Sabbath, the Pharisees could claim that because Jesus broke their rules, his power was not from God. But Jesus made it clear how ridiculous and petty their rules were. God is a God of people, not rules. The best time to reach out to someone is when he or she needs help.

12:10–12 The Pharisees placed their laws above human need. They were so concerned about Jesus' breaking one of their rules that they did not care about the man's shriveled hand. What is your attitude toward others? If your convictions don't allow you to help certain people, your convictions may not be in tune with God's Word. Don't allow dogma to blind you to human need.

12:14 The Pharisees plotted Jesus' death because they were outraged. Jesus had overruled their authority (Luke 6:11) and had exposed their evil attitudes in front of the entire crowd in the synagogue. Jesus had showed that the Pharisees were more loyal to their religious system than to God.

12:15 Up to this point, Jesus had been aggressively confronting the Pharisees' hypocrisy. Here he decided to withdraw from the synagogue before a major confrontation developed because it was not time for him to die. Jesus had many lessons still to teach his disciples and the people.

12:16 Jesus did not want those he healed to tell others about his miracles because he didn't want the people coming to him for the wrong reasons. That would hinder his teaching ministry and arouse false hopes about an earthly kingdom. But the news of Jesus' miracles spread, and many came to see for themselves (see Mark 3:7, 8).

12:17–21 The people expected the Messiah to be a king. This quotation from Isaiah's prophecy (Isaiah 42:1–4) showed that the Messiah was indeed a king, but it illustrated what *kind* of king — a quiet, gentle ruler who brings justice to the nations. Like the crowd in Jesus' day, we may want Christ to rule as a king and bring great and visible victories in our lives. But often Christ's work is quiet, and it happens according to *his* perfect timing, not ours.

I will put my Spirit on him,
    and he will proclaim justice to the nations.
¹⁹He will not quarrel or cry out;
    no one will hear his voice in the streets.
²⁰A bruised reed he will not break,
    and a smoldering wick he will not snuff out,
    till he leads justice to victory.
²¹ In his name the nations will put their hope."ᵘ

Religious Leaders Accuse Jesus of Being under Satan's Power
(74/Mark 3:20–30)

²²Then they brought him a demon-possessed man who was blind and mute, and Jesus healed him, so that he could both talk and see. ᵗ ²³All the people were astonished and said, "Could this be the Son of David?"

12:22
ᵗMt 4:24

²⁴But when the Pharisees heard this, they said, "It is only by Beelzebub,ᵛ the prince of demons, that this fellow drives out demons."ᵘ

12:24
ᵘMt 9:34

²⁵Jesus knew their thoughtsᵛ and said to them, "Every kingdom divided against itself will be ruined, and every city or household divided against itself will not stand. ²⁶If Satan drives out Satan, he is divided against himself. How then can his kingdom stand? ²⁷And if I drive out demons by Beelzebub, by whom do your peopleʷ drive them out? So then, they will be your judges. ²⁸But if I drive out demons by the Spirit of God, then the kingdom of God has come upon you.

12:25
ᵛMt 9:4

12:27
ʷAc 19:13

²⁹"Or again, how can anyone enter a strong man's house and carry off his possessions unless he first ties up the strong man? Then he can rob his house.

³⁰"He who is not with me is against me, and he who does not gather with me scatters. ³¹And so I tell you, every sin and blasphemy will be forgiven men, but the blasphemy against the Spirit will not be forgiven. ˣ ³²Anyone who speaks a word against the Son of Man will be forgiven, but anyone who speaks against the Holy Spirit will not be forgiven, either in this age or in the age to come.

12:31
ˣLk 12:10

³³"Make a tree good and its fruit will be good, or make a tree bad and its fruit will be bad, for a tree is recognized by its fruit. ʸ ³⁴You brood of vipers,ᶻ how can you who are evil say anything good? For out of the overflow of the heart the mouth speaks. ᵃ ³⁵The good man brings good things out of the good stored up in him, and the evil man brings evil things out of the evil stored up in him. ³⁶But I tell you that men will have to give account on the day of judgment for every careless word they

12:33
ʸMt 7:16, 17

12:34
ᶻMt 3:7; 23:33
ᵃLk 6:45

ᵘ 21 Isaiah 42:1-4 ᵛ 24 Greek *Beezeboul* or *Beelzeboul*; also in verse 27

12:24 The Pharisees had already accused Jesus of being in league with the prince of demons (9:34). They were trying to discredit him by using an emotional argument. Refusing to believe that Jesus came from God, they said he was in league with Satan. Jesus easily exposed the foolishness of their argument.

12:25 In the incarnation, Jesus gave up the complete and unlimited use of his supernatural abilities. But he still had profound insight into human nature. His discernment stopped the religious leaders' attempts to trick him. The resurrected Christ knows all our thoughts. This can be comforting because he knows what we really mean when we speak to him. It can be threatening because we cannot hide from him, and he knows our selfish motives.

12:29 At Jesus' birth, Satan's power and control were disrupted. In the desert Jesus overcame the devil's temptations, and at the resurrection he defeated Satan's ultimate weapon, death. Eventually Satan will be constrained forever (Revelation 20:10), and evil will no longer pervade the earth. Jesus has complete power and authority over Satan and all his forces.

12:30 It is impossible to be neutral about Christ. Anyone who is not actively following him has chosen to reject him. Any person who tries to remain neutral in the struggle of good against evil is choosing to be separated from God, who alone is good. To refuse to follow Christ is to choose to be on Satan's team.

12:31, 32 The Pharisees had blasphemed against the Spirit by attributing the power by which Christ did miracles to Satan (12:24) instead of the Holy Spirit. The unpardonable sin is the deliberate refusal to acknowledge God's power in Christ. It indicates a deliberate and irreversible hardness of heart. Sometimes believers worry that they have accidentally committed this unforgivable sin. But only those who have turned their backs on God and rejected all faith have any need to worry. Jesus said they can't be forgiven — not because their sin is worse than any other, but because they will never ask for forgiveness. Whoever rejects the prompting of the Holy Spirit removes himself or herself from the only force that can lead him or her to repentance and restoration to God.

12:34-36 Jesus reminds us that what we say reveals what is in our hearts. What kinds of words come from your mouth? That is an indication of what your heart is really like. You can't solve your heart problem, however, just by cleaning up your speech. You must allow the Holy Spirit to fill you with new attitudes and motives; then your speech will be cleansed at its source.

have spoken. 37For by your words you will be acquitted, and by your words you will be condemned."

Religious Leaders Ask Jesus for a Miracle
(75)

12:38
b Mt 16:1;
Mk 8:11, 12;
Jn 2:18;
1Co 1:22

38Then some of the Pharisees and teachers of the law said to him, "Teacher, we want to see a miraculous sign from you."*b*

12:39
c Mt 16:4

39He answered, "A wicked and adulterous generation asks for a miraculous sign! But none will be given it except the sign of the prophet Jonah. *c* 40For as Jonah was three days and three nights in the belly of a huge fish, *d* so the Son of Man will be

12:40
d Jnh 1:17

three days and three nights in the heart of the earth. 41The men of Nineveh will stand up at the judgment with this generation and condemn it; for they repented at

12:41
e Jnh 3:5

the preaching of Jonah, *e* and now one*w* greater than Jonah is here. 42The Queen of the South will rise at the judgment with this generation and condemn it; for she

12:42
f 1Ki 10:1;
2Ch 9:1

came*f* from the ends of the earth to listen to Solomon's wisdom, and now one greater than Solomon is here.

43"When an evil*x* spirit comes out of a man, it goes through arid places seeking rest and does not find it. 44Then it says, 'I will return to the house I left.' When it arrives, it finds the house unoccupied, swept clean and put in order. 45Then it goes and takes with it seven other spirits more wicked than itself, and they go in and live

12:45
g 2Pe 2:20

there. And the final condition of that man is worse than the first. *g* That is how it will be with this wicked generation."

Jesus Describes His True Family
(76/Mark 3:31–35; Luke 8:19–21)

12:46
h Mt 13:55;
Jn 2:12; 7:3, 5;
Ac 1:14;
1Co 9:5;
Gal 1:19

46While Jesus was still talking to the crowd, his mother and brothers*h* stood outside, wanting to speak to him. 47Someone told him, "Your mother and brothers are standing outside, wanting to speak to you."*y*

48He replied to him, "Who is my mother, and who are my brothers?" 49Pointing to his disciples, he said, "Here are my mother and my brothers. 50For whoever does the will of my Father in heaven is my brother and sister and mother."

w 41 Or *something*; also in verse 42   **x** 43 Greek *unclean*   **y** 47 Some manuscripts do not have verse 47.

12:38–40 The Pharisees were asking for another miraculous sign, but they were not sincerely seeking to know Jesus. Jesus knew they had already seen enough miraculous proof to convince them that he was the Messiah if they would just open their hearts. But they had already decided not to believe in him, and more miracles would not change that.

Many people have said, "If I could just see a real miracle, then I could really believe in God." But Jesus' response to the Pharisees applies to us. We have plenty of evidence — Jesus' birth, death, resurrection, and ascension, and centuries of his work in believers around the world. Instead of looking for additional evidence or miracles, accept what God has already given and move forward. He may use your life as evidence to reach another person.

12:39–41 Jonah was a prophet sent to the Assyrian city of Nineveh (see the book of Jonah). Because Assyria was such a cruel and warlike nation, Jonah tried to run from his assignment and ended up spending three days in the belly of a huge fish. When Jonah got out, he grudgingly went to Nineveh, preached God's message, and saw the city repent. By contrast, when Jesus came to his people, they refused to repent. Here Jesus is clearly saying that his resurrection will prove he is the Messiah. Three days after his death Jesus will come back to life, just as Jonah was given a new chance at life after three days in the fish.

12:41, 42 In Jonah's day, Nineveh was the capital of the Assyrian empire, and it was as powerful as it was evil (Jonah 1:2). But the entire city repented at Jonah's preaching. The Queen of the

South traveled far to see Solomon, king of Israel, and learn about his great wisdom (1 Kings 10:1–10; also see the note on Luke 11:31, 32 for more on the Queen of Sheba). These Gentiles recognized the truth about God when it was presented to them, unlike the religious leaders who ignored the truth even though it stared them in the face. How have you responded to the evidence and truth that you have?

12:43–45 Jesus was describing the attitude of the nation of Israel and the religious leaders in particular. Just cleaning up one's life without filling it with God leaves plenty of room for Satan to enter. The book of Ezra records how the people rid themselves of idolatry, but failed to replace it with love for God and obedience to him. Ridding our lives of sin is the first step. We must also take the second step: filling our lives with God's Word and the Holy Spirit. Unfilled and complacent people are easy targets for Satan.

12:46–50 Jesus was not denying his responsibility to his earthly family. On the contrary, he criticized the religious leaders for not following the Old Testament command to honor their parents (15:1–9). He provided for his mother's security as he hung on the cross (John 19:25–27). His mother and brothers were present in the upper room at Pentecost (Acts 1:14). Instead Jesus was pointing out that spiritual relationships are as binding as physical ones, and he was paving the way for a new community of believers (the universal church), our spiritual family.

Jesus Tells the Parable of the Four Soils
(77/Mark 4:1–9; Luke 8:4–8)

13 That same day Jesus went out of the house and sat by the lake. 2Such large crowds gathered around him that he got into a boat[i] and sat in it, while all the people stood on the shore. 3Then he told them many things in parables, saying: "A farmer went out to sow his seed. 4As he was scattering the seed, some fell along the path, and the birds came and ate it up. 5Some fell on rocky places, where it did not have much soil. It sprang up quickly, because the soil was shallow. 6But when the sun came up, the plants were scorched, and they withered because they had no root. 7Other seed fell among thorns, which grew up and choked the plants. 8Still other seed fell on good soil, where it produced a crop — a hundred,[j] sixty or thirty times what was sown. 9He who has ears, let him hear."[k]

13:2
[i] Lk 5:3

13:8
[j] Ge 26:12

13:9
[k] Mt 11:15

Jesus Explains the Parable of the Four Soils
(78/Mark 4:10–25; Luke 8:9–18)

10The disciples came to him and asked, "Why do you speak to the people in parables?"

11He replied, "The knowledge of the secrets of the kingdom of heaven has been given to you,[l] but not to them. 12Whoever has will be given more, and he will have an abundance. Whoever does not have, even what he has will be taken from him.[m] 13This is why I speak to them in parables:

13:11
[l] 1Co 2:10, 14;
1Jn 2:20, 27

13:12
[m] Mt 25:29

"Though seeing, they do not see;
   though hearing, they do not hear or understand.

14In them is fulfilled the prophecy of Isaiah:

   " 'You will be ever hearing but never understanding;
      you will be ever seeing but never perceiving.
   15For this people's heart has become calloused;
      they hardly hear with their ears,
      and they have closed their eyes.
   Otherwise they might see with their eyes,
      hear with their ears,
      understand with their hearts
   and turn, and I would heal them.'[z][n]

13:15
[n] Isa 6:9, 10;
Jn 12:40;
Ac 28:26, 27

16But blessed are your eyes because they see, and your ears because they hear.[o] 17For I tell you the truth, many prophets and righteous men longed to see what you see[p] but did not see it, and to hear what you hear but did not hear it.

18"Listen then to what the parable of the sower means: 19When anyone hears the message about the kingdom[q] and does not understand it, the evil one comes and snatches away what was sown in his heart. This is the seed sown along the path.

[z] 15 Isaiah 6:9,10

13:16
[o] Mt 16:17

13:17
[p] Heb 11:13;
1Pe 1:10-12

13:19
[q] Mt 4:23

●**13:2, 3** Jesus used many illustrations, or *parables*, when speaking to the crowds. A parable compares something familiar to something unfamiliar. It helps us understand spiritual truth by using everyday objects and relationships. Parables compel listeners to discover truth, while at the same time concealing the truth from those too lazy or too stubborn to see it. To those who are honestly searching, the truth becomes clear. We must be careful not to read too much into parables, forcing them to say what they don't mean. All parables have one meaning unless otherwise specified by Jesus.

●**13:8** This parable should encourage spiritual "sowers" — those who teach, preach, and lead others. The farmer sowed good seed, but not all the seed sprouted, and even the plants that grew had varying yields. Don't be discouraged if you do not always see results as you faithfully teach the Word. Belief cannot be forced to follow a mathematical formula (i.e., a 4:1 ratio of seeds planted to

seeds sprouted). Rather, it is a miracle of God's Holy Spirit as he uses your words to lead others to him.

●**13:9** Human ears hear many sounds, but there is a deeper kind of listening that results in spiritual understanding. If you honestly seek God's will, you have spiritual hearing, and these parables will give you new perspectives.

●**13:10** When speaking in parables, Jesus was not hiding truth from sincere seekers, because those who were receptive to spiritual truth understood the illustrations. To others they were only stories without meaning. This allowed Jesus to give spiritual food to those who hungered for it while preventing his enemies from trapping him sooner than they might otherwise have done.

13:12 This phrase means that we are responsible to use well what we have. When people reject Jesus, their hardness of heart drives away or renders useless even the little understanding they had.

20The one who received the seed that fell on rocky places is the man who hears the word and at once receives it with joy. 21But since he has no root, he lasts only a short time. When trouble or persecution comes because of the word, he quickly falls away. *r* 22The one who received the seed that fell among the thorns is the man who hears the word, but the worries of this life and the deceitfulness of wealth*s* choke it, making it unfruitful. 23But the one who received the seed that fell on good soil is the man who hears the word and understands it. He produces a crop, yielding a hundred, sixty or thirty times what was sown."

13:21
r Mt 11:6
13:22
s Mt 19:23;
1Ti 6:9, 10, 17

Jesus Tells the Parable of the Weeds
(80)

24Jesus told them another parable: "The kingdom of heaven is like a man who sowed good seed in his field. 25But while everyone was sleeping, his enemy came and sowed weeds among the wheat, and went away. 26When the wheat sprouted and formed heads, then the weeds also appeared.

27"The owner's servants came to him and said, 'Sir, didn't you sow good seed in your field? Where then did the weeds come from?'

28" 'An enemy did this,' he replied.

"The servants asked him, 'Do you want us to go and pull them up?'

29" 'No,' he answered, 'because while you are pulling the weeds, you may root up the wheat with them. 30Let both grow together until the harvest. At that time I will tell the harvesters: First collect the weeds and tie them in bundles to be burned; then gather the wheat and bring it into my barn.' "*t*

13:30
t Mt 3:12

Jesus Tells the Parable of the Mustard Seed
(81/Mark 4:30–34)

31He told them another parable: "The kingdom of heaven is like a mustard seed, which a man took and planted in his field. 32Though it is the smallest of all your seeds, yet when it grows, it is the largest of garden plants and becomes a tree, so that the birds of the air come and perch in its branches."*u*

13:32
u Ps 104:12;
Eze 17:23;
Da 4:12

Jesus Tells the Parable of the Yeast
(82)

33He told them still another parable: "The kingdom of heaven is like yeast that a woman took and mixed into a large amount*a* of flour*v* until it worked all through the dough."

34Jesus spoke all these things to the crowd in parables; he did not say anything to them without using a parable. 35So was fulfilled what was spoken through the prophet:

13:33
v Ge 18:6

a 33 Greek *three satas* (probably about 1/2 bushel or 22 liters)

● **13:22** How easy it is to agree with Christ with no intention of obeying. It is easy to denounce worries of this life and the deceitfulness of wealth, and still do nothing to change our ways. In light of eternal life with God, are your present worries justified? If you had everything you could want but forfeited eternal life with God, would those things be so desirable?

● **13:23** The four types of soil represent different responses to God's message. People respond differently because they are in different states of readiness. Some are hardened, others are shallow, others are contaminated by distracting worries, and some are receptive. How has God's Word taken root in your life? What kind of soil are you?

13:24ff Jesus gives the meaning of this parable in verses 36–43. All the parables in this chapter teach us about God and his kingdom. They explain what the kingdom is really like as opposed to our expectations of it. The kingdom of heaven is not a geographic location, but a spiritual realm where God rules and where we share in his eternal life. We join that kingdom when we trust in Christ as Savior.

13:30 The young weeds and the young blades of wheat look the same and can't be distinguished until they are grown and ready for harvest. Weeds (unbelievers) and wheat (believers) must live side by side in this world. God allows unbelievers to remain for a while, just as a farmer allows weeds to remain in his field so the surrounding wheat isn't uprooted with them. At the harvest, however, the weeds will be uprooted and thrown away. God's harvest (judgment) of all people is coming. We are to make ourselves ready by making sure that our faith is sincere.

13:31, 32 The mustard seed was the smallest seed a farmer used. Jesus used this parable to show that the kingdom has small beginnings but will grow and produce great results.

13:33 In other Bible passages, yeast is used as a symbol of evil or uncleanness. Here it is a positive symbol of growth. Although yeast looks like a minor ingredient, it permeates the whole loaf. Although the kingdom began small and was nearly invisible, it would soon grow and have a great impact on the world.

> "I will open my mouth in parables,
> I will utter things hidden since the creation of the world."ᵇʷ

13:35
wPs 78:2;
1Co 2:7

Jesus Explains the Parable of the Weeds
(83)

36Then he left the crowd and went into the house. His disciples came to him and said, "Explain to us the parable of the weeds in the field."

37He answered, "The one who sowed the good seed is the Son of Man. 38The field is the world, and the good seed stands for the sons of the kingdom. The weeds are the sons of the evil one,ˣ 39and the enemy who sows them is the devil. The harvest is the end of the age,ʸ and the harvesters are angels.

13:38
xJn 8:44, 45
13:39
yMt 24:3

40"As the weeds are pulled up and burned in the fire, so it will be at the end of the age. 41The Son of Man will send out his angels, and they will weed out of his kingdom everything that causes sin and all who do evil. 42They will throw them into the fiery furnace, where there will be weeping and gnashing of teeth.ᶻ 43Then the righteous will shine like the sunᵃ in the kingdom of their Father. He who has ears, let him hear.

13:42
zMt 8:12
13:43
aDa 12:3

Jesus Tells the Parable of Hidden Treasure
(84)

44"The kingdom of heaven is like treasure hidden in a field. When a man found it, he hid it again, and then in his joy went and sold all he had and bought that field.ᵇ

13:44
bIsa 55:1;
Php 3:7, 8

Jesus Tells the Parable of the Pearl Merchant
(85)

45"Again, the kingdom of heaven is like a merchant looking for fine pearls. 46When he found one of great value, he went away and sold everything he had and bought it.

Jesus Tells the Parable of the Fishing Net
(86)

47"Once again, the kingdom of heaven is like a net that was let down into the lake and caught all kindsᶜ of fish. 48When it was full, the fishermen pulled it up on the shore. Then they sat down and collected the good fish in baskets, but threw the bad away. 49This is how it will be at the end of the age. The angels will come and separate the wicked from the righteousᵈ 50and throw them into the fiery furnace, where there will be weeping and gnashing of teeth.

13:47
cMt 22:10
13:49
dMt 25:32

51"Have you understood all these things?" Jesus asked.

"Yes," they replied.

52He said to them, "Therefore every teacher of the law who has been instructed

b 35 Psalm 78:2

13:40-43 At the end of the world, angels will separate the evil from the good. There are true and false believers in churches today, but we should be cautious in our judgments because only Christ is qualified to make the final separation. If you start judging, you may damage some of the good "plants." It's more important to judge our own response to God than to analyze others' responses.

13:42 Jesus often uses these terms to refer to the coming judgment. The weeping indicates sorrow or remorse, and gnashing of teeth shows extreme anxiety or pain. Those who say they don't care what happens to them after they die don't realize what they are saying. They will be punished for living in selfishness and indifference to God.

13:43 Those who receive God's favor stand in bright contrast to those who receive his judgment. A similiar illustration is used in Daniel 12:3.

13:44-46 The kingdom of heaven is more valuable than anything else we can have, and a person must be willing to give up everything to obtain it. The man who discovered the treasure in the field stumbled upon it by accident but knew its value when he found it. The merchant was earnestly searching for the pearl of great value, and, when he found it, he sold everything he had to purchase it.

13:47-49 The parable of the fishing net has the same meaning as the parable of the wheat and weeds. We are to obey God and tell others about his grace and goodness, but we cannot dictate who is part of the kingdom of heaven and who is not. This sorting will be done at the last judgment by those infinitely more qualified than we.

13:52 Anyone who understands God's real purpose in the law as revealed in the Old Testament has a real treasure. The Old Testament points the way to Jesus, the Messiah. Jesus always upheld its authority and relevance. But there is a double benefit to those who understand Jesus' teaching about the kingdom of heaven.

about the kingdom of heaven is like the owner of a house who brings out of his storeroom new treasures as well as old."

5. Jesus encounters differing reactions to his ministry

The People of Nazareth Refuse to Believe
(91/Mark 6:1–6)

13:53
e Mt 7:28

13:54
f Mt 4:23
g Mt 7:28

13:55
h Jn 6:42
i Mt 12:46

13:57
j Jn 4:44

53When Jesus had finished these parables, *e* he moved on from there. 54Coming to his hometown, he began teaching the people in their synagogue, *f* and they were amazed. *g* "Where did this man get this wisdom and these miraculous powers?" they asked. 55"Isn't this the carpenter's son? *h* Isn't his mother's *i* name Mary, and aren't his brothers James, Joseph, Simon and Judas? 56Aren't all his sisters with us? Where then did this man get all these things?" 57And they took offense at him.

But Jesus said to them, "Only in his hometown and in his own house is a prophet without honor." *j*

58And he did not do many miracles there because of their lack of faith.

Herod Kills John the Baptist
(95/Mark 6:14–29; Luke 9:7–9)

14:1
k Mk 8:15;
Ac 4:27
l Lk 9:7-9

14 At that time Herod *k* the tetrarch heard the reports about Jesus, *l* 2and he said to his attendants, "This is John the Baptist; he has risen from the dead! That is why miraculous powers are at work in him."

14:3
m Lk 3:19, 20

14:4
n Lev 18:16; 20:21

3Now Herod had arrested John and bound him and put him in prison because of Herodias, his brother Philip's wife, *m* 4for John had been saying to him: "It is not lawful for you to have her." *n* 5Herod wanted to kill John, but he was afraid of the people, because they considered him a prophet.

6On Herod's birthday the daughter of Herodias danced for them and pleased Herod so much 7that he promised with an oath to give her whatever she asked. 8Prompted by her mother, she said, "Give me here on a platter the head of John the

---

This was a new treasure that Jesus was revealing. Both the old and new teaching give practical guidelines for faith and for living in the world. The religious leaders, however, were trapped in the old and blind to the new. They were looking for a future kingdom *preceded* by judgment. Jesus, however, taught that the kingdom was *now* and the judgment was future. The religious leaders were looking for a physical and temporal kingdom (via military rebellion and physical rule), but they were blind to the spiritual significance of the kingdom that Christ brought.

13:55 The residents of Jesus' hometown had known Jesus since he was a young child and were acquainted with his family; they could not bring themselves to believe in his message. They were too close to the situation. Jesus had come to them as a prophet, one who challenged them to respond to unpopular spiritual truth. They did not listen to the timeless message because they could not see beyond the man.

13:57 Jesus was not the first prophet to be rejected in his own country. Jeremiah experienced rejection in his hometown, even by members of his own family (Jeremiah 12:5, 6).

13:58 Jesus did few miracles in his hometown "because of their lack of faith." Lack of faith blinds people to the truth and robs them of hope. These people missed the Messiah. How does your faith measure up? If you can't see God's work, perhaps it is because of your unbelief. Believe, ask God for a mighty work in your life, and expect him to act. Look with the eyes of faith.

14:1 Herod was a tetrarch — one of four rulers over the four districts of Palestine. His territory included the regions of Galilee and Perea. He was the son of Herod the Great, who ordered the killing of the babies in Bethlehem (2:16). Also known as Herod Antipas, he heard Jesus' case before Jesus' crucifixion (Luke 23:6–12). His Profile is found in Mark 6.

NAZARETH REJECTS JESUS
Chronologically, this return to Nazareth occurred after Jesus was in the Gadarene region and healed the demon-possessed men (8:28–34), then recrossed the sea to Capernaum. From there he traveled to Nazareth, where he had grown up, only to discover that the people refused to believe he was the Christ.

14:2 For more information on John the Baptist, see his Profile in John 1.

14:3 Philip, Herod's half brother, was another of Palestine's four rulers. His territories were Iturea and Traconitis, northeast of the Sea of Galilee (Luke 3:1). Philip's wife, Herodias, left Philip to live with Herod Antipas. John the Baptist condemned the two for living immorally (see Mark 6:17, 18).

Baptist." 9The king was distressed, but because of his oaths and his dinner guests, he ordered that her request be granted 10and had John beheaded in the prison. 11His head was brought in on a platter and given to the girl, who carried it to her mother. 12John's disciples came and took his body and buried it. Then they went and told Jesus.

Jesus Feeds Five Thousand
(96/Mark 6:30–44; Luke 9:10–17; John 6:1–15)

13When Jesus heard what had happened, he withdrew by boat privately to a solitary place. Hearing of this, the crowds followed him on foot from the towns. 14When Jesus landed and saw a large crowd, he had compassion on them° and healed their sick.

15As evening approached, the disciples came to him and said, "This is a remote place, and it's already getting late. Send the crowds away, so they can go to the villages and buy themselves some food."

16Jesus replied, "They do not need to go away. You give them something to eat."

17"We have here only five loavesᵖ of bread and two fish," they answered.

18"Bring them here to me," he said. 19And he directed the people to sit down on the grass. Taking the five loaves and the two fish and looking up to heaven, he gave thanks and broke the loaves. �q Then he gave them to the disciples, and the disciples gave them to the people. 20They all ate and were satisfied, and the disciples picked up twelve basketfuls of broken pieces that were left over. 21The number of those who ate was about five thousand men, besides women and children.

Jesus Walks on Water
(97/Mark 6:45–52; John 6:16–21)

22Immediately Jesus made the disciples get into the boat and go on ahead of him to the other side, while he dismissed the crowd. 23After he had dismissed them, he went up on a mountainside by himself to pray. When evening came, he was there

14:14
°Mt 9:36

14:17
ᵖMt 16:9

14:19
q1Sa 9:13;
Lk 24:30

14:9 Herod did not want to kill John the Baptist, but he gave the order so that he wouldn't be embarrassing in front of his guests. How easy it is to give in to the crowd and to let ourselves be pressured into doing wrong. Don't get in a situation where it will be too embarrassing to do what is right. Determine to do what is right, no matter how embarrassing or painful it may be.

14:13, 14 Jesus sought solitude after the news of John's death. Sometimes we may need to deal with our grief alone. Jesus did not dwell on his grief, but returned to the ministry he came to do.

●**14:14** Jesus performed some miracles as signs of his identity. He used other miracles to teach important truths. But here we read that he healed people because he "had compassion on them." Jesus was, and is, a loving, caring, and feeling person. When you are suffering, remember that Jesus hurts with you. He has compassion on you.

●**14:19–21** Jesus multiplied five loaves and two fish to feed over 5,000 people. What he was originally given seemed insufficient, but in his hands it became more than enough. We often feel that our contribution to Jesus is meager, but he can use and multiply whatever we give him, whether it is talent, time, or treasure. It is when we give them to Jesus that our resources are multiplied.

●**14:21** The text states that there were 5,000 men present, *besides* women and children. Therefore, the total number of people Jesus fed could have been 10 to 15 thousand. The number of men is listed separately because in the Jewish culture of the day, men and women usually ate separately when in public. The children ate with the women.

14:23 Seeking solitude was an important priority for Jesus (see also 14:13). He made room in his busy schedule to be alone with the Father. Spending time with God in prayer nurtures a vital relationship and equips us to meet life's challenges and struggles. Develop the discipline of spending time alone with God — it will help you grow spiritually and become more and more like Christ.

JESUS WALKS ON THE SEA
The miraculous feeding of the 5,000 occurred on the shores of the Sea of Galilee near Bethsaida. Jesus then sent his disciples across the lake. Several hours later they encountered a storm, and Jesus came to them— walking on the water. The boat then landed at Gennesaret.

alone, 24but the boat was already a considerable distance[c] from land, buffeted by the waves because the wind was against it.

25During the fourth watch of the night Jesus went out to them, walking on the lake. 26When the disciples saw him walking on the lake, they were terrified. "It's a ghost,"[r] they said, and cried out in fear.

27But Jesus immediately said to them: "Take courage![s] It is I. Don't be afraid."[t]

28"Lord, if it's you," Peter replied, "tell me to come to you on the water."

29"Come," he said.

Then Peter got down out of the boat, walked on the water and came toward Jesus. 30But when he saw the wind, he was afraid and, beginning to sink, cried out, "Lord, save me!"

31Immediately Jesus reached out his hand and caught him. "You of little faith,"[u] he said, "why did you doubt?"

32And when they climbed into the boat, the wind died down. 33Then those who were in the boat worshiped him, saying, "Truly you are the Son of God."[v]

Jesus Heals All Who Touch Him
(98/Mark 6:53–56)

34When they had crossed over, they landed at Gennesaret. 35And when the men of that place recognized Jesus, they sent word to all the surrounding country. People brought all their sick to him 36and begged him to let the sick just touch the edge of his cloak,[w] and all who touched him were healed.

Jesus Teaches about Inner Purity
(102/Mark 7:1–23)

15 Then some Pharisees and teachers of the law came to Jesus from Jerusalem and asked, 2"Why do your disciples break the tradition of the elders? They don't wash their hands before they eat!"[x]

c 24 Greek *many stadia*

14:26 [r]Lk 24:37
14:27 [s]Mt 9:2 [t]Mt 17:7; 28:10; Rev 1:17
14:31 [u]Mt 6:30
14:33 [v]Ps 2:7
14:36 [w]Mt 9:20
15:2 [x]Lk 11:38

●**14:28** Peter was not putting Jesus to the test, something we are told not to do (4:7). Instead he was the only one in the boat to react in faith. His impulsive request led him to experience a rather unusual demonstration of God's power. Peter started to sink because he took his eyes off Jesus and focused on the high waves around him. His faith wavered when he realized what he was doing. We may not walk on water, but we do walk through tough situations. If we focus on the waves of difficult circumstances around us without looking to Jesus for help, we too may despair and sink. To maintain your faith when situations are difficult, keep your eyes on Jesus' power rather than on your inadequacies.

●**14:30, 31** Although we start out with good intentions, sometimes our faith falters. This doesn't necessarily mean we have failed. When Peter's faith faltered, he reached out to Christ, the only one who could help. He was afraid, but he still looked to Christ. When you are apprehensive about the troubles around you and doubt Christ's presence or ability to help, you must remember that he is the *only* one who can really help.

14:34 Gennesaret was located on the west side of the Sea of Galilee in a fertile, well-watered area.

●**14:35, 36** The people recognized Jesus as a great healer, but how many understood who he truly was? They came to Jesus for physical healing, but did they come for spiritual healing? They came to prolong their lives on earth, but did they come to secure their eternal lives? People may seek Jesus to learn valuable lessons from his life or in hopes of finding relief from pain. But we miss Jesus' whole message if we seek him only to heal our bodies but not our souls, if we look to him for help only in this life, rather than for his eternal plan for us. Only when we understand the real Jesus Christ can we appreciate how he can truly change our lives.

●**14:36** Jewish men wore tassels on the lower edges of their robes according to God's command (Deuteronomy 22:12). By Jesus' day, these tassels were seen as signs of holiness (23:5). It was natural that people seeking healing should reach out and touch these. But as one sick woman learned, healing came from faith and not from Jesus' cloak (9:19–22).

15:1, 2 The Pharisees and teachers of the law came from Jerusalem, the center of Jewish authority, to scrutinize Jesus' activities. Over the centuries since the Jews' return from Babylonian captivity, hundreds of religious traditions had been added to God's laws. The Pharisees and teachers of the law considered them all equally important. Many traditions are not bad in themselves. Certain religious traditions can add richness and meaning to life. But we must not assume that because our traditions have been practiced for years they should be elevated to a sacred standing. God's principles never change, and his law doesn't need additions. Traditions should help us understand God's laws better, not become laws themselves.

3Jesus replied, "And why do you break the command of God for the sake of your tradition? 4For God said, 'Honor your father and mother'dy and 'Anyone who curses his father or mother must be put to death.'ez 5But you say that if a man says to his father or mother, 'Whatever help you might otherwise have received from me is a gift devoted to God,' 6he is not to 'honor his fatherf' with it. Thus you nullify the word of God for the sake of your tradition. 7You hypocrites! Isaiah was right when he prophesied about you:

8" 'These people honor me with their lips,
>   but their hearts are far from me.
9They worship me in vain;
>   their teachings are but rules taught by men.a' gb"

10Jesus called the crowd to him and said, "Listen and understand. 11What goes into a man's mouth does not make him 'unclean,'c but what comes out of his mouth, that is what makes him 'unclean.' "

12Then the disciples came to him and asked, "Do you know that the Pharisees were offended when they heard this?"

13He replied, "Every plant that my heavenly Father has not plantedd will be pulled up by the roots. 14Leave them; they are blind guides.he If a blind man leads a blind man, both will fall into a pit."f

15Peter said, "Explain the parable to us."g

16"Are you still so dull?"h Jesus asked them. 17"Don't you see that whatever enters the mouth goes into the stomach and then out of the body? 18But the things that come out of the mouth come from the heart,i and these make a man 'unclean.' 19For out of the heart come evil thoughts, murder, adultery, sexual immorality,

d4 Exodus 20:12; Deut. 5:16   e4 Exodus 21:17; Lev. 20:9   f6 Some manuscripts father or his mother
g9 Isaiah 29:13   h14 Some manuscripts guides of the blind

15:4
yEx 20:12;
Dt 5:16
zLev 20:9

15:9
aCol 2:20-22
bIsa 29:13

15:11
cAc 10:14, 15

15:13
dIsa 60:21

15:14
eMt 23:16, 24
fLk 6:39

15:15
gMt 13:36

15:16
hMt 16:9

15:18
iMt 12:34;
Jas 3:6

MINISTRY IN PHOENICIA

After preaching again in Capernaum, Jesus left Galilee for Phoenicia, where he preached in Tyre and Sidon. On his return, he traveled through the region of the Decapolis (Ten Cities), fed the 4,000 beside the sea, then crossed to Magadan.

for needy parents. These religious leaders were ignoring God's clear command to honor their parents.

15:8, 9 The prophet Isaiah also criticized hypocrites (Isaiah 29:13), and Jesus applied Isaiah's words to these religious leaders. When we claim to honor God while our hearts are far from him, our worship means nothing. It is not enough to act religious. Our actions and our attitudes must be sincere. If they are not, Isaiah's words also describe us.

15:9 The Pharisees knew a lot about God, but they didn't know God. It is not enough to study about religion or even to study the Bible. We must respond to God himself.

15:11 Jesus was referring to the Jewish regulations concerning food and drink. This verse could be paraphrased: "You aren't made unclean by eating nonkosher food! It is what you say and think that makes you unclean!" This statement offended the Pharisees who were very concerned about what people ate and drank.

15:13, 14 Jesus told his disciples to leave the Pharisees alone because the Pharisees were blind to God's truth. Anyone who listened to their teaching would risk spiritual blindness as well. Not all religious leaders clearly see God's truth. Make sure that those you listen to and learn from are those with good spiritual eyesight — they teach and follow the principles of Scripture.

15:15 Later Peter would be faced with the issue of clean and unclean food (see the notes on 15:11 and Acts 10:12). Then he would learn that nothing should be a barrier to proclaiming the gospel to the Gentiles (non-Jews).

15:16-20 We work hard to keep our outward appearance attractive, but what is in our hearts is even more important. The way we are deep down (where others can't see) matters much to God. What are you like inside? When people become Christians, God makes them different on the inside. He will continue the process of change inside them if they only ask. God wants us to seek healthy thoughts and motives, not just healthy food and exercise.

15:5, 6 This was the practice of Corban (literally, "offering"; see Mark 7:11). Anyone who made a Corban vow was required to dedicate money to God's temple that otherwise would have gone to support his parents. Corban had become a religiously acceptable way to neglect parents, circumventing the child's responsibility to them. Although the action — giving money to God — seemed worthy and no doubt conferred prestige on the giver, many people who took the Corban vow were disregarding God's command to care

15:19
/Gal 5:19-21

theft, false testimony, slander./ 20These are what make a man 'unclean'; but eating with unwashed hands does not make him 'unclean.' "

Jesus Sends a Demon Out of a Girl
(103/Mark 7:24–30)

21Leaving that place, Jesus withdrew to the region of Tyre and Sidon. 22A Ca-

15:22
k Mt 9:27
/ Mt 4:24

naanite woman from that vicinity came to him, crying out, "Lord, Son of David,k have mercy on me! My daughter is suffering terribly from demon-possession."/

23Jesus did not answer a word. So his disciples came to him and urged him, "Send her away, for she keeps crying out after us."

15:24
m Mt 10:6, 23

24He answered, "I was sent only to the lost sheep of Israel."m

15:25
n Mt 8:2

25The woman came and knelt before him.n "Lord, help me!" she said.

26He replied, "It is not right to take the children's bread and toss it to their dogs."

27"Yes, Lord," she said, "but even the dogs eat the crumbs that fall from their masters' table."

15:28
o Mt 9:22

28Then Jesus answered, "Woman, you have great faith!o Your request is granted." And her daughter was healed from that very hour.

The Crowd Marvels at Jesus' Healings
(104/Mark 7:31–37)

29Jesus left there and went along the Sea of Galilee. Then he went up on a mountainside and sat down. 30Great crowds came to him, bringing the lame, the blind, the crippled, the mute and many others, and laid them at his feet; and he healed

15:30
p Mt 4:23

them.p 31The people were amazed when they saw the mute speaking, the crippled made well, the lame walking and the blind seeing. And they praised the God of

15:31
q Mt 9:8

Israel.q

Jesus Feeds Four Thousand
(105/Mark 8:1–10)

32Jesus called his disciples to him and said, "I have compassion for these peo-

15:32
r Mt 9:36

ple;r they have already been with me three days and have nothing to eat. I do not want to send them away hungry, or they may collapse on the way."

15:22 This woman is called a "Greek, born in Syrian Phoenicia" in Mark's Gospel (7:26), indicating that she was from the territory northwest of Galilee where the cities of Tyre and Sidon were located. Matthew calls her a Canaanite, naming her ancient ancestors who were enemies of Israel. Matthew's Jewish audience would have immediately understood the significance of Jesus helping this woman.

• **15:23** The disciples asked Jesus to get rid of the woman because she was bothering them with her nagging persistence. They showed no compassion for her or sensitivity to her needs. It is possible to become so occupied with spiritual matters that we miss real needs right around us. This is especially likely if we are prejudiced against needy people or if they cause us inconvenience. Instead of being bothered, be aware of the opportunities that surround you. Be open to the beauty of God's message for all people, and make an effort not to shut out those who are different from you.

• **15:24** Jesus' words do not contradict the truth that God's message is for all people (Psalm 22:27; Isaiah 56:7; Matthew 28:19; Romans 15:9–12). After all, when Jesus said these words, he was in Gentile territory on a mission to Gentile people. He ministered to Gentiles on many other occasions also. Jesus was simply telling the woman that Jews were to have the first opportunity to accept him as the Messiah because God wanted them to present the mes-

sage of salvation to the rest of the world (see Genesis 12:3). Jesus was not rejecting the Canaanite woman. He may have wanted to test her faith, or he may have wanted to use the situation as another opportunity to teach that faith is available to all people.

15:26–28 Dog was a term the Jews commonly applied to Gentiles because the Jews considered these pagan people no more likely than dogs to receive God's blessing. Jesus was not degrading the woman by using this term, he was reflecting the Jews' attitude so as to contrast it with his own. The woman did not argue. Instead, using Jesus' choice of words, she agreed to be considered a dog as long as she could receive God's blessing for her daughter. Ironically, many Jews would lose God's blessing and salvation because they rejected Jesus, and many Gentiles would find salvation because they recognized and accepted him.

• **15:29–31** A great crowd was brought to Jesus to be healed, and he healed them all. Jesus is still able to heal broken lives, and we can be the ones who bring suffering people to him. Who do you know that needs Christ's healing touch? You can bring them to Jesus through prayer or through explaining to them the reason for the hope that you have (1 Peter 3:15). Then let Christ do the healing.

• **15:32ff** This feeding of 4,000 is a separate event from the feeding of the 5,000 (14:13–21), confirmed by Mark 8:19, 20. This was the beginning of Jesus' expanded ministry to the Gentiles.

33His disciples answered, "Where could we get enough bread in this remote place to feed such a crowd?"

34"How many loaves do you have?" Jesus asked.

"Seven," they replied, "and a few small fish."

35He told the crowd to sit down on the ground. 36Then he took the seven loaves and the fish, and when he had given thanks, he broke them*s* and gave them to the disciples, and they in turn to the people. 37They all ate and were satisfied. Afterward the disciples picked up seven basketfuls of broken pieces that were left over.*t* 38The number of those who ate was four thousand, besides women and children. 39After Jesus had sent the crowd away, he got into the boat and went to the vicinity of Magadan.

15:36
*s*Mt 14:19

15:37
*t*Mt 16:10

Religious Leaders Ask for a Sign in the Sky
(106/Mark 8:11–13)

16 The Pharisees and Sadducees came to Jesus and tested him by asking him to show them a sign from heaven. *u*

2He replied,*i* "When evening comes, you say, 'It will be fair weather, for the sky is red,' 3and in the morning, 'Today it will be stormy, for the sky is red and overcast.' You know how to interpret the appearance of the sky, but you cannot interpret the signs of the times. *v* 4A wicked and adulterous generation looks for a miraculous sign, but none will be given it except the sign of Jonah."*w* Jesus then left them and went away.

16:1
*u*Mt 12:38

16:3
*v*Lk 12:54-56
16:4
*w*Mt 12:39

Jesus Warns against Wrong Teaching
(107/Mark 8:14–21)

5When they went across the lake, the disciples forgot to take bread. 6"Be careful," Jesus said to them. "Be on your guard against the yeast of the Pharisees and Sadducees."*x*

7They discussed this among themselves and said, "It is because we didn't bring any bread."

8Aware of their discussion, Jesus asked, "You of little faith,*y* why are you talking among yourselves about having no bread? 9Do you still not understand? Don't you remember the five loaves for the five thousand, and how many basketfuls you gathered?*z* 10Or the seven loaves for the four thousand, and how many basketfuls you gathered?*a* 11How is it you don't understand that I was not talking to you about bread? But be on your guard against the yeast of the Pharisees and Sadducees."

16:6
*x*Lk 12:1

16:8
*y*Mt 6:30

16:9
*z*Mt 14:17-21
16:10
*a*Mt 15:34-38

i 2 Some early manuscripts do not have the rest of verse 2 and all of verse 3.

●**15:33** Jesus had already fed more than 5,000 people with five loaves and two fish. Here, in a similar situation, the disciples were again perplexed. How easily we throw up our hands in despair when faced with difficult situations. Like the disciples, we often forget that if God has cared for us in the past, he will do the same now. When facing a difficult situation, remember how God cared for you and trust him to work faithfully again.

15:39 Magadan was located on the west shore of the Sea of Galilee. Also known as Dalmanutha (Mark 8:10), this was Mary Magdalene's hometown.

16:1 The Pharisees and Sadducees were Jewish religious leaders of two different parties, and their views were diametrically opposed on many issues. The Pharisees carefully followed their religious rules and traditions, believing that this was the way to God. They also believed in the authority of all Scripture and in the resurrection of the dead. The Sadducees accepted only the books of Moses as Scripture and did not believe in life after death. In Jesus, however, these two groups had a common enemy, and they joined forces to try to kill him. For more information on the Pharisees and Sadducees, see the charts in chapter 3 and Mark 2.

16:1 The Pharisees and Sadducees demanded a sign *from heaven.* They tried to explain away Jesus' other miracles as sleight

of hand, coincidence, or use of evil power, but they believed that only God could do a sign in the sky. This, they were sure, would be a feat beyond Jesus' power. Although Jesus could have easily impressed them, he refused. He knew that even a miracle in the sky would not convince them he was the Messiah because they had already decided not to believe in him.

16:4 By using the sign of Jonah, who was inside a great fish for three days, Jesus was predicting his death and resurrection (see also 12:38–42).

16:4 Many people, like these Jewish leaders, say they want to see a miracle so that they can believe. But Jesus knew that miracles never convince the skeptical. Jesus had been healing, raising people from the dead, and feeding thousands, and still people wanted him to prove himself. Do you doubt Christ because you haven't *seen* a miracle? Do you expect God to prove himself to you personally before you believe? Jesus says, "Blessed are those who have not seen and yet have believed" (John 20:29). We have all the miracles recorded in the Old and New Testaments, 2,000 years of church history, and the witness of thousands. With all this evidence, those who won't believe are either too proud or too stubborn. If you simply step forward in faith and believe, then you will begin to see the miracles that God can do with your life!

¹²Then they understood that he was not telling them to guard against the yeast used in bread, but against the teaching of the Pharisees and Sadducees.

Peter Says Jesus Is the Messiah
(109/Mark 8:27–30; Luke 9:18–20)

¹³When Jesus came to the region of Caesarea Philippi, he asked his disciples, "Who do people say the Son of Man is?"

16:14
b Mt 3:1
c Mk 6:15;
Jn 1:21

¹⁴They replied, "Some say John the Baptist;[b] others say Elijah; and still others, Jeremiah or one of the prophets."[c]

¹⁵"But what about you?" he asked. "Who do you say I am?"

¹⁶Simon Peter answered, "You are the Christ,[j] the Son of the living God."

¹⁷Jesus replied, "Blessed are you, Simon son of Jonah, for this was not revealed to you by man,[d] but by my Father in heaven. ¹⁸And I tell you that you are Peter,[k][e] and on this rock I will build my church, and the gates of Hades[l] will not overcome it.[m] ¹⁹I will give you the keys of the kingdom of heaven; whatever you bind on earth will be[n] bound in heaven, and whatever you loose on earth will be[n] loosed in heaven."[f] ²⁰Then he warned his disciples not to tell anyone that he was the Christ.

16:17
d 1Co 15:50

16:18
e Jn 1:42

16:19
f Mt 18:18;
Jn 20:23

j 16 *Or* Messiah; *also in verse 20* k 18 Peter *means* rock. l 18 *Or* hell m 18 *Or* not prove stronger than it n 19 *Or* have been

---

16:12 Yeast is put into bread to make it rise, and it takes only a little to affect a whole batch of dough. Jesus used yeast as an example of how a small amount of evil can affect a large group of people. The wrong teachings of the Pharisees and Sadducees were leading many people astray. Beware of the tendency to say, "How can this little wrong possibly affect anyone?"

16:13 Caesarea Philippi was located several miles north of the Sea of Galilee, in the territory ruled by Philip. The influence of Greek and Roman culture was everywhere, and pagan temples and idols abounded. When Philip became ruler, he rebuilt and renamed the city after the emperor (Caesar) and himself. The city was originally called Caesarea, the same name as the capital city of Philip's brother Herod's territory.

● **16:13–17** The disciples answered Jesus' question with the common view — that Jesus was one of the great prophets come back to life. This belief may have stemmed from Deuteronomy 18:18, where God said he would raise up a prophet from among the people. (John the Baptist's Profile is in John 1; Elijah's Profile is in 1 Kings 18; and Jeremiah's Profile is in Jeremiah 2.) Peter, however, confessed Jesus as divine and as the promised and long-awaited Messiah. If Jesus were to ask you this question, how would you answer? Is he your Lord and Messiah?

● **16:18** The rock on which Jesus would build his church has been identified as: (1) Jesus himself (his work of salvation by dying for us on the cross); (2) Peter (the first great leader in the church at Jerusalem); (3) the confession of faith that Peter gave and that all subsequent true believers would give. It seems most likely that the rock refers to Peter as the leader of the church (for his function, not necessarily his character). Just as Peter had revealed the true identity of Christ, so Jesus revealed Peter's identity and role.

Later, Peter reminds Christians that they are the church built on the foundation of the apostles and prophets, with Jesus Christ as the cornerstone (1 Peter 2:4–6). All believers are joined into this church by faith in Jesus Christ as Savior, the same faith that Peter expressed here (see also Ephesians 2:20, 21). Jesus praised Peter for his confession of faith. It is faith like Peter's that is the foundation of Christ's kingdom.

16:19 The meaning of this verse has been a subject of debate for centuries. Some say the keys represent the authority to carry out church discipline, legislation, and administration (18:15–18); while others say the keys give the authority to announce the forgiveness

of sins (John 20:23). Still others say the keys may be the opportunity to bring people to the kingdom of heaven by presenting them with the message of salvation found in God's Word (Acts 15:7–9). The religious leaders thought they held the keys of the kingdom, and they tried to shut some people out. We cannot decide to open or close the kingdom of heaven for others, but God uses us to help others find the way inside. To all who believe in Christ and obey his words, the kingdom doors are swung wide open.

JOURNEY TO CAESAREA PHILIPPI
Jesus left Magadan, crossed the lake, and landed in Bethsaida. There he healed a man who had been born blind. From there, he and his disciples went to Caesarea Philippi, where Peter confessed Jesus as the Messiah and Son of God.

● **16:20** Jesus warned the disciples not to publicize Peter's confession because they did not yet fully understand the kind of Messiah he had come to be — not a military commander but a suffering servant. They needed to come to a full understanding of Jesus and their mission as disciples before they could proclaim it to others in a way that would not cause a rebellion. They would have a difficult time understanding what Jesus came to do until his earthly mission was complete.

Jesus Predicts His Death the First Time
(110/Mark 8:31—9:1; Luke 9:21–27)

21From that time on Jesus began to explain to his disciples that he must go to Jerusalem and suffer many things*g* at the hands of the elders, chief priests and teachers of the law, and that he must be killed and on the third day be raised to life.*h*

16:21
*g*Lk 17:25
*h*Mk 9:31

22Peter took him aside and began to rebuke him. "Never, Lord!" he said. "This shall never happen to you!"

23Jesus turned and said to Peter, "Get behind me, Satan! You are a stumbling block to me; you do not have in mind the things of God, but the things of men."

24Then Jesus said to his disciples, "If anyone would come after me, he must deny himself and take up his cross and follow me.*i* 25For whoever wants to save his life*o* will lose it, but whoever loses his life for me will find it. 26What good will it be for a man if he gains the whole world, yet forfeits his soul? Or what can a man give in exchange for his soul? 27For the Son of Man is going to come in his Father's glory with his angels, and then he will reward each person according to what he has done.*j* 28I tell you the truth, some who are standing here will not taste death before they see the Son of Man coming in his kingdom."

16:24
*i*Mt 10:38;
Lk 14:27

16:27
*j*2Co 5:10;
Rev 22:12

Jesus Is Transfigured on the Mountain
(111/Mark 9:2–13; Luke 9:28–36)

17 After six days Jesus took with him Peter, James and John the brother of James, and led them up a high mountain by themselves. 2There he was transfigured before them. His face shone like the sun, and his clothes became as white as the light. 3Just then there appeared before them Moses and Elijah, talking with Jesus.

o 25 The Greek word means either *life* or *soul*; also in verse 26.

●**16:21** The phrase "From that time on" marks a turning point. In 4:17 it signaled Jesus' announcement of the kingdom of heaven. Here it points to his new emphasis on his death and resurrection. The disciples still didn't grasp Jesus' true purpose because of their preconceived notions about what the Messiah should be. This is the first of three times that Jesus predicted his death (see 17:22, 23; 20:18 for others).

16:21-28 This passage corresponds to Daniel's prophecies: the Messiah would be cut off (Daniel 9:26); there would be a period of trouble (9:27); and the king would come in glory (7:13, 14). The disciples would endure the same suffering as their King and, like him, would be rewarded in the end.

●**16:22** Peter, Jesus' friend and devoted follower who had just eloquently proclaimed Jesus' true identity, sought to protect him from the suffering he prophesied. But if Jesus hadn't suffered and died, Peter (and we) would have died in his sins. Great temptations can come from those who love us and seek to protect us. Be cautious of advice from a friend who says, "Surely God doesn't want you to face this." Often our most difficult temptations come from those who are only trying to protect us from discomfort.

16:23 In his desert temptations, Jesus heard the message that he could achieve greatness without dying (4:6). Here he heard the same message from Peter. Peter had just recognized Jesus as Messiah; here, however, he forsook God's perspective and evaluated the situation from a human one. Satan is always trying to get us to leave God out of the picture. Jesus rebuked Peter for this attitude.

16:24 When Jesus used this picture of his followers taking up their crosses to follow him, the disciples knew what he meant. Crucifixion was a common Roman method of execution, and condemned criminals had to carry their crosses through the streets to the execution site. Following Jesus, therefore, meant a true commitment, the risk of death, and no turning back (see 10:39).

16:25 The possibility of losing their lives was very real for the disciples as well as for Jesus. Real discipleship implies real commitment—pledging our whole existence to his service. If we try to save our physical life from death, pain, or discomfort, we may risk losing our true eternal life. If we protect ourselves from pain, we begin to die spiritually and emotionally. Our lives turn inward, and we lose our intended purpose. When we give our lives in service to Christ, however, we discover the real purpose of living.

●**16:26** When we don't know Christ, we make choices as though this life were all we have. In reality, this life is just the introduction to eternity. How we live this brief span, however, determines our eternal state. What we accumulate on earth has no value in purchasing eternal life. Even the highest social or civic honors cannot earn us entrance into heaven. Evaluate all that happens from an eternal perspective, and you will find your values and decisions changing.

16:27 Jesus Christ has been given the authority to judge all the earth (Romans 14:9–11; Philippians 2:9–11). Although his judgment is already working in our lives, there is a future, final judgment when Christ returns (25:31–46) and everyone's life is reviewed and evaluated. This will not be confined to unbelievers; Christians too will face a judgment. Their eternal destiny is secure, but Jesus will look at how they handled gifts, opportunities, and responsibilities in order to determine their heavenly rewards. At the time of judgment, God will deliver the righteous and condemn the wicked. We should not judge others' salvation; that is God's work.

16:28 Because all the disciples died *before* Christ's return, many believe that Jesus' words were fulfilled at the transfiguration when Peter, James, and John saw his glory (17:1-3). Others say this statement refers to Pentecost (Acts 2) and the beginning of Christ's church. In either case, certain disciples were eyewitnesses to the power and glory of Christ's kingdom.

17:1ff The transfiguration was a vision, a brief glimpse of the true glory of the King (16:27, 28). This was a special revelation of Jesus' divinity to three of the disciples, and it was God's divine affirmation of everything Jesus had done and was about to do.

4Peter said to Jesus, "Lord, it is good for us to be here. If you wish, I will put up three shelters — one for you, one for Moses and one for Elijah."

17:5
k Mt 3:17
l Ac 3:22, 23

5While he was still speaking, a bright cloud enveloped them, and a voice from the cloud said, "This is my Son, whom I love; with him I am well pleased.k Listen to him!"l

6When the disciples heard this, they fell facedown to the ground, terrified. 7But Jesus came and touched them. "Get up," he said. "Don't be afraid."m 8When they looked up, they saw no one except Jesus.

17:7
m Mt 14:27

9As they were coming down the mountain, Jesus instructed them, "Don't tell anyone what you have seen, until the Son of Man has been raised from the dead."n

17:9
n Mt 16:21

10The disciples asked him, "Why then do the teachers of the law say that Elijah must come first?"

11Jesus replied, "To be sure, Elijah comes and will restore all things.o 12But I tell you, Elijah has already come,p and they did not recognize him, but have done to him everything they wished.q In the same way the Son of Man is going to suffer r at their hands." 13Then the disciples understood that he was talking to them about John the Baptist.

17:11
o Mal 4:6;
Lk 1:16, 17

17:12
p Mt 11:14
q Mt 14:3, 10
r Mt 16:21

Jesus Heals a Demon-Possessed Boy
(112/Mark 9:14–29; Luke 9:37–43)

14When they came to the crowd, a man approached Jesus and knelt before him. 15"Lord, have mercy on my son," he said. "He has seizures and is suffering greatly. He often falls into the fire or into the water. 16I brought him to your disciples, but they could not heal him."

17"O unbelieving and perverse generation," Jesus replied, "how long shall I stay with you? How long shall I put up with you? Bring the boy here to me." 18Jesus rebuked the demon, and it came out of the boy, and he was healed from that moment.

19Then the disciples came to Jesus in private and asked, "Why couldn't we drive it out?"

20He replied, "Because you have so little faith. I tell you the truth, if you have

---

17:3–5 Moses and Elijah were the two greatest prophets in the Old Testament. Moses represents the law, or the old covenant. He wrote the Pentateuch, and he predicted the coming of a great prophet (Deuteronomy 18:15–19). Elijah represents the prophets who foretold the coming of the Messiah (Malachi 4:5, 6). Moses' and Elijah's presence with Jesus confirmed Jesus' Messianic mission — to fulfill God's law and the words of God's prophets. Just as God's voice in the cloud over Mount Sinai gave authority to his law (Exodus 19:9), God's voice at the transfiguration gave authority to Jesus' words.

17:4 Peter wanted to build three shelters for these three great men to stay to show how the Feast of Tabernacles was fulfilled in the coming of God's kingdom. Peter had the right idea about Christ, but his timing was wrong. Peter wanted to act, but this was a time for worship and adoration. He wanted to capture the moment, but he was supposed to learn and move on.

● **17:5** Jesus is more than just a great leader, a good example, a good influence, or a great prophet. He is the Son of God. When you understand this profound truth, the only adequate response is worship. When you have a correct understanding of Christ, you will obey him.

● **17:9** Jesus told Peter, James, and John not to tell anyone what they had seen until after his resurrection because Jesus knew that they didn't fully understand it and could not explain what they didn't understand. Their question (17:10ff) revealed their misunderstandings. They knew that Jesus was the Messiah, but they had much more to learn about the significance of his death and resurrection.

17:10–12 Based on Malachi 4:5, 6, the teachers of the Old Testament law believed that Elijah must appear before the Messiah would appear. Jesus referred to John the Baptist, not to the Old Testament prophet Elijah. John the Baptist took on Elijah's prophetic role — boldly confronting sin and pointing people to God. Malachi had prophesied that a prophet like Elijah would come (Malachi 4:5).

17:17 The disciples had been given the authority to do the healing, but they had not yet learned how to appropriate the power of God. Jesus' frustration is with the unbelieving and unresponsive generation. His disciples were merely a reflection of that attitude in this instance. Jesus' purpose was not to criticize the disciples, but to encourage them to greater faith.

17:17–20 The disciples were unable to drive out this demon, and they asked Jesus why. He pointed to their lack of faith. It is the power of God, not our faith, that moves mountains, but faith must be present to do so. The mustard seed was the smallest particle imaginable. Even small or undeveloped faith would have been sufficient. Perhaps the disciples had tried to drive out the demon with their own ability rather than God's. There is great power in even a little faith when God is with us. If we feel weak or powerless as Christians, we should examine our faith, making sure we are trusting not in our own abilities to produce results, but in God's.

17:20 Jesus wasn't condemning the disciples for substandard faith; he was trying to show how important faith would be in their future ministry. If you are facing a problem that seems as big and immovable as a mountain, turn your eyes from the mountain and look to Christ for more faith. Only then will your work for him become useful and vibrant.

faith^s as small as a mustard seed,^{t} you can say to this mountain, 'Move from here to there' and it will move. ^{u} Nothing will be impossible for you.^{p}"

17:20
^{s}Mt 21:21
^{t}Lk 17:6
^{u}1Co 13:2

Jesus Predicts His Death the Second Time
(113/Mark 9:30–32; Luke 9:44, 45)

22When they came together in Galilee, he said to them, "The Son of Man is going to be betrayed into the hands of men. 23They will kill him, and on the third day he will be raised to life." And the disciples were filled with grief.

Peter Finds the Coin in the Fish's Mouth
(114)

24After Jesus and his disciples arrived in Capernaum, the collectors of the two-drachma tax^v came to Peter and asked, "Doesn't your teacher pay the temple tax^q?"

17:24
^{v}Ex 30:13

25"Yes, he does," he replied.

When Peter came into the house, Jesus was the first to speak. "What do you think, Simon?" he asked. "From whom do the kings of the earth collect duty and taxes^w — from their own sons or from others?"

17:25
^{w}Mt 22:17-21;
Ro 13:7

26"From others," Peter answered.

"Then the sons are exempt," Jesus said to him. 27"But so that we may not offend^x them, go to the lake and throw out your line. Take the first fish you catch; open its mouth and you will find a four-drachma coin. Take it and give it to them for my tax and yours."

17:27
^{x}Jn 6:61

The Disciples Argue about Who Would Be the Greatest
(115/Mark 9:33–37; Luke 9:46–48)

18 At that time the disciples came to Jesus and asked, "Who is the greatest in the kingdom of heaven?"

2He called a little child and had him stand among them. 3And he said: "I tell you the truth, unless you change and become like little children,^{y} you will never enter

18:3
^{y}Mt 19:14;
1Pe 2:2

p 20 Some manuscripts you. 21But this kind does not go out except by prayer and fasting. **q 24** Greek the two drachmas

---

• **17:22, 23** Once again Jesus predicted his death (see also 16:21); but more important, he told of his resurrection. Unfortunately, the disciples heard only the first part of Jesus' words and became discouraged. They couldn't understand why Jesus wanted to go back to Jerusalem where he would walk right into trouble.

The disciples didn't fully comprehend the purpose of Jesus' death and resurrection until Pentecost (Acts 2). We shouldn't get upset at ourselves for being slow to understand everything about Jesus. After all, the disciples were with him, saw his miracles, heard his words, and still had difficulty understanding. Despite their questions and doubts, however, they believed. We should do no less.

• **17:22, 23** The disciples didn't understand why Jesus kept talking about his death because they expected him to set up a political kingdom. His death, they thought, would dash their hopes. They didn't know that Jesus' death and resurrection would make his kingdom possible.

17:24 All Jewish males had to pay a temple tax to support temple upkeep (Exodus 30:11–16). Tax collectors set up booths to collect these taxes. Only Matthew records this incident — perhaps because he had been a tax collector himself.

17:24–27 As usual, Peter answered a question without really knowing the answer, putting Jesus and the disciples in an awkward position. Jesus used this situation, however, to emphasize his kingly role. Just as kings pay no taxes and collect none from their

family, Jesus, the King, owed no taxes. But Jesus supplied the tax payment for both himself and Peter rather than offend those who didn't understand his kingship. Although Jesus supplied the tax money, Peter had to go and get it. Ultimately all that we have comes to us from God's supply, but he may want us to be active in the process.

17:24–27 As God's people, we are foreigners on earth because our loyalty is always to our real King — Jesus. Still we have to cooperate with the authorities and be responsible citizens. An ambassador to another country keeps the local laws in order to represent well the one who sent him. We are Christ's ambassadors (2 Corinthians 5:20). Are you being a good foreign ambassador for him to this world?

18:1 From Mark's Gospel we learn that Jesus precipitated this conversation by asking the disciples what they had been discussing among themselves earlier (Mark 9:33, 34).

18:1–4 Jesus used a child to help his self-centered disciples get the point. We are not to be childish (like the disciples, arguing over petty issues), but rather childlike, with humble and sincere hearts. Are you being childlike or childish?

18:3, 4 The disciples had become so preoccupied with the organization of Jesus' earthly kingdom that they had lost sight of its divine purpose. Instead of seeking a place of service, they sought positions of advantage. It is easy to lose our eternal perspective and compete for promotions or status in the church. It is difficult to identify with "children" — weak and dependent people with no status or influence.

the kingdom of heaven. 4Therefore, whoever humbles himself like this child is the greatest in the kingdom of heaven.

5"And whoever welcomes a little child like this in my name welcomes me. 6But if anyone causes one of these little ones who believe in me to sin, it would be better for him to have a large millstone hung around his neck and to be drowned in the depths of the sea.z

Jesus Warns against Temptation
(117/Mark 9:42–50)

7"Woe to the world because of the things that cause people to sin! Such things must come, but woe to the man through whom they come!a 8If your hand or your foot causes you to sin,b cut it off and throw it away. It is better for you to enter life maimed or crippled than to have two hands or two feet and be thrown into eternal fire. 9And if your eye causes you to sin,c gouge it out and throw it away. It is better for you to enter life with one eye than to have two eyes and be thrown into the fire of hell.

Jesus Warns against Looking Down on Others
(118)

10"See that you do not look down on one of these little ones. For I tell you that their angelsd in heaven always see the face of my Father in heaven.r

12"What do you think? If a man owns a hundred sheep, and one of them wanders away, will he not leave the ninety-nine on the hills and go to look for the one that wandered off? 13And if he finds it, I tell you the truth, he is happier about that one sheep than about the ninety-nine that did not wander off. 14In the same way your Father in heaven is not willing that any of these little ones should be lost.

Jesus Teaches How to Treat a Believer Who Sins
(119)

15"If your brother sins against you,s go and show him his fault,e just between the two of you. If he listens to you, you have won your brother over. 16But if he will not listen, take one or two others along, so that 'every matter may be established by the testimony of two or three witnesses.'tf 17If he refuses to listen to them, tell it

18:6 zLk 17:2

18:7 aLk 17:1

18:8 bMt 5:29

18:9 cMt 5:29

18:10 dPs 34:7

18:15 eLev 19:17; Lk 17:3; Jas 5:19, 20

18:16 fDt 19:15; Jn 8:17; 2Co 13:1; Heb 10:28

r 10 Some manuscripts *heaven.* 11 *The Son of Man came to save what was lost.* s 15 Some manuscripts do not have *against you.* t 16 Deut. 19:15

18:6 Children are trusting by nature. They trust adults, and through that trust their capacity to trust God grows. God holds parents and other adults who influence young children accountable for how they affect these little ones' ability to trust. Jesus warned that anyone who turns little children away from faith will receive severe punishment.

18:7ff Jesus warned the disciples about two ways to cause "little ones" to sin: tempting them (18:7–9) and neglecting or demeaning them (18:10–14). As leaders, we are to help young people or new believers avoid anything or anyone that could cause them to stumble in their faith and lead them to sin. We must never take lightly the spiritual education and protection of the young in age and in the faith.

18:8, 9 We must remove stumbling blocks that cause us to sin. This does not mean to cut off a part of the body; it means that any person, program, or teaching in the church that threatens the spiritual growth of the body must be removed. For the individual, any relationship, practice, or activity that leads to sin should be stopped. Jesus says it would be better to go to heaven with one hand than to hell with both. Sin, of course, affects more than our hands; it affects our minds and hearts.

18:10 Our concern for children must match God's treatment of them. Certain angels are assigned to watch over children, and they have direct access to God. These words ring out sharply in cultures where children are taken lightly, ignored, or aborted. If their

angels have constant access to God, the least we can do is to allow children to approach us easily in spite of our far too busy schedules.

18:14 Just as a shepherd is concerned enough about one lost sheep to go search the hills for it, so God is concerned about every human being he has created (he is "not wanting anyone to perish," 2 Peter 3:9). You come in contact with children who need Christ at home, at school, in church, and in the neighborhood. Steer them toward Christ by your example, your words, and your acts of kindness.

18:15–17 These are Jesus' guidelines for dealing with those who sin against us. They were meant for (1) Christians, not unbelievers, (2) sins committed against *you* and not others, and (3) conflict resolution in the context of the church, not the community at large. Jesus' words are not a license for a frontal attack on every person who hurts or slights us. They are not a license to start a destructive gossip campaign or to call for a church trial. They are designed to reconcile those who disagree so that all Christians can live in harmony.

When someone wrongs us, we often do the opposite of what Jesus recommends. We turn away in hatred or resentment, seek revenge, or engage in gossip. By contrast, we should go to that person *first*, as difficult as that may be. Then we should forgive that person as often as he or she needs it (18:21, 22). This will create a much better chance of restoring the relationship.

to the church; and if he refuses to listen even to the church, treat him as you would a pagan or a tax collector.

18"I tell you the truth, whatever you bind on earth will be[u] bound in heaven, and whatever you loose on earth will be[u] loosed in heaven.[g]

19"Again, I tell you that if two of you on earth agree about anything you ask for, it will be done for you by my Father in heaven. 20For where two or three come together in my name, there am I with them."

Jesus Tells the Parable of the Unforgiving Debtor
(120)

21Then Peter came to Jesus and asked, "Lord, how many times shall I forgive my brother when he sins against me? Up to seven times?"[h]

22Jesus answered, "I tell you, not seven times, but seventy-seven times.[v][i]

23"Therefore, the kingdom of heaven is like a king who wanted to settle accounts[j] with his servants. 24As he began the settlement, a man who owed him ten thousand talents[w] was brought to him. 25Since he was not able to pay,[k] the master ordered that he and his wife and his children and all that he had be sold[l] to repay the debt.

26"The servant fell on his knees before him.[m] 'Be patient with me,' he begged, 'and I will pay back everything.' 27The servant's master took pity on him, canceled the debt and let him go.

28"But when that servant went out, he found one of his fellow servants who owed him a hundred denarii.[x] He grabbed him and began to choke him. 'Pay back what you owe me!' he demanded.

29"His fellow servant fell to his knees and begged him, 'Be patient with me, and I will pay you back.'

30"But he refused. Instead, he went off and had the man thrown into prison until he could pay the debt. 31When the other servants saw what had happened, they were greatly distressed and went and told their master everything that had happened.

32"Then the master called the servant in. 'You wicked servant,' he said, 'I canceled all that debt of yours because you begged me to. 33Shouldn't you have had mercy on your fellow servant just as I had on you?' 34In anger his master turned him over to the jailers to be tortured, until he should pay back all he owed.

35"This is how my heavenly Father will treat each of you unless you forgive your brother from your heart."[n]

u 18 Or have been   v 22 Or seventy times seven   w 24 That is, millions of dollars   x 28 That is, a few dollars

18:18
gMt 16:19;
Jn 20:23

18:21
hLk 17:4

18:22
iGe 4:24

18:23
jMt 25:19

18:25
kLk 7:42
l2Ki 4:1;
Ne 5:5, 8

18:26
mMt 8:2

18:35
nMt 6:14

18:18 This *binding* and *loosing* refers to the decisions of the church in conflicts. Among believers, there is no court of appeals beyond the church. Ideally, the church's decisions should be God-guided and based on discernment of his Word. Believers have the responsibility, therefore, to bring their problems to the church, and the church has the responsibility to use God's guidance in seeking to resolve conflicts. Handling problems God's way will have an impact now and for eternity.

18:19, 20 Jesus looked ahead to a new day when he would be present with his followers not in body, but through his Holy Spirit. In the body of believers (the church), the sincere agreement of two people is more powerful than the superficial agreement of thousands, because Christ's Holy Spirit is with them. Two or more believers, *filled with the Holy Spirit,* will pray according to God's will, not their own; thus their requests will be granted.

18:22 The rabbis taught that people should forgive those who of-

fend them — but only three times. Peter, trying to be especially generous, asked Jesus if seven (the "perfect" number) was enough times to forgive someone. But Jesus answered, "Seventy-seven times," meaning that we shouldn't even keep track of how many times we forgive someone. We should always forgive those who are truly repentant, no matter how many times they ask.

18:30 In Bible times, serious consequences awaited those who could not pay their debts. A person lending money could seize the borrower who couldn't pay and force him or his family to work until the debt was paid. The debtor could also be thrown into prison, or his family could be sold into slavery to help pay off the debt. It was hoped that the debtor, while in prison, would sell off his landholdings or that relatives would pay the debt. If not, the debtor could remain in prison for life.

18:35 Because God has forgiven all our sins, we should not withhold forgiveness from others. Realizing how completely Christ has forgiven us should produce a free and generous attitude of forgiveness toward others. When we don't forgive others, we are setting ourselves outside and above Christ's law of love.

19:3–12 John was put in prison and killed, at least in part, for his

6. Jesus faces conflict with the religious leaders

Jesus Teaches about Marriage and Divorce
(173/Mark 10:1–12)

19 When Jesus had finished saying these things, he left Galilee and went into the region of Judea to the other side of the Jordan. 2Large crowds followed him, and he healed them^o there.

3Some Pharisees came to him to test him. They asked, "Is it lawful for a man to divorce his wife^p for any and every reason?"

4"Haven't you read," he replied, "that at the beginning the Creator 'made them male and female,'^{yq} 5and said, 'For this reason a man will leave his father and mother and be united to his wife, and the two will become one flesh'$^{z?r}$ 6So they are no longer two, but one. Therefore what God has joined together, let man not separate."

7"Why then," they asked, "did Moses command that a man give his wife a certificate of divorce and send her away?"^{s}

8Jesus replied, "Moses permitted you to divorce your wives because your hearts were hard. But it was not this way from the beginning. 9I tell you that anyone who divorces his wife, except for marital unfaithfulness, and marries another woman commits adultery."^{t}

y 4 Gen. 1:27   *z 5* Gen. 2:24

19:2
^{o}Mt 4:23

19:3
^{p}Mt 5:31

19:4
^{q}Ge 1:27; 5:2

19:5
^{r}Ge 2:24;
1Co 6:16;
Eph 5:31

19:7
^{s}Dt 24:1-4

19:9
^{t}Lk 16:18

JESUS AND FORGIVENESS

Jesus forgave	*Reference*
the paralytic lowered on a mat through the roof.	Matthew 9:2–8
the woman caught in adultery.	John 8:3–11
the woman who anointed his feet with oil.	Luke 7:47–50
Peter, for denying he knew Jesus.	John 18:15–18, 25–27; 21:15–19
the criminal on the cross.	Luke 23:39–43
the people who crucified him.	Luke 23:34

Jesus not only taught frequently about forgiveness, he also demonstrated his own willingness to forgive. Here are several examples that should be an encouragement to recognize his willingness to forgive us also.

---

public opinions on marriage and divorce, so the Pharisees hoped to trap Jesus too. They were trying to trick Jesus by having him choose sides in a theological controversy. Two schools of thought represented two opposing views of divorce. One group supported divorce for almost any reason. The other believed that divorce could be allowed only for marital unfaithfulness. This conflict hinged on how each group interpreted Deuteronomy 24:1–4. In his answer, however, Jesus focused on marriage rather than divorce. He pointed out that God intended marriage to be permanent and gave four reasons for the importance of marriage (19:4–6).

19:7, 8 This law is found in Deuteronomy 24:1–4. In Moses' day, as well as in Jesus' day, the practice of marriage fell far short of God's intention. The same is true today. Jesus said that Moses gave this law only because of the people's hard hearts – permanent marriage was God's intention. But because sinful human nature made divorce inevitable, Moses instituted some laws to help its victims. These were civil laws designed especially to protect the women who, in that culture, were quite vulnerable when living alone. Because of Moses' law, a man could no longer just throw his wife out – he had to write a formal letter of dismissal. This was a radical step toward civil rights, for it made men think twice about divorce. God designed marriage to be indissoluble. Instead of looking for reasons to leave each other, married couples should concentrate on how to stay together (19:3–9).

JESUS TRAVELS TOWARD JERUSALEM
Jesus left Galilee for the last time — heading toward his death in Jerusalem. He again crossed the Jordan, spending some time in Perea before going on to Jericho.

¹⁰The disciples said to him, "If this is the situation between a husband and wife, it is better not to marry."

¹¹Jesus replied, "Not everyone can accept this word, but only those to whom it has been given. ᵘ ¹²For some are eunuchs because they were born that way; others were made that way by men; and others have renounced marriageᵃ because of the kingdom of heaven. The one who can accept this should accept it."

19:11
ᵘMt 13:11;
1Co 7:7-9, 17

Jesus Blesses Little Children
(174/Mark 10:13–16; Luke 18:15–17)

¹³Then little children were brought to Jesus for him to place his hands on them and pray for them. But the disciples rebuked those who brought them.

¹⁴Jesus said, "Let the little children come to me, and do not hinder them, for the kingdom of heaven belongs to such as these."ᵛ ¹⁵When he had placed his hands on them, he went on from there.

19:14
ᵛMt 18:3;
1Pe 2:2

Jesus Speaks to the Rich Young Man
(175/Mark 10:17–31; Luke 18:18–30)

¹⁶Now a man came up to Jesus and asked, "Teacher, what good thing must I do to get eternal lifeʷ?"ˣ

¹⁷"Why do you ask me about what is good?" Jesus replied. "There is only One who is good. If you want to enter life, obey the commandments."

19:16
ʷMt 25:46
ˣLk 10:25

¹⁸"Which ones?" the man inquired.

Jesus replied, " 'Do not murder, do not commit adultery,ʸ do not steal, do not give false testimony, ¹⁹honor your father and mother,'ᵇ and 'love your neighbor as yourself.' ᶜ"ᶻ

19:18
ʸJas 2:11

19:19
ᶻLev 19:18

²⁰"All these I have kept," the young man said. "What do I still lack?"

²¹Jesus answered, "If you want to be perfect, go, sell your possessions and give to the poor, ᵃ and you will have treasure in heaven. ᵇ Then come, follow me."

²²When the young man heard this, he went away sad, because he had great wealth.

19:21
ᵃAc 2:45
ᵇMt 6:20

ᵃ 12 Or have made themselves eunuchs　ᵇ 19 Exodus 20:12-16; Deut. 5:16-20　ᶜ 19 Lev. 19:18

19:10–12 Although divorce was relatively easy in Old Testament times (19:7), it is not what God originally intended. Couples should decide against divorce from the start and build their marriage on mutual commitment. There are also many good reasons for not marrying, one being to have more time to work for God's kingdom. Don't assume that God wants everyone to marry. For many it may be better if they don't. Be sure that you prayerfully seek God's will before you plunge into the lifelong commitment of marriage.

19:12 A "eunuch" is an emasculated male — a man with no testicles.

19:12 Some have physical limitations that prevent their marrying, while others choose not to marry because, in their particular situation, they can serve God better as single people. Jesus was not teaching us to avoid marriage because it is inconvenient or takes away our freedom. That would be selfishness. A good reason to remain single is to use the time and freedom to serve God. Paul elaborates on this in 1 Corinthians 7.

19:13–15 The disciples must have forgotten what Jesus had said about children (18:4–6). Jesus wanted little children to come because he loves them and because they have the kind of attitude needed to approach God. He didn't mean that heaven is only for children, but that people need childlike attitudes of trust in God. The receptiveness of little children was a great contrast to the stubbornness of the religious leaders who let their education and sophistication stand in the way of the simple faith needed to believe in Jesus.

19:16 To this man seeking assurance of eternal life, Jesus pointed out that salvation does not come from good deeds unac-

companied by love for God. The man needed a whole new starting point. Instead of adding another commandment to keep or good deed to perform, the young man needed to submit humbly to the lordship of Christ.

19:17 In response to the young man's question about how to have eternal life, Jesus told him to keep God's Ten Commandments. Jesus then listed six of them, all referring to relationships with others. When the young man replied that he had kept the commandments, Jesus told him that he must do something more — sell everything and give the money to the poor. Jesus' statement exposed the man's weakness. In reality, his wealth was his god, his idol, and he would not give it up. Thus he violated the first and greatest commandment (Exodus 20:3; Matthew 22:36–40).

19:21 When Jesus told this young man that he would "be perfect" if he gave everything he had to the poor, Jesus wasn't speaking in the temporal, human sense. He was explaining how to be justified and made whole or complete in God's sight.

19:21 Should all believers sell everything they own? No. We are responsible to care for our own needs and the needs of our families so as not to be a burden on others. We should, however, be willing to give up anything if God asks us to do so. This kind of attitude allows nothing to come between us and God and keeps us from using our God-given wealth selfishly. If you are comforted by the fact that Christ did not tell all his followers to sell all their possessions, then you may be too attached to what you have.

19:22 We cannot love God with all our hearts and yet keep our money to ourselves. Loving him totally means using our money in ways that please him.

19:23
c Mt 13:22

23 Then Jesus said to his disciples, "I tell you the truth, it is hard for a rich man c to enter the kingdom of heaven. 24 Again I tell you, it is easier for a camel to go through the eye of a needle than for a rich man to enter the kingdom of God."

25 When the disciples heard this, they were greatly astonished and asked, "Who then can be saved?"

19:26
d Ge 18:14;
Job 42:2;
Jer 32:17

26 Jesus looked at them and said, "With man this is impossible, but with God all things are possible." d

27 Peter answered him, "We have left everything to follow you! What then will there be for us?"

28 Jesus said to them, "I tell you the truth, at the renewal of all things, when the Son of Man sits on his glorious throne, you who have followed me will also sit on twelve thrones, judging the twelve tribes of Israel. e 29 And everyone who has left houses or brothers or sisters or father or mother**d** or children or fields for my sake will receive a hundred times as much and will inherit eternal life. 30 But many who are first will be last, and many who are last will be first. f

19:28
e Lk 22:28-30;
Rev 3:21

19:30
f Mt 20:16;
Lk 13:30

Jesus Tells the Parable of the Workers Paid Equally
(176)

20:1
g Mt 13:24

20 "For the kingdom of heaven is like g a landowner who went out early in the morning to hire men to work in his vineyard. 2 He agreed to pay them a denarius for the day and sent them into his vineyard.

3 "About the third hour he went out and saw others standing in the marketplace doing nothing. 4 He told them, 'You also go and work in my vineyard, and I will pay you whatever is right.' 5 So they went.

"He went out again about the sixth hour and the ninth hour and did the same thing. 6 About the eleventh hour he went out and found still others standing around. He asked them, 'Why have you been standing here all day long doing nothing?'

7 " 'Because no one has hired us,' they answered.

"He said to them, 'You also go and work in my vineyard.'

20:8
h Lev 19:13

8 "When evening came, h the owner of the vineyard said to his foreman, 'Call the workers and pay them their wages, beginning with the last ones hired and going on to the first.'

9 "The workers who were hired about the eleventh hour came and each received a denarius. 10 So when those came who were hired first, they expected to receive more. But each one of them also received a denarius. 11 When they received it, they began to grumble against the landowner. 12 'These men who were hired last worked only one hour,' they said, 'and you have made them equal to us who have borne the burden of the work and the heat i of the day.'

20:12
i Jnh 4:8;
Jas 1:11

d 29 Some manuscripts *mother or wife*

19:24 Because it is impossible for a camel to go through the eye of a needle, it appears impossible for a rich person to get into the kingdom of God. Jesus explained, however, that "with God all things are possible" (19:26). Even rich people can enter the kingdom if God brings them in. Faith in Christ, not in self or riches, is what counts. On what are you counting for salvation?

19:25, 26 The disciples were astonished. They thought that if anyone could be saved, it would be the rich, whom their culture considered especially blessed by God.

19:27 In the Bible, God gives rewards to his people according to his justice. In the Old Testament, obedience often brought reward in this life (Deuteronomy 28), but obedience and immediate reward are not always linked. If they were, good people would always be rich, and suffering would always be a sign of sin. As believers, our true reward is God's presence and power through the Holy Spirit. Later, in eternity, we will be rewarded for our faith and service. If material rewards in this life came to us for every faithful deed, we would be tempted to boast about our achievements and act out of wrong motivations.

19:29 Jesus assured the disciples that anyone who gives up

something valuable for his sake will be repaid many times over in this life, although not necessarily in the same form. For example, a person may be rejected by his or her family for accepting Christ, but he or she will gain the larger family of believers.

19:30 Jesus turned the world's values upside down. Consider the most powerful or well-known people in our world — how many got where they are by being humble, self-effacing, and gentle? Not many! But in the life to come, the last will be first — if they got in last place by choosing to follow Jesus. Don't forfeit eternal rewards for temporary benefits. Be willing to make sacrifices now for greater rewards later. Be willing to accept human disapproval, while knowing that you have God's approval.

20:1ff Jesus further clarified the membership rules of the kingdom of heaven — entrance is by God's grace alone. In this parable, God is the landowner, and believers are the workers. This parable speaks especially to those who feel superior because of heritage or favored position, to those who feel superior because they have spent so much time with Christ, and to new believers as reassurance of God's grace.

13"But he answered one of them, 'Friend, I am not being unfair to you. Didn't you agree to work for a denarius? 14Take your pay and go. I want to give the man who was hired last the same as I gave you. 15Don't I have the right to do what I want with my own money? Or are you envious because I am generous?'*i*

16"So the last will be first, and the first will be last."*k*

20:15
i Dt 15:9;
Mk 7:22

20:16
k Mt 19:30

Jesus Predicts His Death the Third Time
(177/Mark 10:32-34; Luke 18:31-34)

17Now as Jesus was going up to Jerusalem, he took the twelve disciples aside and said to them, 18"We are going up to Jerusalem, and the Son of Man will be betrayed to the chief priests and the teachers of the law.*l* They will condemn him to death 19and will turn him over to the Gentiles to be mocked and flogged*m* and crucified.*n* On the third day he will be raised to life!"

20:18
l Mt 27:1, 2

20:19
m Mt 16:21
n Ac 2:23

Jesus Teaches about Serving Others
(178/Mark 10:35-45)

20Then the mother of Zebedee's sons*o* came to Jesus with her sons and, kneeling down, asked a favor of him.

20:20
o Mt 4:21

21"What is it you want?" he asked.

She said, "Grant that one of these two sons of mine may sit at your right and the other at your left in your kingdom."*p*

20:21
p Mt 19:28

22"You don't know what you are asking," Jesus said to them. "Can you drink the cup*q* I am going to drink?"

"We can," they answered.

20:22
q Mt 26:39, 42;
Lk 22:42;
Jn 18:11

23Jesus said to them, "You will indeed drink from my cup,*r* but to sit at my right or left is not for me to grant. These places belong to those for whom they have been prepared by my Father."

20:23
r Ac 12:2;
Rev 1:9

24When the ten heard about this, they were indignant with the two brothers. 25Jesus called them together and said, "You know that the rulers of the Gentiles lord it over them, and their high officials exercise authority over them. 26Not so with you. Instead, whoever wants to become great among you must be your servant,*s* 27and whoever wants to be first must be your slave — 28just as the Son of

20:26
s Mk 9:35

20:15 This parable is not about rewards but about salvation. It is a strong teaching about *grace,* God's generosity. We shouldn't begrudge those who turn to God in the last moments of life, because, in reality, *no one* deserves eternal life.

Many people we don't expect to see in the kingdom will be there. The criminal who repented as he was dying (Luke 23:40-43) will be there along with people who have believed and served God for many years. Do you resent God's gracious acceptance of the despised, the outcast, and the sinners who have turned to him for forgiveness? Are you ever jealous of what God has given to another person? Instead, focus on God's gracious benefits to you, and be thankful for what you have.

20:17-19 Jesus predicted his death and resurrection for the third time (see 16:21 and 17:22, 23 for the first two times). But the disciples still didn't understand what he meant. They continued to argue greedily over their positions in Christ's kingdom (20:20-28).

20:20 The mother of James and John came to Jesus and "kneeling down, asked a favor of him." She gave Jesus worship, but her real motive was to get something from him. Too often this happens in our churches and in our lives. We play religious games, expecting God to give us something in return. True worship, however, adores and praises Christ for who he is and for what he has done.

20:20 The mother of James and John asked Jesus to give her sons special positions in his kingdom. Parents naturally want to see their children promoted and honored, but this desire is dangerous if it causes them to lose sight of God's specific will for their children. God may have different work in mind — not as glamorous, but just as important. Thus parents' desires for their children's ad-

vancement must be held in check as they pray that God's will be done in their children's lives.

20:20 According to 27:56, the mother of James and John was at the cross when Jesus was crucified. Some have suggested that she was the sister of Mary, the mother of Jesus. A close family relationship could have prompted her to make this request for her sons.

20:22 James, John, and their mother failed to grasp Jesus' previous teachings on rewards (19:16-30) and eternal life (20:1-16). They failed to understand the suffering they must face before living in the glory of God's kingdom. The "cup" was the suffering and crucifixion that Christ faced. Both James and John would also face great suffering. James would be put to death for his faith, and John would be exiled.

20:23 Jesus was showing that he was under the authority of the Father, who alone makes the decisions about leadership in heaven. Such rewards are not granted as favors. They are for those who have maintained their commitment to Jesus in spite of severe trials.

20:24 The other disciples were upset with James and John for trying to grab the top positions. *All* the disciples wanted to be the greatest (18:1), but Jesus taught them that the greatest person in God's kingdom is the servant of all. Authority is given not for self-importance, ambition, or respect, but for useful service to God and his creation.

20:27 Jesus described leadership from a new perspective. Instead of using people, we are to serve them. Jesus' mission was to serve others and to give his life away. A real leader has a servant's

20:28
t Jn 13:13-16;
Php 2:7
u Mt 26:28;
1Ti 2:6;
Tit 2:14;
Heb 9:28

20:30
v Mt 9:27

21:5
w Zec 9:9;
Isa 62:11

Man did not come to be served, but to serve,*t* and to give his life as a ransom*u* for many."

Jesus Heals a Blind Beggar
(179/Mark 10:46–52; Luke 18:35–43)

29 As Jesus and his disciples were leaving Jericho, a large crowd followed him. 30 Two blind men were sitting by the roadside, and when they heard that Jesus was going by, they shouted, "Lord, Son of David,*v* have mercy on us!"

31 The crowd rebuked them and told them to be quiet, but they shouted all the louder, "Lord, Son of David, have mercy on us!"

32 Jesus stopped and called them. "What do you want me to do for you?" he asked.

33 "Lord," they answered, "we want our sight."

34 Jesus had compassion on them and touched their eyes. Immediately they received their sight and followed him.

Jesus Rides into Jerusalem on a Donkey
(183/Mark 11:1–11; Luke 19:28–44; John 12:12–19)

21 As they approached Jerusalem and came to Bethphage on the Mount of Olives, Jesus sent two disciples, 2 saying to them, "Go to the village ahead of you, and at once you will find a donkey tied there, with her colt by her. Untie them and bring them to me. 3 If anyone says anything to you, tell him that the Lord needs them, and he will send them right away."

4 This took place to fulfill what was spoken through the prophet:

5 "Say to the Daughter of Zion,
    'See, your king comes to you,
  gentle and riding on a donkey,
    on a colt, the foal of a donkey.' "*e w*

6 The disciples went and did as Jesus had instructed them. 7 They brought the

e 5 Zech. 9:9

---

heart. Servant leaders appreciate others' worth and realize that they're not above any job. If you see something that needs to be done, don't wait to be asked. Take the initiative and do it like a faithful servant.

20:28 A ransom was the price paid to release a slave from bondage. Jesus often told his disciples that he must die, but here he told them why — to redeem all people from the bondage of sin and death. The disciples thought that as long as Jesus was alive, he could save them. But Jesus revealed that only his death would save them and the world.

20:29-34 Matthew records that there were two blind men, while Mark and Luke mention only one. This is probably the same event, but Mark and Luke singled out the more vocal of the two men.

20:30 The blind men called Jesus "Son of David" because the Jews knew that the Messiah would be a descendant of David (see Isaiah 9:6, 7; 11:1; Jeremiah 23:5, 6). These blind beggars could *see* that Jesus was the long-awaited Messiah, while the religious leaders who witnessed Jesus' miracles were blind to his identity, refusing to open their eyes to the truth. Seeing with your eyes doesn't guarantee seeing with your heart.

20:32, 33 Although Jesus was concerned about the coming events in Jerusalem, he demonstrated what he had just told the disciples about service (20:28) by stopping to care for the blind men.

21:2-5 Matthew mentions a donkey and a colt, while the other Gospels mention only the colt. This was the same event, but Matthew focuses on the prophecy in Zechariah 9:9, where a donkey and a colt are mentioned. He shows how Jesus' actions fulfilled the

prophet's words, thus giving another indication that Jesus was indeed the Messiah. When Jesus entered Jerusalem on a donkey's colt, he affirmed his Messianic royalty as well as his humility.

PREPARATION FOR THE TRIUMPHAL ENTRY
On their way from Jericho, Jesus and the disciples neared Bethphage, on the slope of the Mount of Olives just outside Jerusalem. Two disciples went into the village, as Jesus told them, to bring back a donkey and its colt. Jesus rode into Jerusalem on the donkey, an unmistakable sign of his kingship.

donkey and the colt, placed their cloaks on them, and Jesus sat on them. 8A very large crowd spread their cloaks on the road, while others cut branches from the trees and spread them on the road. 9The crowds that went ahead of him and those that followed shouted,

> "Hosanna𝑓 to the Son of David!"

> "Blessed is he who comes in the name of the Lord!"𝘨ˣ

> "Hosanna𝑓 in the highest!"

21:9
ˣPs 118:26

10When Jesus entered Jerusalem, the whole city was stirred and asked, "Who is this?"

11The crowds answered, "This is Jesus, the prophet𝑦 from Nazareth in Galilee."

21:11
𝑦Jn 6:14; 7:40

Jesus Clears the Temple Again
(184/Mark 11:12–19; Luke 19:45–48)

12Jesus entered the temple area and drove out all who were buying and selling there. He overturned the tables of the money changers and the benches of those selling doves. 13"It is written," he said to them, " 'My house will be called a house of prayer,'ʰᶻ but you are making it a 'den of robbers.'ⁱᵃ

21:13
ᶻIsa 56:7
ᵃJer 7:11

14The blind and the lame came to him at the temple, and he healed them. 15But when the chief priests and the teachers of the law saw the wonderful things he did and the children shouting in the temple area, "Hosanna to the Son of David," they were indignant.

16"Do you hear what these children are saying?" they asked him.

"Yes," replied Jesus, "have you never read,

> " 'From the lips of children and infants
>   you have ordained praise'ʲ?" ᵇ

21:16
ᵇPs 8:2

17And he left them and went out of the city to Bethany, where he spent the night.

Jesus Says the Disciples Can Pray for Anything
(188/Mark 11:20–26)

18Early in the morning, as he was on his way back to the city, he was hungry. 19Seeing a fig tree by the road, he went up to it but found nothing on it except leaves. Then he said to it, "May you never bear fruit again!" Immediately the tree withered.

20When the disciples saw this, they were amazed. "How did the fig tree wither so quickly?" they asked.

21Jesus replied, "I tell you the truth, if you have faith and do not doubt,ᶜ not

21:21
ᶜMt 17:20;
Lk 17:6;
Jas 1:6

𝑓 9 A Hebrew expression meaning "Save!" which became an exclamation of praise; also in verse 15 𝘨 9 Psalm 118:26 ʰ 13 Isaiah 56:7 ⁱ 13 Jer. 7:11 ʲ 16 Psalm 8:2

21:8 This verse is one of the few places where the Gospels record that Jesus' glory is recognized on earth. Jesus boldly declared himself King, and the crowd gladly joined him. But these same people would bow to political pressure and desert him in just a few days. Today we celebrate this event on Palm Sunday. That day should remind us to guard against superficial acclaim for Christ.

21:12 This is the second time Jesus cleared the temple (see John 2:13–17). Merchants and money changers set up their booths in the court of the Gentiles in the temple, crowding out the Gentiles who had come from all over the civilized world to worship God. The merchants sold sacrificial animals at high prices, taking advantage of those who had come long distances. The money changers exchanged all international currency for the special temple coins—the only money the merchants would accept. They often deceived foreigners who didn't know the exchange rates. Their commercialism in God's house frustrated people's attempts at worship. This, of course, greatly angered Jesus. Any practice that

interferes with worshiping God should be stopped.

21:19 Why did Jesus curse the fig tree? This was not a thoughtless, angry act, but an acted-out parable. Jesus was showing his anger at religion without substance. Just as the fig tree looked good from a distance but was fruitless on close examination, so the temple looked impressive at first glance, but its sacrifices and other activities were hollow because they were not done to worship God sincerely (see 21:43). If you only appear to have faith without putting it to work in your life, you are like the fig tree that withered and died because it bore no fruit. Genuine faith means bearing fruit for God's kingdom. For more information about the fig tree, see the note on Mark 11:13–26.

21:21 Many have wondered about Jesus' statement that if we have faith and don't doubt, we can move mountains. Jesus, of course, was not suggesting that his followers use prayer as "magic" and perform capricious "mountain-moving" acts. Instead, he was making a strong point about the disciples' (and our) lack of faith. What kinds of mountains do you face? Have you talked to

only can you do what was done to the fig tree, but also you can say to this mountain, 'Go, throw yourself into the sea,' and it will be done. 22If you believe, you will receive whatever you ask for*d* in prayer."

21:22
d Mt 7:7

Religious Leaders Challenge Jesus' Authority
(189/Mark 11:27–33; Luke 20:1–8)

21:23
e Ac 4:7

23Jesus entered the temple courts, and, while he was teaching, the chief priests and the elders of the people came to him. "By what authority*e* are you doing these things?" they asked. "And who gave you this authority?"

24Jesus replied, "I will also ask you one question. If you answer me, I will tell you by what authority I am doing these things. 25John's baptism — where did it come from? Was it from heaven, or from men?"

They discussed it among themselves and said, "If we say, 'From heaven,' he will ask, 'Then why didn't you believe him?' 26But if we say, 'From men' — we are afraid of the people, for they all hold that John was a prophet."

27So they answered Jesus, "We don't know."

Then he said, "Neither will I tell you by what authority I am doing these things.

Jesus Tells the Parable of the Two Sons
(190)

21:28
f ver 33

28"What do you think? There was a man who had two sons. He went to the first and said, 'Son, go and work today in the vineyard.'*f*

29" 'I will not,' he answered, but later he changed his mind and went.

30"Then the father went to the other son and said the same thing. He answered, 'I will, sir,' but he did not go.

31"Which of the two did what his father wanted?"

"The first," they answered.

21:31
g Lk 7:29
h Lk 7:50
21:32
i Mt 3:1-12
j Lk 3:12, 13

Jesus said to them, "I tell you the truth, the tax collectors*g* and the prostitutes*h* are entering the kingdom of God ahead of you. 32For John came to you to show you the way of righteousness,*i* and you did not believe him, but the tax collectors*j* and the prostitutes did. And even after you saw this, you did not repent and believe him.

Jesus Tells the Parable of the Wicked Tenants
(191/Mark 12:1–12; Luke 20:9–19)

21:33
k Ps 80:8
l Isa 5:1-7
m Mt 25:14, 15

33"Listen to another parable: There was a landowner who planted*k* a vineyard. He put a wall around it, dug a winepress in it and built a watchtower.*l* Then he rented the vineyard to some farmers and went away on a journey.*m* 34When the harvest time approached, he sent his servants to the tenants to collect his fruit.

God about them? How strong is your faith?

21:22 This verse is not a guarantee that we can get *anything* we want simply by asking Jesus and believing. God does not grant requests that would hurt us or others or that would violate his own nature or will. Jesus' statement is not a blank check. To be fulfilled, our requests must be in harmony with the principles of God's kingdom. The stronger our belief, the more likely our prayers will be in line with God's will, and then God will be happy to grant them.

21:23-25 In Jesus' world, as in ours, people looked for the outward sign of authority — education, title, position, connections. But Jesus' authority came from who he was, not from any outward and superficial trappings. As followers of Christ, God has given us authority — we can confidently speak and act on his behalf because he has authorized us. Are you exercising your authority?

21:23-27 The Pharisees demanded to know where Jesus got his authority. If Jesus said his authority came from God, they would accuse him of blasphemy. If he said that he was acting on his own authority, the crowds would be convinced that the Pharisees had the greater authority. But Jesus answered them with a seemingly

unrelated question that exposed their real motives. They didn't really want an answer to their question; they only wanted to trap him. Jesus showed that the Pharisees wanted the truth only if it supported their own views and causes.

21:25 For more information on John the Baptist, see Matthew 3 and his Profile in John 1.

● **21:30** The son who said he would obey and then didn't represented the nation of Israel in Jesus' day. They said they wanted to do God's will, but they constantly disobeyed. They were phony, just going through the motions. It is dangerous to pretend to obey God when our hearts are far from him because God knows our true intentions. Our actions must match our words.

● **21:33ff** The main elements in this parable are (1) the landowner — God, (2) the vineyard — Israel, (3) the tenants — the Jewish religious leaders, (4) the landowner's servants — the prophets and priests who remained faithful to God and preached to Israel, (5) the son — Jesus (21:38), and (6) the other tenants — the Gentiles. Jesus was exposing the religious leaders' murderous plot (21:45).

35"The tenants seized his servants; they beat one, killed another, and stoned a
third.[n] 36Then he sent other servants to them, more than the first time, and the
tenants treated them the same way. 37Last of all, he sent his son to them. 'They will
respect my son,' he said.

38"But when the tenants saw the son, they said to each other, 'This is the heir.[o]
Come, let's kill him and take his inheritance.'[p] 39So they took him and threw him
out of the vineyard and killed him.

40"Therefore, when the owner of the vineyard comes, what will he do to those
tenants?"

41"He will bring those wretches to a wretched end," they replied, "and he will
rent the vineyard to other tenants,[q] who will give him his share of the crop at
harvest time."

42Jesus said to them, "Have you never read in the Scriptures:

" 'The stone the builders rejected
has become the capstone[k];
the Lord has done this,
and it is marvelous in our eyes'[l]?[r]

43"Therefore I tell you that the kingdom of God will be taken away from you[s]
and given to a people who will produce its fruit. 44He who falls on this stone will
be broken to pieces, but he on whom it falls will be crushed."[m]

45When the chief priests and the Pharisees heard Jesus' parables, they knew he
was talking about them. 46They looked for a way to arrest him, but they were afraid
of the crowd because the people held that he was a prophet.[t]

21:35 [n]2Ch 24:21; Mt 23:34, 37; Heb 11:36, 37
21:38 [o]Heb 1:2 [p]Ps 2:8
21:41 [q]Ac 13:46
21:42 [r]Ps 118:22, 23; Ac 4:11
21:43 [s]Mt 8:12
21:46 [t]ver 11, 26

Jesus Tells the Parable of the Wedding Feast
(192)

22 Jesus spoke to them again in parables, saying: 2"The kingdom of heaven is
like[u] a king who prepared a wedding banquet for his son. 3He sent his servants[v] to those who had been invited to the banquet to tell them to come, but they
refused to come.

4"Then he sent some more servants[w] and said, 'Tell those who have been invited
that I have prepared my dinner: My oxen and fattened cattle have been butchered,
and everything is ready. Come to the wedding banquet.'

5"But they paid no attention and went off—one to his field, another to his business. 6The rest seized his servants, mistreated them and killed them. 7The king was
enraged. He sent his army and destroyed those murderers[x] and burned their city.

8"Then he said to his servants, 'The wedding banquet is ready, but those I invited
did not deserve to come. 9Go to the street corners and invite to the banquet anyone
you find.' 10So the servants went out into the streets and gathered all the people
they could find, both good and bad, and the wedding hall was filled with guests.

11"But when the king came in to see the guests, he noticed a man there who was

22:2 [u]Mt 13:24
22:3 [v]Mt 21:34
22:4 [w]Mt 21:36
22:7 [x]Lk 19:27

[k] 42 Or *cornerstone* [l] 42 Psalm 118:22,23 [m] 44 Some manuscripts do not have verse 44.

21:37 In trying to reach us with his love, God finally sent his own Son. Jesus' perfect life, his words of truth, and his sacrifice of love are meant to cause us to listen to him and to follow him as Lord. If we ignore God's gracious gift of his Son, we reject God himself.

21:42 Jesus refers to himself as "the stone the builders rejected." Although Jesus was rejected by many of his people, he will become the capstone, or cornerstone, of his new building, the church (see Acts 4:11; 1 Peter 2:7).

21:44 Jesus used this metaphor to show that one stone can affect people different ways, depending on how they relate to it (see Isaiah 8:14, 15; 28:16; Daniel 2:34, 44, 45). Ideally they will build on it; many, however, will trip over it. And at the last judgment God's enemies will be crushed by it. In the end, Christ, the "building block," will become the "crushing stone." He offers mercy and forgiveness *now* and promises judgment later. We should choose him now!

22:1–14 In this culture, two invitations were expected when banquets were given. The first asked the guests to attend; the second announced that all was ready. In this story the king invited his guests three times—and each time they rejected his invitation. God wants us to join him at his banquet, which will last for eternity. That's why he sends us invitations again and again. Have you accepted his invitation?

22:11, 12 It was customary for wedding guests to be given garments to wear to the banquet. It was unthinkable to refuse to wear these garments. That would insult the host, who could only assume that the guest was arrogant and thought he didn't need these garments, or that he did not want to take part in the wedding celebration. The wedding clothes picture the righteousness needed to

22:12
y Mt 20:13; 26:50

22:13
z Mt 8:12

not wearing wedding clothes. 12'Friend,'y he asked, 'how did you get in here without wedding clothes?' The man was speechless.

13"Then the king told the attendants, 'Tie him hand and foot, and throw him outside, into the darkness, where there will be weeping and gnashing of teeth.'z

14"For many are invited, but few are chosen."

Religious Leaders Question Jesus about Paying Taxes
(193/Mark 12:13–17; Luke 20:20–26)

22:16
a Mk 3:6

22:17
b Mt 17:25

15Then the Pharisees went out and laid plans to trap him in his words. 16They sent their disciples to him along with the Herodians.a "Teacher," they said, "we know you are a man of integrity and that you teach the way of God in accordance with the truth. You aren't swayed by men, because you pay no attention to who they are. 17Tell us then, what is your opinion? Is it right to pay taxesb to Caesar or not?"

18But Jesus, knowing their evil intent, said, "You hypocrites, why are you trying to trap me? 19Show me the coin used for paying the tax." They brought him a denarius, 20and he asked them, "Whose portrait is this? And whose inscription?"

21"Caesar's," they replied.

22:21
c Ro 13:7

Then he said to them, "Give to Caesar what is Caesar's,c and to God what is God's."

22When they heard this, they were amazed. So they left him and went away.

Religious Leaders Question Jesus about the Resurrection
(194/Mark 12:18–27; Luke 20:27–40)

22:23
d Ac 23:8

22:24
e Dt 25:5, 6

23That same day the Sadducees, who say there is no resurrection,d came to him with a question. 24"Teacher," they said, "Moses told us that if a man dies without having children, his brother must marry the widow and have children for him.e 25Now there were seven brothers among us. The first one married and died, and since he had no children, he left his wife to his brother. 26The same thing happened to the second and third brother, right on down to the seventh. 27Finally, the woman died. 28Now then, at the resurrection, whose wife will she be of the seven, since all of them were married to her?"

---

enter God's kingdom — the total acceptance in God's eyes that Christ gives every believer. Christ has provided this garment of righteousness for everyone, but each person must choose to put it on in order to enter the King's banquet (eternal life). There is an open invitation, but we must be ready. For more on the imagery of clothes of righteousness and salvation, see Psalm 132:16; Isaiah 61:10; Zechariah 3:3–5; Revelation 3:4, 5; 19:7, 8.

22:15–17 The Pharisees, a religious group, opposed the Roman occupation of Palestine. The Herodians, a political party, supported Herod Antipas and the policies instituted by Rome. Normally these two groups were bitter enemies, but here they united against Jesus. Thinking they had a foolproof plan to corner him, together their representatives asked Jesus about paying Roman taxes. If Jesus agreed that it was right to pay taxes to Caesar, the Pharisees would say he was opposed to God, the only King they recognized. If Jesus said the taxes should not be paid, the Herodians would hand him over to Herod on the charge of rebellion. In this case the Pharisees were not motivated by love for God's laws, and the Herodians were not motivated by love for Roman justice. Jesus' answer exposed their evil motives and embarrassed them both.

22:17 The Jews were required to pay taxes to support the Roman government. They hated this taxation because the money went directly into Caesar's treasury, where some of it went to support the pagan temples and decadent life-style of the Roman aristocracy.

Caesar's image on the coins was a constant reminder of Israel's subjection to Rome.

22:19 The denarius was the usual day's wage for a laborer.

22:21 Jesus avoided this trap by showing that we have dual citizenship (1 Peter 2:17). Our citizenship in the nation requires that we pay money for the services and benefits we receive. Our citizenship in the kingdom of heaven requires that we pledge to God our primary obedience and commitment.

22:23ff After the Pharisees and Herodians had failed to trap Jesus, the Sadducees smugly stepped in to try. They did not believe in the resurrection because the Pentateuch (Genesis — Deuteronomy) has no direct teaching on it. The Pharisees had never been able to come up with a convincing argument from the Pentateuch for the resurrection, and the Sadducees thought they had trapped Jesus for sure. But Jesus was about to show them otherwise (see 22:31, 32 for Jesus' answer).

22:24 For more information on Moses, see his Profile in Exodus 14.

22:24 The law said that when a woman's husband died without having a son, the man's brother had a responsibility to marry and care for the widow (Deuteronomy 25:5, 6). This law protected women who were left alone, because in that culture they usually had no other means to support themselves.

29Jesus replied, "You are in error because you do not know the Scriptures[f] or the power of God. 30At the resurrection people will neither marry nor be given in marriage; they will be like the angels in heaven. 31But about the resurrection of the dead — have you not read what God said to you, 32'I am the God of Abraham, the God of Isaac, and the God of Jacob'[n]?[g] He is not the God of the dead but of the living."

33When the crowds heard this, they were astonished at his teaching.[h]

Religious Leaders Question Jesus about the Greatest Commandment
(195/Mark 12:28–34)

34Hearing that Jesus had silenced the Sadducees, the Pharisees got together. 35One of them, an expert in the law,[i] tested him with this question: 36"Teacher, which is the greatest commandment in the Law?"

37Jesus replied: " 'Love the Lord your God with all your heart and with all your soul and with all your mind.'[o][j] 38This is the first and greatest commandment. 39And the second is like it: 'Love your neighbor as yourself.'[p][k] 40All the Law and the Prophets hang on these two commandments."[l]

Religious Leaders Cannot Answer Jesus' Question
(196/Mark 12:35–37; Luke 20:41–44)

41While the Pharisees were gathered together, Jesus asked them, 42"What do you think about the Christ[q]? Whose son is he?"

"The son of David," they replied.

43He said to them, "How is it then that David, speaking by the Spirit, calls him 'Lord'? For he says,

44 " 'The Lord said to my Lord:
"Sit at my right hand
until I put your enemies
under your feet." '[r][m]

45If then David calls him 'Lord,' how can he be his son?" 46No one could say a word in reply, and from that day on no one dared to ask him any more questions.[n]

n *32* Exodus 3:6   o *37* Deut. 6:5   p *39* Lev. 19:18   q *42* Or *Messiah*   r *44* Psalm 110:1

22:29
f Jn 20:9

22:32
g Ex 3:6;
Ac 7:32

22:33
h Mt 7:28

22:35
i Lk 7:30; 10:25;
11:45

22:37
j Dt 6:5

22:39
k Lev 19:18;
Mt 5:43

22:40
l Mt 7:12

22:44
m Ps 110:1;
Ac 2:34, 35;
Heb 1:13; 10:13

22:46
n Mk 12:34

22:29, 30 The Sadducees asked Jesus what marriage would be like in heaven. Jesus said it was more important to understand God's power than know what heaven will be like. In every generation and culture, ideas of eternal life tend to be based on images and experiences of present life. Jesus answered that these faulty ideas are caused by ignorance of God's Word. We must not make up our own ideas about eternity and heaven by thinking of it and God in human terms. We should concentrate more on our relationship with God than about what heaven will look like. Eventually we will find out, and it will be far beyond our greatest expectations.

22:31, 32 Because the Sadducees accepted only the Pentateuch as God's divine Word, Jesus answered them from the book of Exodus (3:6). God would not have said, "I am the God of Abraham, the God of Isaac, and the God of Jacob" if God thought of Abraham, Isaac, and Jacob as dead. From God's perspective, they are alive. Jesus' use of the present tense pointed to the resurrection and the eternal life that all believers enjoy in him.

22:34 We might think the Pharisees would have been glad to see the Sadducees silenced. The question that the Sadducees had always used to trap them was finally answered by Jesus. But the Pharisees were too proud to be impressed. Jesus' answer gave them a theological victory over the Sadducees, but they were more interested in defeating Jesus than in learning the truth.

22:35-40 The Pharisees, who had classified over 600 laws, often tried to distinguish the more important from the less important. So one of them, an "expert in the law," asked Jesus to identify the most important law. Jesus quoted from Deuteronomy 6:5 and Leviticus 19:18. By fulfilling these two commands, a person keeps all the others. They summarize the Ten Commandments and the other Old Testament moral laws.

22:37-40 Jesus says that if we truly love God and our neighbor, we will naturally keep the commandments. This is looking at God's law positively. Rather than worrying about all we should *not* do, we should concentrate on all we *can* do to show our love for God and others.

22:41-45 The Pharisees, Herodians, and Sadducees had asked their questions. Then Jesus turned the tables and asked them a penetrating question — who they thought the Messiah was. The Pharisees knew that the Messiah would be a descendant of David, but they did not understand that he would be God himself. Jesus quoted from Psalm 110:1 to show that the Messiah would be greater than David. (Hebrews 1:13 uses the same text as proof of Christ's deity.) The most important question we will ever answer is what we believe about Christ. Other theological questions are irrelevant until we believe that Jesus is who he said he is.

Jesus Warns against the Religious Leaders
(197/Mark 12:38–40; Luke 20:45–47)

23 Then Jesus said to the crowds and to his disciples: 2"The teachers of the law and the Pharisees sit in Moses' seat. 3So you must obey them and do everything they tell you. But do not do what they do, for they do not practice what they preach. 4They tie up heavy loads and put them on men's shoulders, but they themselves are not willing to lift a finger to move them. *o*

5"Everything they do is done for men to see:*p* They make their phylacteries**s** *q* wide and the tassels on their garments long; 6they love the place of honor at banquets and the most important seats in the synagogues;*r* 7they love to be greeted in the marketplaces and to have men call them 'Rabbi.'

8"But you are not to be called 'Rabbi,' for you have only one Master and you are all brothers. 9And do not call anyone on earth 'father,' for you have one Father, and he is in heaven. 10Nor are you to be called 'teacher,' for you have one Teacher, the Christ.*t* 11The greatest among you will be your servant. 12For whoever exalts himself will be humbled, and whoever humbles himself will be exalted. *s*

Jesus Condemns the Religious Leaders
(198)

13"Woe to you, teachers of the law and Pharisees, you hypocrites! You shut the kingdom of heaven in men's faces. You yourselves do not enter, nor will you let those enter who are trying to.*u* *t*

15"Woe to you, teachers of the law and Pharisees, you hypocrites! You travel over land and sea to win a single convert, and when he becomes one, you make him twice as much a son of hell as you are.

16"Woe to you, blind guides!*u* You say, 'If anyone swears by the temple, it means nothing; but if anyone swears by the gold of the temple, he is bound by his oath.' *v* 17You blind fools! Which is greater: the gold, or the temple that makes the gold sacred?*w* 18You also say, 'If anyone swears by the altar, it means nothing; but if anyone swears by the gift on it, he is bound by his oath.' 19You blind men! Which is greater: the gift, or the altar that makes the gift sacred?*x* 20Therefore, he who swears by the altar swears by it and by everything on it. 21And he who swears by

23:4
*o*Lk 11:46

23:5
*p*Mt 6:1, 2, 5, 16
*q*Dt 6:8

23:6
*r*Lk 11:43

23:12
*s*Lk 14:11

23:13
*t*Lk 11:52

23:16
*u*ver 24
*v*Mt 5:33-35

23:17
*w*Ex 30:29

23:19
*x*Ex 29:37

s *5* That is, boxes containing Scripture verses, worn on forehead and arm   **t** *10* Or *Messiah*   **u** *13* Some manuscripts *to. 14Woe to you, teachers of the law and Pharisees, you hypocrites! You devour widows' houses and for a show make lengthy prayers. Therefore you will be punished more severely.*

● **23:2, 3**   The Pharisees' traditions and their interpretations and applications of the laws had become as important to them as God's law itself. Their laws were not all bad — some were beneficial. The problem arose when the religious leaders (1) took manmade rules as seriously as God's laws, (2) told the people to obey these rules but did not do so themselves, or (3) obeyed the rules not to honor God but to make themselves look good. Usually Jesus did not condemn what the Pharisees taught, but what they *were* — hypocrites.

● **23:5**   Phylacteries were little leather boxes containing Scripture verses. Very religious people wore these boxes on their forehead and arms in order to obey Deuteronomy 6:8 and Exodus 13:9, 16. But the phylacteries had become more important for the status they gave than for the truth they contained.

● **23:5–7**   Jesus again exposed the hypocritical attitudes of the religious leaders. They knew the Scriptures but did not live by them. They didn't care about *being* holy — just *looking* holy in order to receive the people's admiration and praise. Today, like the Pharisees, many people who know the Bible do not let it change their lives. They say they follow Jesus, but they don't live by his standards of love. People who live this way are hypocrites. We must make sure that our actions match our beliefs.

● **23:5–7**   People desire positions of leadership not only in business but also in the church. It is dangerous when love for the position grows stronger than loyalty to God. This is what happened to the Pharisees and teachers of the law. Jesus is not against all leadership — we need Christian leaders — but against leadership that serves itself rather than others.

23:11, 12   Jesus challenged society's norms. To him, greatness comes from serving — giving of yourself to help God and others. Service keeps us aware of others' needs, and it stops us from focusing only on ourselves. Jesus came as a servant. What kind of greatness do you seek?

● **23:13, 14**   Being a religious leader in Jerusalem was very different from being a pastor in a secular society today. Israel's history, culture, and daily life centered around its relationship with God. The religious leaders were the best known, most powerful, and most respected of all leaders. Jesus made these stinging accusations because the leaders' hunger for more power, money, and status had made them lose sight of God, and their blindness was spreading to the whole nation.

● **23:15**   The Pharisees' converts were attracted to Pharisaism, not to God. By getting caught up in the details of their additional laws and regulations, they completely missed God, to whom the laws pointed. A religion of deeds puts pressure on people to surpass others in what they know and do. Thus, a hypocritical teacher was likely to have students who were even more hypocritical. We must make sure we are not creating Pharisees by emphasizing outward obedience at the expense of inner renewal.

the temple swears by it and by the one who dwells in it. 22And he who swears by heaven swears by God's throne and by the one who sits on it.*y*

23"Woe to you, teachers of the law and Pharisees, you hypocrites! You give a tenth of your spices — mint, dill and cummin. But you have neglected the more important matters of the law — justice, mercy and faithfulness.*z* You should have practiced the latter, without neglecting the former. 24You blind guides! You strain out a gnat but swallow a camel.

25"Woe to you, teachers of the law and Pharisees, you hypocrites! You clean the outside of the cup and dish,*a* but inside they are full of greed and self-indulgence.*b* 26Blind Pharisee! First clean the inside of the cup and dish, and then the outside also will be clean.

27"Woe to you, teachers of the law and Pharisees, you hypocrites! You are like whitewashed tombs,*c* which look beautiful on the outside but on the inside are full of dead men's bones and everything unclean. 28In the same way, on the outside you appear to people as righteous but on the inside you are full of hypocrisy and wickedness.

29"Woe to you, teachers of the law and Pharisees, you hypocrites! You build tombs for the prophets*d* and decorate the graves of the righteous. 30And you say, 'If we had lived in the days of our forefathers, we would not have taken part with them in shedding the blood of the prophets.' 31So you testify against yourselves that you are the descendants of those who murdered the prophets. 32Fill up, then, the measure of the sin of your forefathers!

33"You snakes! You brood of vipers!*e* How will you escape being condemned to hell? 34Therefore I am sending you prophets and wise men and teachers. Some of them you will kill and crucify;*f* others you will flog in your synagogues*g* and pursue from town to town. 35And so upon you will come all the righteous blood that has been shed on earth, from the blood of righteous Abel*h* to the blood of Zechariah son of Berekiah, whom you murdered between the temple and the altar.*i* 36I tell you the truth, all this will come upon this generation.

Jesus Grieves over Jerusalem Again
(199)

37"O Jerusalem, Jerusalem, you who kill the prophets and stone those sent to you,*j* how often I have longed to gather your children together, as a hen gathers her chicks under her wings, but you were not willing. 38Look, your house is left to

23:22
yMt 5:34

23:23
zLk 11:42

23:25
aMk 7:4
bLk 11:39

23:27
cLk 11:44

23:29
dLk 11:47, 48

23:33
eMt 3:7

23:34
fLk 11:49
gMt 10:17

23:35
hGe 4:8
i2Ch 24:21

23:37
i2Ch 24:21

• **23:23, 24** It's possible to obey the details of the laws but still be disobedient in our general behavior. For example, we could be very precise and faithful about giving 10 percent of our money to God, but refuse to give one minute of our time in helping others. Tithing is important, but giving a tithe does not exempt us from fulfilling God's other directives.

• **23:24** The Pharisees strained their water so they wouldn't accidentally swallow a gnat — an unclean insect according to the law. Meticulous about the details of ceremonial cleanliness, they nevertheless had lost their perspective on inner purity. Ceremonially clean on the outside, they had corrupt hearts.

• **23:25-28** Jesus condemned the Pharisees and religious leaders for outwardly appearing saintly and holy but inwardly remaining full of corruption and greed. Living our Christianity merely as a show for others is like washing a cup on the outside only. When we are clean on the inside, our cleanliness on the outside won't be a sham.

• **23:34-36** These prophets, wise men, and teachers were probably leaders in the early church who were persecuted, scourged, and killed, as Jesus predicted. The people of Jesus' generation said they would not act as their fathers did in killing the prophets whom God had sent to them (23:30), but they were about to kill the

Messiah himself and his faithful followers. Thus they would become guilty of all the righteous blood shed through the centuries.

23:35 Jesus was giving a brief history of Old Testament martyrdom. Abel was the first martyr (Genesis 4); Zechariah was the last mentioned in the Hebrew Bible, which ended with 2 Chronicles. Zechariah is a classic example of a man of God who was killed by those who claimed to be God's people (see 2 Chronicles 24:20, 21).

23:37 Jesus wanted to gather his people together as a hen protects her chicks under her wings, but they wouldn't let him. Jesus also wants to protect us if we will just come to him. Many times we hurt and don't know where to turn. We reject Christ's help because we don't think he can give us what we need. But who knows our needs better than our Creator? Those who turn to Jesus will find that he helps and comforts as no one else can.

23:37 Jerusalem was the capital city of God's chosen people, the ancestral home of David, Israel's greatest king, and the location of the temple, the earthly dwelling place of God. It was intended to be the center of worship of the true God and a symbol of justice to all people. But Jerusalem had become blind to God and insensitive to human need. Here we see the depth of Jesus' feelings for lost people and for his beloved city, which would soon be destroyed.

23:39
kPs 118:26;
Mt 21:9

you desolate. 39For I tell you, you will not see me again until you say, 'Blessed is he who comes in the name of the Lord.'v"k

7. Jesus teaches on the Mount of Olives

Jesus Tells about the Future
(201/Mark 13:1–23; Luke 21:5–24)

24 Jesus left the temple and was walking away when his disciples came up to him to call his attention to its buildings. 2"Do you see all these things?" he

24:2
lLk 19:44

asked. "I tell you the truth, not one stone here will be left on another;l every one will be thrown down."

3As Jesus was sitting on the Mount of Olives, the disciples came to him privately. "Tell us," they said, "when will this happen, and what will be the sign of your coming and of the end of the age?"

4Jesus answered: "Watch out that no one deceives you. 5For many will come in

24:5
mver 11, 23, 24

my name, claiming, 'I am the Christ,w' and will deceive many.m 6You will hear of wars and rumors of wars, but see to it that you are not alarmed. Such things must happen, but the end is still to come. 7Nation will rise against nation, and kingdom

24:7
nIsa 19:2

against kingdom.n There will be famines and earthquakes in various places. 8All these are the beginning of birth pains.

24:9
oMt 10:17
pJn 16:2

9"Then you will be handed over to be persecutedo and put to death,p and you will be hated by all nations because of me. 10At that time many will turn away from

v 39 Psalm 118:26   w 5 Or Messiah; also in verse 23

THE SEVEN WOES	23:14	Not letting others enter the kingdom of heaven and not entering yourselves
	23:15	Converting people away from God to be like yourselves
	23:16–22	Blindly leading God's people to follow man-made traditions instead of God's Word
	23:23, 24	Involving yourself in every last detail and ignoring what is really important: justice, mercy, and faith
	23:25, 26	Keeping up appearances while your private world is corrupt
	23:27, 28	Acting spiritual to cover up sin
	23:29–36	Pretending to have learned from past history, but your present behavior shows you have learned nothing

Jesus mentioned seven ways to guarantee God's anger, often called the "seven woes." These seven statements about the religious leaders must have been spoken with a mixed tone of judgment and sorrow. They were strong and unforgettable. They are still applicable any time we become so involved in perfecting the practice of religion that we forget that God is also concerned with mercy, real love, and forgiveness.

24:1, 2 Although no one knows exactly what this temple looked like, it must have been beautiful. Herod had helped the Jews remodel and beautify it, no doubt to stay on friendly terms with his subjects. Next to the inner temple, where the sacred objects were kept and the sacrifices offered, there was a large area called the court of the Gentiles (this was where the money changers and merchants had their booths). Outside these courts were long porches. Solomon's porch was 1,562 feet long; the royal portico was decorated with 160 columns stretching along its 921-foot length. Gazing at this glorious and massive structure, the disciples found Jesus' words about its destruction difficult to believe. But the temple was indeed destroyed only 40 years later when the Romans sacked Jerusalem in A.D. 70.

● **24:3ff** Jesus was sitting on the Mount of Olives, the very place where the prophet Zechariah had predicted that the Messiah would stand when he came to establish his kingdom (Zechariah 14:4). It was a fitting place for the disciples to ask Jesus when he would come in power and what they could expect then. Jesus' reply emphasized the events that would take place before the end of the age. He pointed out that his disciples should be less con-

cerned with knowing the exact date and more concerned with being prepared — living God's way consistently so that no matter when Jesus came in glory, he would claim them as his own.

24:4 The disciples asked Jesus for the sign of his coming and of the end of the age. Jesus' first response was "Watch out that no one deceives you." The fact is that whenever we look for signs, we become very susceptible to being deceived. There are many "false prophets" (24:11, 24) around with counterfeit signs of spiritual power and authority. The only sure way to keep from being deceived is to focus on Christ and his words. Don't look for special signs, and don't spend time looking at other people. Look at Christ.

24:9-13 You may not be facing intense persecution now, but Christians in other parts of the world are. As you hear about Christians suffering for their faith, remember that they are your brothers and sisters in Christ. Pray for them. Ask God what you can do to help them in their troubles. When one part suffers, the *whole* body suffers. But when all the parts join together to ease the suffering, the whole body benefits (1 Corinthians 12:26).

the faith and will betray and hate each other, 11and many false prophets will appear and deceive many people. 12Because of the increase of wickedness, the love of most will grow cold, 13but he who stands firm to the end will be saved. q 14And this gospel of the kingdom will be preached in the whole world r as a testimony to all nations, and then the end will come.

15"So when you see standing in the holy place 'the abomination that causes desolation,' x s spoken of through the prophet Daniel — let the reader understand — 16then let those who are in Judea flee to the mountains. 17Let no one on the roof of his house go down to take anything out of the house. 18Let no one in the field go back to get his cloak. 19How dreadful it will be in those days for pregnant women and nursing mothers! t 20Pray that your flight will not take place in winter or on the Sabbath. 21For then there will be great distress, unequaled from the beginning of the world until now — and never to be equaled again. u 22If those days had not been cut short, no one would survive, but for the sake of the elect those days will be shortened. 23At that time if anyone says to you, 'Look, here is the Christ!' or, 'There he is!' do not believe it. v 24For false Christs and false prophets will appear and perform great signs and miracles w to deceive even the elect — if that were possible. 25See, I have told you ahead of time.

Jesus Tells about His Return
(202/Mark 13:24–31; Luke 21:25–33)

26"So if anyone tells you, 'There he is, out in the desert,' do not go out; or, 'Here he is, in the inner rooms,' do not believe it. 27For as lightning x that comes from the east is visible even in the west, so will be the coming of the Son of Man. 28Wherever there is a carcass, there the vultures will gather. y

29"Immediately after the distress of those days

> " 'the sun will be darkened,
> and the moon will not give its light;
> the stars will fall from the sky,
> and the heavenly bodies will be shaken.' y z

x 15 Daniel 9:27; 11:31; 12:11   y 29 Isaiah 13:10; 34:4

24:13
q Mt 10:22

24:14
r Ro 10:18

24:15
s Da 9:27; 12:11

24:19
t Lk 23:29

24:21
u Joel 2:2

24:23
v Lk 17:23; 21:8

24:24
w 2Th 2:9-11

24:27
x Lk 17:24

24:28
y Lk 17:37

24:29
z Eze 32:7;
Joel 2:10, 31

24:11 The Old Testament frequently mentions false prophets (see 2 Kings 3:13; Isaiah 44:25; Jeremiah 23:16; Ezekiel 13:2, 3; Micah 3:5; Zechariah 13:2). False prophets claimed to receive messages from God, but they preached a "health and wealth" message. They said what the people wanted to hear, even when the nation was not following God as it should. There were false prophets in Jesus' day, and we have them today. They are the popular leaders who tell people what they want to hear — such as "God wants you to be rich," "Do whatever your desires tell you," or "There is no such thing as sin or hell." Jesus said false teachers would come, and he warned his disciples, as he warns us, not to listen to their dangerous words.

24:12 With false teaching and loose morals comes a particularly destructive disease — the loss of true love for God and others. Sin cools your love for God and others by turning your focus on yourself. You cannot truly love if you think only of yourself.

24:13 Jesus predicted that his followers would be severely persecuted by those who hated what he stood for. In the midst of terrible persecutions, however, they could have hope, knowing that salvation was theirs. Times of trial serve to sift true Christians from false or fair-weather Christians. When you are pressured to give up and turn your back on Christ, don't do it. Remember the benefits of standing firm, and continue to live for Christ.

24:14 Jesus said that before he returns, the gospel of the kingdom (the message of salvation) would be preached throughout the world. This was the disciples' mission — and it is ours today. Jesus

talked about the end times and final judgment to show his followers the urgency of spreading the good news of salvation to everyone.

24:15, 16 What was this "abomination that causes desolation" mentioned by both Daniel and Jesus? Rather than one specific object, event, or person, it could be seen as any deliberate attempt to mock and deny the reality of God's presence. Daniel's prediction came true in 168 B.C. when Antiochus Epiphanes sacrificed a pig to Zeus on the sacred temple altar (Daniel 9:27; 11:30, 31). Jesus' words were remembered in A.D. 70 when Titus placed an idol on the site of the burned temple after destroying Jerusalem. In the end times the antichrist will set up an image of himself and order everyone to worship it (2 Thessalonians 2:4; Revelation 13:14, 15). These are all "abominations" that mock God.

24:21, 22 Jesus, talking about the end times, telescoped near future and far future events, as did the Old Testament prophets. Many of these persecutions have already occurred; more are yet to come. But God is in control of even the length of persecutions. He will not forget his people. This is all we need to know about the future to motivate us to live rightly now.

24:23, 24 Jesus' warnings about false teachers still hold true. Upon close examination it becomes clear that many nice-sounding messages don't agree with God's message in the Bible. Only a solid foundation in God's Word can equip us to perceive the errors and distortions in false teaching.

24:24-28 In times of persecution even strong believers will find it difficult to be loyal. To keep from being deceived by false mes-

24:30
aRev 1:7

24:31
bIsa 27:13;
1Co 15:52

24:33
cJas 5:9

24:34
dMt 16:28

24:36
eAc 1:7

24:37
fGe 6:5

24:40
gLk 17:34

24:42
hMt 25:13

24:43
iLk 12:39

24:45
jMt 25:21, 23

24:46
kRev 16:15

24:47
lMt 25:21, 23

24:51
mMt 8:12

30"At that time the sign of the Son of Man will appear in the sky, and all the nations of the earth will mourn. They will see the Son of Man coming on the clouds of the sky, a with power and great glory. 31And he will send his angels with a loud trumpet call, b and they will gather his elect from the four winds, from one end of the heavens to the other.

32"Now learn this lesson from the fig tree: As soon as its twigs get tender and its leaves come out, you know that summer is near. 33Even so, when you see all these things, you know that itz is near, right at the door. c 34I tell you the truth, this generationa will certainly not pass away until all these things have happened. d 35Heaven and earth will pass away, but my words will never pass away.

Jesus Tells about Remaining Watchful
(203/Mark 13:32–37; Luke 21:34–38)

36"No one knows about that day or hour, not even the angels in heaven, nor the Son, b but only the Father. e 37As it was in the days of Noah, f so it will be at the coming of the Son of Man. 38For in the days before the flood, people were eating and drinking, marrying and giving in marriage, up to the day Noah entered the ark; 39and they knew nothing about what would happen until the flood came and took them all away. That is how it will be at the coming of the Son of Man. 40Two men will be in the field; one will be taken and the other left. g 41Two women will be grinding with a hand mill; one will be taken and the other left.

42"Therefore keep watch, because you do not know on what day your Lord will come. h 43But understand this: If the owner of the house had known at what time of night the thief was coming, i he would have kept watch and would not have let his house be broken into. 44So you also must be ready, because the Son of Man will come at an hour when you do not expect him.

45"Who then is the faithful and wise servant, j whom the master has put in charge of the servants in his household to give them their food at the proper time? 46It will be good for that servant whose master finds him doing so when he returns. k 47I tell you the truth, he will put him in charge of all his possessions. l 48But suppose that servant is wicked and says to himself, 'My master is staying away a long time,' 49and he then begins to beat his fellow servants and to eat and drink with drunkards. 50The master of that servant will come on a day when he does not expect him and at an hour he is not aware of. 51He will cut him to pieces and assign him a place with the hypocrites, where there will be weeping and gnashing of teeth. m

z 33 Or he   a 34 Or race   b 36 Some manuscripts do not have *nor the Son.*

---

siahs, we must understand that Jesus' return will be unmistakable (Mark 13:26); no one will doubt that it is he. If you have to be told that the Messiah has come, then he hasn't (24:27). Christ's coming will be obvious to everyone.

24:30 The nations of the earth will mourn because unbelievers will suddenly realize they have chosen the wrong side. Everything they have scoffed about will be happening, and it will be too late for them.

24:36 It is good that we don't know exactly when Christ will return. If we knew the precise date, we might be tempted to be lazy in our work for Christ. Worse yet, we might plan to keep sinning and then turn to God right at the end. Heaven is not our only goal; we have work to do here. And we must keep on doing it until death or until we see the unmistakable return of our Savior.

24:40–42 Christ's second coming will be swift and sudden. There will be no opportunity for last-minute repentance or bargaining. The choice we have already made will determine our eternal destiny.

24:44 Jesus' purpose in telling about his return is not to stimulate predictions and calculations about the date, but to warn us to be

prepared. Will you be ready? The only safe choice is to obey him *today* (24:46).

24:45–47 Jesus asks us to spend the time of waiting taking care of his people and doing his work here on earth, both within the church and outside it. This is the best way to prepare for Christ's return.

24:50 Knowing that Christ's return will be sudden and unexpected should motivate us always to be prepared. We are not to live irresponsibly — sitting and waiting, doing nothing; seeking self-serving pleasure; using his tarrying as an excuse not to do God's work of building his kingdom; developing a false security based on precise calculations of events; or letting our curiosity about the end times divert us from doing God's work.

24:51 "Weeping and gnashing of teeth" is a phrase used to describe despair. God's coming judgment is as certain as Jesus' return to earth.

Jesus Tells the Parable of the Ten Bridesmaids
(204)

25 "At that time the kingdom of heaven will be like[n] ten virgins who took their lamps and went out to meet the bridegroom.[o] 2Five of them were foolish and five were wise. 3The foolish ones took their lamps but did not take any oil with them. 4The wise, however, took oil in jars along with their lamps. 5The bridegroom was a long time in coming, and they all became drowsy and fell asleep.[p]

6"At midnight the cry rang out: 'Here's the bridegroom! Come out to meet him!'

7"Then all the virgins woke up and trimmed their lamps. 8The foolish ones said to the wise, 'Give us some of your oil; our lamps are going out.'

9" 'No,' they replied, 'there may not be enough for both us and you. Instead, go to those who sell oil and buy some for yourselves.'

10"But while they were on their way to buy the oil, the bridegroom arrived. The virgins who were ready went in with him to the wedding banquet. And the door was shut.

11"Later the others also came. 'Sir! Sir!' they said. 'Open the door for us!'

12"But he replied, 'I tell you the truth, I don't know you.'

13"Therefore keep watch, because you do not know the day or the hour.[q]

25:1
[n]Mt 13:24
[o]Rev 19:7

25:5
[p]1Th 5:6

25:13
[q]Mt 24:42, 44

Jesus Tells the Parable of the Loaned Money
(205)

14"Again, it will be like a man going on a journey,[r] who called his servants and entrusted his property to them. 15To one he gave five talents[c] of money, to another two talents, and to another one talent, each according to his ability.[s] Then he went on his journey. 16The man who had received the five talents went at once and put his money to work and gained five more. 17So also, the one with the two talents gained two more. 18But the man who had received the one talent went off, dug a hole in the ground and hid his master's money.

19"After a long time the master of those servants returned and settled accounts with them.[t] 20The man who had received the five talents brought the other five. 'Master,' he said, 'you entrusted me with five talents. See, I have gained five more.'

21"His master replied, 'Well done, good and faithful servant! You have been faithful with a few things; I will put you in charge of many things.[u] Come and share your master's happiness!'

22"The man with the two talents also came. 'Master,' he said, 'you entrusted me with two talents; see, I have gained two more.'

23"His master replied, 'Well done, good and faithful servant! You have been

25:14
[r]Mt 21:33;
Lk 19:12

25:15
[s]Mt 18:24, 25

25:19
[t]Mt 18:23

25:21
[u]Mt 24:45, 47

c 15 A talent was worth more than a thousand dollars.

• **25:1ff** Jesus told the following parables to clarify further what it means to be ready for his return and how to live until he comes. In the story of the ten virgins (25:1–13), we are taught that every person is responsible for his or her own spiritual condition. The story of the talents (25:14–30) shows the necessity of using well what God has entrusted to us. The parable of the sheep and goats (25:31–46) stresses the importance of serving others in need. No parable by itself *completely* describes our preparation. Instead, each paints one part of the whole picture.

25:1ff This parable is about a wedding. On the wedding day the bridegroom went to the bride's house for the ceremony; then the bride and groom, along with a great procession, returned to the groom's house where a feast took place, often lasting a full week.

These ten virgins were waiting to join the procession, and they hoped to take part in the wedding banquet. But when the groom didn't come at the expected time, five of them were out of lamp oil. By the time they had purchased extra oil, it was too late to join the feast.

When Jesus returns to take his people to heaven, we must be ready. Spiritual preparation cannot be bought or borrowed at the last minute. Our relationship with God must be our own.

25:15 The master divided the money (talents) among his servants according to their abilities. No one received more or less than he could handle. If he failed in his assignment, his excuse could not be that he was overwhelmed. Failure could come only from laziness or hatred toward the master. The talents represent any kind of resource we are given. God gives us time, gifts, and other resources according to our abilities, and he expects us to invest them wisely until he returns. We are responsible to use well what God has given us. The issue is not how much we have, but how well we use what we have.

25:21 Jesus is coming back — we know this is true. Does this mean we must quit our jobs in order to serve God? No, it means we are to use our time, talents, and treasures diligently in order to serve God completely in whatever we do. For a few people, this may mean changing professions. For most of us, it means doing our daily work out of love for God.

25:23
v ver 21

faithful with a few things; I will put you in charge of many things.ᵛ Come and share your master's happiness!'

24"Then the man who had received the one talent came. 'Master,' he said, 'I knew that you are a hard man, harvesting where you have not sown and gathering where you have not scattered seed. 25So I was afraid and went out and hid your talent in the ground. See, here is what belongs to you.'

26"His master replied, 'You wicked, lazy servant! So you knew that I harvest where I have not sown and gather where I have not scattered seed? 27Well then, you should have put my money on deposit with the bankers, so that when I returned I would have received it back with interest.

28" 'Take the talent from him and give it to the one who has the ten talents. 29For everyone who has will be given more, and he will have an abundance. Whoever does not have, even what he has will be taken from him.ʷ 30And throw that worthless servant outside, into the darkness, where there will be weeping and gnashing of teeth.'ˣ

25:29
w Mt 13:12

25:30
x Mt 8:12

Jesus Tells about the Final Judgment
(206)

31"When the Son of Man comes in his glory, and all the angels with him, he will sit on his throneʸ in heavenly glory. 32All the nations will be gathered before him, and he will separate the people one from another as a shepherd separates the sheep from the goats.ᶻ 33He will put the sheep on his right and the goats on his left.

25:31
y Mt 19:28

25:32
z Eze 34:17, 20

34"Then the King will say to those on his right, 'Come, you who are blessed by my Father; take your inheritance, the kingdomᵃ prepared for you since the creation of the world.ᵇ 35For I was hungry and you gave me something to eat, I was thirsty and you gave me something to drink, I was a stranger and you invited me in,ᶜ 36I needed clothes and you clothed me,ᵈ I was sick and you looked after me, I was in prison and you came to visit me.'ᵉ

25:34
a 1Co 15:50
b Rev 13:8

25:35
c Heb 13:2

25:36
d Jas 2:15, 16
e 2Ti 1:16

37"Then the righteous will answer him, 'Lord, when did we see you hungry and feed you, or thirsty and give you something to drink? 38When did we see you a stranger and invite you in, or needing clothes and clothe you? 39When did we see you sick or in prison and go to visit you?'

40"The King will reply, 'I tell you the truth, whatever you did for one of the least of these brothers of mine, you did for me.'ᶠ

25:40
f Mt 10:40, 42

41"Then he will say to those on his left, 'Depart from me,ᵍ you who are cursed, into the eternal fireʰ prepared for the devil and his angels.ⁱ 42For I was hungry and you gave me nothing to eat, I was thirsty and you gave me nothing to drink, 43I was

25:41
g Mt 7:23
h Mk 9:43, 48; Jude 7
i 2Pe 2:4

25:24-30 This last man was thinking only of himself. He hoped to play it safe and protect himself from his hard master, but he was judged for his self-centeredness. We must not make excuses to avoid doing what God calls us to do. If God truly is our Master, we must obey willingly. Our time, abilities, and money aren't ours in the first place — we are caretakers, not owners. When we ignore, squander, or abuse what we are given, we are rebellious and deserve to be punished.

● **25:29, 30** This parable describes the consequences of two attitudes to Christ's return. The person who diligently prepares for it by investing his or her time and talent to serve God will be rewarded. The person who has no heart for the work of the kingdom will be punished. God rewards faithfulness. Those who bear no fruit for God's kingdom cannot expect to be treated the same as those who are faithful.

● **25:31-46** God will separate his obedient followers from pretenders and unbelievers. The real evidence of our belief is the way we act. To treat all persons we encounter as if they are Jesus is no easy task. What we do for others demonstrates what we really think about Jesus' words to us — feed the hungry, give the homeless a place to stay, look after the sick. How well do your actions

separate you from pretenders and unbelievers?

● **25:32** Jesus used sheep and goats to picture the division between believers and unbelievers. Sheep and goats often grazed together but were separated when it came time to shear the sheep. Ezekiel 34:17-24 also refers to the separation of sheep and goats.

● **25:34-40** This parable describes acts of mercy we all can do every day. These acts do not depend on wealth, ability, or intelligence; they are simple acts freely given and freely received. We have no excuse to neglect those who have deep needs, and we cannot hand over this responsibility to the church or government. Jesus demands our personal involvement in caring for others' needs (Isaiah 58:7).

● **25:40** There has been much discussion about the identity of the "brothers." Some have said they are the Jews; others say they are all Christians; still others say they are suffering people everywhere. Such a debate is much like the lawyer's earlier question to Jesus, "Who is my neighbor?" (Luke 10:29). The point of this parable is not the *who*, but the *what* — the importance of serving where service is needed. The focus of this parable is that we should love every person and serve anyone we can. Such love for others glorifies God by reflecting our love for him.

a stranger and you did not invite me in, I needed clothes and you did not clothe me, I was sick and in prison and you did not look after me.'

44"They also will answer, 'Lord, when did we see you hungry or thirsty or a stranger or needing clothes or sick or in prison, and did not help you?'

45"He will reply, 'I tell you the truth, whatever you did not do for one of the least of these, you did not do for me.'[j]

46"Then they will go away to eternal punishment, but the righteous to eternal life."[k]

25:45
[j] Pr 14:31

25:46
[k] Da 12:2;
Jn 5:29

C. DEATH AND RESURRECTION OF JESUS, THE KING (26:1 – 28:20)

After facing much opposition for his teaching, Jesus is betrayed by Judas, disowned by the disciples, crucified, and buried. Three days later he rises from the dead and appears to the disciples, confirming that he is indeed King over life and death. The long-awaited King has brought in his kingdom, but it is different than expected, for he reigns in our hearts until the day he comes again to establish a new and perfect world.

Religious Leaders Plot to Kill Jesus
(207/Mark 14:1, 2; Luke 22:1, 2)

26 When Jesus had finished saying all these things,[l] he said to his disciples, 2"As you know, the Passover[m] is two days away — and the Son of Man will be handed over to be crucified."

3Then the chief priests and the elders of the people assembled[n] in the palace of the high priest, whose name was Caiaphas,[o] 4and they plotted to arrest Jesus in some sly way and kill him. 5"But not during the Feast," they said, "or there may be a riot among the people."

26:1
[l] Mt 7:28

26:2
[m] Jn 11:55

26:3
[n] Ps 2:2
[o] Jn 11:47-53

A Woman Anoints Jesus with Perfume
(182/Mark 14:3–9; John 12:1–11)

6While Jesus was in Bethany[p] in the home of a man known as Simon the Leper, 7a woman came to him with an alabaster jar of very expensive perfume, which she poured on his head as he was reclining at the table.

8When the disciples saw this, they were indignant. "Why this waste?" they asked. 9"This perfume could have been sold at a high price and the money given to the poor."

10Aware of this, Jesus said to them, "Why are you bothering this woman? She has done a beautiful thing to me. 11The poor you will always have with you,[q] but

26:6
[p] Mt 21:17

26:11
[q] Dt 15:11

25:46 Eternal punishment takes place in hell (the lake of fire, or Gehenna), the place of punishment after death for all those who refuse to repent. In the Bible, three words are used in connection with eternal punishment.

(1) *Sheol,* or "the grave," is used in the Old Testament to mean the place of the dead, generally thought to be under the earth. (See Job 24:19; Psalm 16:10; Isaiah 38:10.)

(2) *Hades* is the Greek word for the underworld, the realm of the dead. It is the word used in the New Testament for Sheol. (See Matthew 16:18; Revelation 1:18; 20:13, 14.)

(3) *Gehenna,* or hell, was named after the Valley of Hinnom near Jerusalem where children were sacrificed by fire to the pagan gods (see 2 Kings 23:10; 2 Chronicles 28:3). This is the place of eternal fire (Matthew 5:22; 10:28; Mark 9:43; Luke 12:5; James 3:6; Revelation 19:20) prepared for the devil, his angels, and all those who do not believe in God (25:46; Revelation 20:9, 10). This is the final and eternal state of the wicked after the resurrection and the last judgment.

When Jesus warns against unbelief, he is trying to save us from agonizing punishment.

26:3 Caiaphas was the ruling high priest during Jesus' ministry. He was the son-in-law of Annas, the previous high priest. The Roman government had taken over the process of appointing all political and religious leaders. Caiaphas served for 18 years, longer than most high priests, suggesting that he was gifted at coopera-

ting with the Romans. He was the first to recommend Jesus' death in order to "save" the nation (John 11:49, 50).

26:3-5 This was a deliberate plot to kill Jesus. Without this plot, there would have been no groundswell of popular opinion against him. In fact, because of Jesus' popularity, the religious leaders were afraid to arrest him during the Passover. They did not want their actions to incite a riot.

● **26:6-13** Matthew and Mark put this event just before the Last Supper, while John has it just before the Triumphal Entry. Of the three, John places this event in the most likely chronological order. We must remember that the main purpose of the Gospel writers was to give an accurate record of Jesus' message, not to present an exact chronological account of his life. Matthew and Mark may have chosen to place this event here to contrast the complete devotion of Mary with the betrayal of Judas, the next event they record in their Gospels.

● **26:7** This woman was Mary, the sister of Martha and Lazarus, who lived in Bethany (John 12:1–3). Alabaster jars were carved from a translucent gypsum. These jars were used to hold perfumed oil.

● **26:8** All the disciples were indignant, but John's Gospel singles out Judas Iscariot as especially so (John 12:4).

● **26:11** Here Jesus brought back to mind Deuteronomy 15:11: "There will always be poor people in the land." This statement does not justify ignoring the needs of the poor. Scripture continually calls

you will not always have me. [12]When she poured this perfume on my body, she did it to prepare me for burial. [13]I tell you the truth, wherever this gospel is preached throughout the world, what she has done will also be told, in memory of her."

Judas Agrees to Betray Jesus
(208/Mark 14:10, 11; Luke 22:3–6)

[14]Then one of the Twelve — the one called Judas Iscariot — went to the chief priests [15]and asked, "What are you willing to give me if I hand him over to you?"

MARY / LAZARUS'S SISTER

Hospitality is an art. Making sure a guest is welcomed, warmed, and well fed requires creativity, organization, and teamwork. Their ability to accomplish these goals makes Mary and her sister Martha one of the best hospitality teams in the Bible. Their frequent guest was Jesus Christ.

For Mary, hospitality meant giving more attention to the guest himself than to the needs he might have. She would rather talk than cook. She was more interested in her guest's words than in the cleanliness of her home or the timeliness of her meals. She let her older sister Martha take care of those details. Mary's approach to events shows her to be mainly a "responder." She did little preparation — her role was participation. Unlike her sister, who had to learn to stop and listen, Mary needed to learn that action is often appropriate and necessary.

We first meet Mary during a visit Jesus paid to her home. She simply sat at his feet and listened. When Martha became irritated at her sister's lack of help, Jesus stated that Mary's choice to enjoy his company was the most appropriate response at the time. Our last glimpse of Mary shows her to have become a woman of thoughtful and worshipful action. Again she was at Jesus' feet, washing them with perfume and wiping them with her hair. She seemed to understand, better even than the disciples, why Jesus was going to die. Jesus said her act of worship would be told everywhere, along with the gospel, as an example of costly service.

What kind of hospitality does Jesus receive in your life? Are you so busy planning and running your life that you neglect precious time with him? Or do you respond to him by listening to his Word, then finding ways to worship him with your life? It is that kind of hospitality he longs for from each of us.

Strengths and accomplishments:
• Perhaps the only person who understood and accepted Jesus' coming death, taking time to anoint his body while he was still living
• Learned when to listen and when to act

Lessons from her life:
• The busyness of serving God can become a barrier to knowing him personally
• Small acts of obedience and service have widespread effects

Vital statistics:
• Where: Bethany
• Relatives: Sister: Martha. Brother: Lazarus

Key verses:
"When she poured this perfume on my body, she did it to prepare me for burial. I tell you the truth, wherever this gospel is preached throughout the world, what she has done will also be told, in memory of her" (Matthew 26:12, 13).

Mary's story is told in Matthew 26:6–13; Mark 14:3–9; Luke 10:38–42; John 11:17–45; 12:1–11.

---

us to care for the needy. The passage in Deuteronomy continues: "Therefore I command you to be openhanded toward your brothers and toward the poor and needy in your land.'" Rather, by saying this, Jesus highlighted the special sacrifice Mary made for him.

● **26:14, 15** Why would Judas want to betray Jesus? Judas, like the other disciples, expected Jesus to start a political rebellion and overthrow Rome. As treasurer, Judas certainly assumed (as did the other disciples — see Mark 10:35–37) that he would be given an important position in Jesus' new government. But when Jesus praised Mary for pouring out perfume worth a year's salary, Judas

may have realized that Jesus' kingdom was not physical or political, but spiritual. Judas's greedy desire for money and status could not be realized if he followed Jesus, so he betrayed Jesus in exchange for money and favor from the religious leaders.

● **26:15** Matthew alone records the exact amount of money Judas accepted to betray Jesus — 30 silver coins, the price of a slave (Exodus 21:32). The religious leaders had planned to wait until after the Passover to take Jesus, but with Judas's unexpected offer, they accelerated their plans.

So they counted out for him thirty silver coins. [r] 16From then on Judas watched for an opportunity to hand him over.

Disciples Prepare for the Passover
(209/Mark 14:12–16; Luke 22:7–13)

17On the first day of the Feast of Unleavened Bread, [s] the disciples came to Jesus and asked, "Where do you want us to make preparations for you to eat the Passover?"

18He replied, "Go into the city to a certain man and tell him, 'The Teacher says: My appointed time is near. I am going to celebrate the Passover with my disciples at your house.' " 19So the disciples did as Jesus had directed them and prepared the Passover.

Jesus and the Disciples Have the Last Supper
(211/Mark 14:17–26; Luke 22:14–30; John 13:21–30)

20When evening came, Jesus was reclining at the table with the Twelve. 21And while they were eating, he said, "I tell you the truth, one of you will betray me."

22They were very sad and began to say to him one after the other, "Surely not I, Lord?"

23Jesus replied, "The one who has dipped his hand into the bowl with me will betray me. [t] 24The Son of Man will go just as it is written about him. [u] But woe to that man who betrays the Son of Man! It would be better for him if he had not been born."

25Then Judas, the one who would betray him, said, "Surely not I, Rabbi?" Jesus answered, "Yes, it is you." [d]

26While they were eating, Jesus took bread, gave thanks and broke it, and gave it to his disciples, saying, "Take and eat; this is my body."

26:15
[r]Zec 11:12

26:17
[s]Ex 12:18-20

26:23
[t]Jn 13:18

26:24
[u]Isa 53;
Mk 9:12;
Lk 24:25-27, 46;
Ac 17:2, 3

d 25 Or "You yourself have said it"

VISIT IN BETHANY
Chronologically, the events of Matthew 26:6–13 precede the events of 21:1ff. In 20:29, Jesus left Jericho, heading toward Jerusalem. Then he arrived in Bethany, where a woman anointed him. From there he went toward Bethphage, where two of his disciples got the donkey that he would ride into Jerusalem.

26:17 The Passover took place on one night and at one meal, but the Feast of Unleavened Bread, which was celebrated with it, continued for a week. The people removed all yeast from their homes in commemoration of their ancestors' exodus from Egypt, when they did not have time to let the bread dough rise. Thousands of people poured into Jerusalem from all over the Roman empire for this feast. For more information on how the Passover was celebrated, see the notes on Mark 14:1 and in Exodus 12.

26:23 In Jesus' time, some food was eaten from a common bowl into which everyone dipped their hand.

26:26 Each name we use for this sacrament brings out a different dimension to it. It is the Lord's Supper because it commemorates the Passover meal Jesus ate with his disciples; it is the Eucharist (thanksgiving) because in it we thank God for Christ's work for us; it is Communion because through it we commune with God and with other believers. As we eat the bread and drink the wine, we should be quietly reflective as we recall Jesus' death and his promise to come again, grateful for God's wonderful gift to us, and joyful as we meet with Christ and the body of believers.

26:28 How does Jesus' blood relate to the new covenant? People under the old covenant (those who lived before Jesus) could approach God only through a priest and an animal sacrifice. Now all people can come directly to God through faith because Jesus' death has made us acceptable in God's eyes (Romans 3:21–24).

The old covenant was a shadow of the new (Jeremiah 31:31; Hebrews 8:1ff), pointing forward to the day when Jesus himself would be the final and ultimate sacrifice for sin. Rather than an unblemished lamb slain on the altar, the perfect Lamb of God was slain on the cross, a sinless sacrifice so that our sins could be forgiven once and for all. All those who believe in Christ receive that forgiveness.

27Then he took the cup, gave thanks and offered it to them, saying, "Drink from it, all of you. 28This is my blood of the[e] covenant,[v] which is poured out for many for the forgiveness of sins.[w] 29I tell you, I will not drink of this fruit of the vine from now on until that day when I drink it anew with you in my Father's kingdom."

30When they had sung a hymn, they went out to the Mount of Olives.

26:28
[v] Heb 9:20
[w] Mt 20:28

Jesus Again Predicts Peter's Denial
(222/Mark 14:27–31)

31Then Jesus told them, "This very night you will all fall away on account of me, for it is written:

26:31
[x] Zec 13:7;
Jn 16:32

> " 'I will strike the shepherd,
>   and the sheep of the flock will be scattered.'[f][x]

32But after I have risen, I will go ahead of you into Galilee."[y]

33Peter replied, "Even if all fall away on account of you, I never will."

34"I tell you the truth," Jesus answered, "this very night, before the rooster crows, you will disown me three times."[z]

35But Peter declared, "Even if I have to die with you,[a] I will never disown you." And all the other disciples said the same.

26:32
[y] Mt 28:7, 10, 16

26:34
[z] Jn 13:38

26:35
[a] Jn 13:37

Jesus Agonizes in the Garden
(223/Mark 14:32–42; Luke 22:39–46)

36Then Jesus went with his disciples to a place called Gethsemane, and he said to them, "Sit here while I go over there and pray." 37He took Peter and the two sons of Zebedee[b] along with him, and he began to be sorrowful and troubled. 38Then he

26:37
[b] Mt 4:21

e 28 Some manuscripts *the new*   f 31 Zech. 13:7

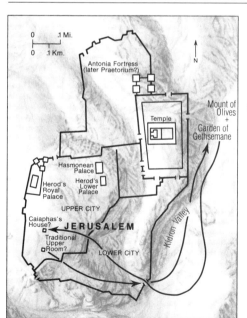

26:29 Again Jesus assured his disciples of victory over death and of their future with him. The next few hours would bring apparent defeat, but soon they would experience the power of the Holy Spirit and witness the great spread of the gospel message. And one day, they would all be together again in God's new kingdom.

26:30 It is possible that the hymn the disciples sang was from Psalms 115 – 118, the traditional psalms sung as part of the Passover meal.

●**26:35** All the disciples declared that they would die before disowning Jesus. A few hours later, however, they all scattered. Talk is cheap. It is easy to say we are devoted to Christ, but our claims are meaningful only when they are tested in the crucible of persecution. How strong is your faith? Is it strong enough to stand up under intense trial?

26:37, 38 Jesus was in great anguish over his approaching physical pain, separation from the Father, and death for the sins of the world. The divine course was set, but he, in his human nature, still struggled (Hebrews 5:7–9). Because of the anguish Jesus experienced, he can relate to our suffering. Jesus' strength to obey came from his relationship with God the Father, who is also the source of our strength (John 17:11, 15, 16, 21, 26).

THE PASSOVER MEAL AND GETHSEMANE Jesus, who would soon be the final Passover Lamb, ate the traditional Passover meal with his disciples in the upper room of a house in Jerusalem. During the meal they partook of the wine and bread, which would be the elements of future communion celebrations, and then went out to the Garden of Gethsemane on the Mount of Olives.

said to them, "My soul is overwhelmed with sorrow^c to the point of death. Stay here and keep watch with me."

^{39}Going a little farther, he fell with his face to the ground and prayed, "My Father, if it is possible, may this cup^d be taken from me. Yet not as I will, but as you will."^{e}

^{40}Then he returned to his disciples and found them sleeping. "Could you men not keep watch with me^f for one hour?" he asked Peter. ^{41}"Watch and pray so that you will not fall into temptation. The spirit is willing, but the body is weak."

^{42}He went away a second time and prayed, "My Father, if it is not possible for this cup to be taken away unless I drink it, may your will be done."

^{43}When he came back, he again found them sleeping, because their eyes were heavy. ^{44}So he left them and went away once more and prayed the third time, saying the same thing.

^{45}Then he returned to the disciples and said to them, "Are you still sleeping and resting? Look, the hour is near, and the Son of Man is betrayed into the hands of sinners. ^{46}Rise, let us go! Here comes my betrayer!"

Jesus Is Betrayed and Arrested
(224/Mark 14:43–52; Luke 22:47–53; John 18:1–11)

^{47}While he was still speaking, Judas, one of the Twelve, arrived. With him was a large crowd armed with swords and clubs, sent from the chief priests and the elders of the people. ^{48}Now the betrayer had arranged a signal with them: "The one I kiss is the man; arrest him." ^{49}Going at once to Jesus, Judas said, "Greetings, Rabbi!"^{g} and kissed him.

^{50}Jesus replied, "Friend,^{h} do what you came for."^{g}

Then the men stepped forward, seized Jesus and arrested him. ^{51}With that, one of Jesus' companions reached for his sword, drew it out and struck the servant of the high priest, cutting off his ear.^{i}

^{52}"Put your sword back in its place," Jesus said to him, "for all who draw the sword will die by the sword.^{j} ^{53}Do you think I cannot call on my Father, and he will at once put at my disposal more than twelve legions of angels?^{k} ^{54}But how then would the Scriptures be fulfilled^l that say it must happen in this way?"

^{55}At that time Jesus said to the crowd, "Am I leading a rebellion, that you have come out with swords and clubs to capture me? Every day I sat in the temple courts teaching, and you did not arrest me. ^{56}But this has all taken place that the writings of the prophets might be fulfilled." Then all the disciples deserted him and fled.

g 50 Or "Friend, why have you come?"

26:38
c Jn 12:27

26:39
d Mt 20:22
e Jn 6:38

26:40
f ver 38

26:49
g ver 25
26:50
h Mt 20:13; 22:12

26:51
i Jn 18:10

26:52
j Ge 9:6;
Rev 13:10

26:53
k 2Ki 6:17;
Da 7:10

26:54
l ver 24

26:39 Jesus was not rebelling against his Father's will when he asked that the cup of suffering and separation be taken away. In fact, he reaffirmed his desire to do God's will by saying, "Yet not as I will, but as you will." His prayer reveals to us his terrible suffering. His agony was worse than death because he paid for *all* sin by being separated from God. The sinless Son of God took our sins upon himself to save us from suffering and separation.

26:39 In times of suffering people sometimes wish they knew the future, or they wish then they could understand the reason for their anguish. Jesus knew what lay ahead of him, and he knew the reason. Even so, his struggle was intense — more wrenching than any struggle we will ever have to face. What does it take to be able to say "as you will"? It takes firm trust in God's plans; it takes prayer and obedience each step of the way.

26:40, 41 Jesus used Peter's drowsiness to warn him about the kinds of temptation he would soon face. The way to overcome temptation is to keep watch and pray. Watching means being aware of the possibilities of temptation, sensitive to the subtleties, and spiritually equipped to fight it. Because temptation strikes where we are most vulnerable, we can't resist it alone. Prayer is es-

sential because God's strength can shore up our defenses and defeat Satan's power.

● **26:48** Judas had told the crowd to arrest the man he kissed. This was not an arrest by Roman soldiers under Roman law, but an arrest by the religious leaders. Judas pointed Jesus out not because Jesus was hard to recognize, but because Judas had agreed to be the formal accuser in case a trial was called. Judas was able to lead the group to one of Jesus' retreats where no onlookers would interfere with the arrest.

26:51-53 The man who cut off the servant's ear was Peter (John 18:10). Peter was trying to prevent what he saw as *defeat*. He didn't realize that Jesus had to die in order to gain *victory*. But Jesus demonstrated perfect commitment to his Father's will. His kingdom would not be advanced with swords, but with faith and obedience.

26:55 Although the religious leaders could have arrested Jesus at any time, they came at night because they were afraid of the crowds that followed him each day (see 26:5).

● **26:56** A few hours earlier, this band of men had said they would rather die than desert their Lord (see the note on 26:35).

Caiaphas Questions Jesus
(226/Mark 14:53–65)

57Those who had arrested Jesus took him to Caiaphas, the high priest, where the teachers of the law and the elders had assembled. 58But Peter followed him at a distance, right up to the courtyard of the high priest. *m* He entered and sat down with the guards to see the outcome.

59The chief priests and the whole Sanhedrin were looking for false evidence against Jesus so that they could put him to death. 60But they did not find any, though many false witnesses*n* came forward.

Finally two*o* came forward 61and declared, "This fellow said, 'I am able to destroy the temple of God and rebuild it in three days.' "

62Then the high priest stood up and said to Jesus, "Are you not going to answer? What is this testimony that these men are bringing against you?" 63But Jesus remained silent.

The high priest said to him, "I charge you under oath*p* by the living God: Tell us if you are the Christ,*h* the Son of God."

64"Yes, it is as you say," Jesus replied. "But I say to all of you: In the future you will see the Son of Man sitting at the right hand of the Mighty One and coming on the clouds of heaven."

65Then the high priest tore his clothes and said, "He has spoken blasphemy! Why do we need any more witnesses? Look, now you have heard the blasphemy. 66What do you think?"

"He is worthy of death,"*q* they answered.

67Then they spit in his face and struck him with their fists.*r* Others slapped him 68and said, "Prophesy to us, Christ. Who hit you?"*s*

26:58
m Jn 18:15

26:60
n Ps 27:12; 35:11;
Ac 6:13
o Dt 19:15

26:63
p Lev 5:1

26:66
q Lev 24:16;
Jn 19:7

26:67
r Mt 16:21

26:68
s Lk 22:63-65

h 63 Or *Messiah*; also in verse 68

BETRAYED!

Delilah betrayed Samson to the Philistines.	Judges 16:16–21
Absalom betrayed David, his father.	2 Samuel 15:10–17
Jehu betrayed Joram and killed him.	2 Kings 9:14–27
Officials betrayed Joash and killed him.	2 Kings 12:20, 21
Judas betrayed Jesus.	Matthew 26:46–56

Scripture records a number of occasions in which a person or group was betrayed. The tragedies caused by these violations of trust are a strong lesson about the importance of keeping our commitments.

26:57 Earlier in the evening, Jesus had been questioned by Annas (the former high priest and father-in-law of Caiaphas). Annas then sent Jesus to Caiaphas's home to be questioned (John 18:12–24). Because of their haste to complete the trial and see Jesus die before the Sabbath, less than 24 hours away, the religious leaders met in Caiaphas's home at night instead of waiting for daylight and meeting in the temple.

26:59 The Sanhedrin was the most powerful religious and political body of the Jewish people. Although the Romans controlled Israel's government, they gave the people power to handle religious disputes and some civil disputes, so the Sanhedrin made many of the local decisions affecting daily life. But a death sentence had to be approved by the Romans (John 18:31).

26:60, 61 The Sanhedrin tried to find witnesses who would distort some of Jesus' teachings. Finally they found two witnesses who distorted Jesus' words about the temple (see John 2:19). They claimed that Jesus had said he could destroy the temple — a blasphemous boast. Actually Jesus had said, "Destroy this temple, and I will raise it again in three days." Jesus, of course, was talking

about his body, not the building. Ironically, the religious leaders were about to destroy Jesus' body just as he had said, and three days later he would rise from the dead.

26:64 Jesus declared his royalty in no uncertain terms. In saying he was the Son of Man, Jesus was claiming to be the Messiah, as his listeners well knew. He knew this declaration would be his undoing, but he did not panic. He was calm, courageous, and determined.

26:65, 66 The high priest accused Jesus of blasphemy — calling himself God. To the Jews, this was a great crime, punishable by death (Leviticus 24:16). The religious leaders refused even to consider that Jesus' words might be true. They had decided against Jesus, and in so doing, they sealed their own fate as well as his. Like the members of the Sanhedrin, you must decide whether Jesus' words are blasphemy or truth. Your decision has eternal implications.

Peter Denies Knowing Jesus
(227/Mark 14:66–72; Luke 22:54–65; John 18:25–27)

69Now Peter was sitting out in the courtyard, and a servant girl came to him. "You also were with Jesus of Galilee," she said.

70But he denied it before them all. "I don't know what you're talking about," he said.

71Then he went out to the gateway, where another girl saw him and said to the people there, "This fellow was with Jesus of Nazareth."

72He denied it again, with an oath: "I don't know the man!"

73After a little while, those standing there went up to Peter and said, "Surely you are one of them, for your accent gives you away."

74Then he began to call down curses on himself and he swore to them, "I don't know the man!"

Immediately a rooster crowed. 75Then Peter remembered the word Jesus had spoken: "Before the rooster crows, you will disown me three times."*t* And he went outside and wept bitterly.

26:75
t ver 34;
Jn 13:38

The Council of Religious Leaders Condemns Jesus
(228/Mark 15:1; Luke 22:66–71)

27 Early in the morning, all the chief priests and the elders of the people came to the decision to put Jesus to death. *u* 2They bound him, led him away and handed him over*v* to Pilate, the governor. *w*

27:1
u Mk 15:1;
Lk 22:66

27:2
v Mt 20:19
w Ac 3:13

JESUS' TRIAL After Judas singled Jesus out for arrest, the mob took Jesus first to Caiaphas, the high priest. This trial, a mockery of justice, ended at daybreak with their decision to kill him—but the Jews needed Rome's permission for the death sentence. Jesus was taken to Pilate (who was probably in the Praetorium), then to Herod (Luke 23:5–12), and back to Pilate, who sentenced him to die.

● **26:69ff** There were three stages to Peter's denial. First he acted confused and tried to divert attention from himself by changing the subject. Second, using an oath he denied that he knew Jesus. Third, he began to curse and swear. Believers who deny Christ often begin doing so subtly by pretending not to know him. When opportunities to discuss religious issues come up, they walk away or pretend they don't know the answers. With only a little more pressure, they can be induced to deny flatly their relationship with Christ. If you find yourself subtly diverting conversation so you don't have to talk about Christ, watch out. You may be on the road to disowning him.

● **26:72–74** That Peter denied that he knew Jesus, using an oath and calling down curses, does not mean he used foul language. This was the kind of swearing that a person does in a court of law. Peter was swearing that he did not know Jesus and was invoking a curse on himself if his words were untrue. In effect he was saying, "May God strike me dead if I am lying."

27:1, 2 The religious leaders had to persuade the Roman government to sentence Jesus to death because they did not have the authority to do it themselves. The Romans had taken away the religious leaders' authority to inflict capital punishment. Politically, it looked better for the religious leaders anyway if someone else was responsible for killing Jesus. They wanted the death to appear Roman-sponsored so the crowds couldn't blame them. The Jewish leaders had arrested Jesus on theological grounds—blasphemy; but because this charge would be thrown out of a Roman court, they had to come up with a political reason for Jesus' death. Their strategy was to show Jesus as a rebel who claimed to be a king and thus a threat to Caesar.

27:2 Pilate was the Roman governor for the regions of Samaria and Judea from A.D. 26–36. Jerusalem was located in Judea. Pilate took special pleasure in demonstrating his authority over the Jews; for example, he impounded money from the temple treasuries to build an aqueduct. Pilate was not popular, but the religious leaders had no other way to get rid of Jesus than to go to him. Ironically, when Jesus, a Jew, came before him for trial, Pilate found him innocent. He could not find a single fault in Jesus, nor could he contrive one.

Judas Kills Himself
(229)

27:3
×Mt 26:14, 15

27:4
yver 24

27:5
zAc 1:18

3When Judas, who had betrayed him, saw that Jesus was condemned, he was seized with remorse and returned the thirty silver coins× to the chief priests and the elders. 4"I have sinned," he said, "for I have betrayed innocent blood."

"What is that to us?" they replied. "That's your responsibility."y

5So Judas threw the money into the temple and left. Then he went away and hanged himself. z

6The chief priests picked up the coins and said, "It is against the law to put this into the treasury, since it is blood money." 7So they decided to use the money to buy the potter's field as a burial place for foreigners. 8That is why it has been called

PETER

Jesus' first words to Simon Peter were "Come, follow me" (Mark 1:17). His last words to him were "You must follow me" (John 21:22). Every step of the way between those two challenges, Peter never failed to follow—even though he often stumbled.

When Jesus entered Peter's life, this plain fisherman became a new person with new goals and new priorities. He did not become a perfect person, however, and he never stopped being Simon Peter. We may wonder what Jesus saw in Simon that made him greet this potential disciple with a new name, Peter—the "rock." Impulsive Peter certainly didn't act like a rock much of the time. But when Jesus chose his followers, he wasn't looking for models; he was looking for real people. He chose people who could be changed by his love, and then he sent them out to communicate that his acceptance was available to anyone—even to those who often fail.

We may wonder what Jesus sees in us when he calls us to follow him. But we know Jesus accepted Peter, and, in spite of his failures, Peter went on to do great things for God. Are you willing to keep following Jesus, even when you fail?

Strengths and accomplishments:
● Became the recognized leader among Jesus' disciples—one of the inner group of three
● Was the first great voice of the gospel during and after Pentecost
● Probably knew Mark and gave him information for the Gospel of Mark
● Wrote 1 and 2 Peter

Weaknesses and mistakes:
● Often spoke without thinking; was brash and impulsive
● During Jesus' trial, denied three times that he even knew Jesus
● Later found it hard to treat Gentile Christians as equals

Lessons from his life:
● Enthusiasm has to be backed up by faith and understanding, or it fails
● God's faithfulness can compensate for our greatest unfaithfulness
● It is better to be a follower who fails than one who fails to follow

Vital statistics:
● Occupations: Fisherman, disciple
● Relatives: Father: John. Brother: Andrew
● Contemporaries: Jesus, Pilate, Herod

Key verse:
"And I tell you that you are Peter, and on this rock I will build my church, and the gates of Hades will not overcome it" (Matthew 16:18).

Peter's story is told in the Gospels and the book of Acts. He is mentioned in Galatians 1:18 and 2:7–14; and he wrote the books of 1 and 2 Peter.

27:3, 4 Jesus' formal accuser (see 26:48 note) wanted to drop his charges, but the religious leaders refused to halt the trial. When he betrayed Jesus, perhaps Judas was trying to force Jesus' hand to get him to lead a revolt against Rome. This did not work, of course. Whatever his reason, Judas changed his mind, but it was too late. Many of the plans we set into motion cannot be reversed. It is best to think of the potential consequences before we launch into an action we may later regret.

27:4 The priests' job was to teach people about God and act as intercessors for them, helping administer the sacrifices to cover their sins. Judas returned to the priests, exclaiming that he had sinned. Rather than helping him find forgiveness, however, the

priests said, "That's your responsibility." Not only had they rejected the Messiah, they had rejected their role as priests.

●**27:5** According to Matthew, Judas hanged himself. Acts 1:18, however, says that he fell and burst open. The best explanation is that the limb from which he was hanging broke, and the resulting fall split open his body.

27:6 These chief priests felt no guilt in giving Judas money to betray an innocent man, but when Judas returned the money, the priests couldn't accept it because it was wrong to accept blood money—payment for murder! Their hatred for Jesus had caused them to lose all sense of justice.

the Field of Blood[a] to this day. 9Then what was spoken by Jeremiah the prophet
was fulfilled: "They took the thirty silver coins, the price set on him by the people
of Israel, 10and they used them to buy the potter's field, as the Lord commanded
me."[i]

27:8
a Ac 1:19

Jesus Stands Trial before Pilate
(230/Mark 15:2–5; Luke 23:1–5; John 18:28–37)

11Meanwhile Jesus stood before the governor, and the governor asked him, "Are
you the king of the Jews?"

"Yes, it is as you say," Jesus replied.

12When he was accused by the chief priests and the elders, he gave no answer.
13Then Pilate asked him, "Don't you hear the testimony they are bringing against
you?"[b] 14But Jesus made no reply, not even to a single charge — to the great
amazement of the governor.

27:13
b Mt 26:62

Pilate Hands Jesus Over to Be Crucified
(232/Mark 15:6–15; Luke 23:13–25; John 18:39 – 19:16)

15Now it was the governor's custom at the Feast to release a prisoner[c] chosen by
the crowd. 16At that time they had a notorious prisoner, called Barabbas. 17So
when the crowd had gathered, Pilate asked them, "Which one do you want me to
release to you: Barabbas, or Jesus who is called Christ?" 18For he knew it was out
of envy that they had handed Jesus over to him.

27:15
c Jn 18:39

19While Pilate was sitting on the judge's seat, his wife sent him this message:
"Don't have anything to do with that innocent[d] man, for I have suffered a great
deal today in a dream because of him."

27:19
d ver 24

20But the chief priests and the elders persuaded the crowd to ask for Barabbas
and to have Jesus executed. [e]

27:20
e Ac 3:14

21"Which of the two do you want me to release to you?" asked the governor.

"Barabbas," they answered.

22"What shall I do, then, with Jesus who is called Christ?" Pilate asked.

They all answered, "Crucify him!"

23"Why? What crime has he committed?" asked Pilate.

But they shouted all the louder, "Crucify him!"

24When Pilate saw that he was getting nowhere, but that instead an uproar[f] was

27:24
f Mt 26:5

i 10 See Zech. 11:12,13; Jer. 19:1-13; 32:6-9.

27:9, 10 This prophecy is found specifically in Zechariah 11:12,
13, but may also have been taken from Jeremiah 17:2, 3; 18:1–4;
19:1–11; or 32:6–15. In Old Testament times, Jeremiah was considered the collector of some of the prophets' writings, so perhaps
his name is cited rather than Zechariah.

27:12 Standing before Pilate, the religious leaders accused Jesus of a different crime than the ones for which they had arrested
him. They arrested him for blasphemy (claiming to be God), but
that charge would mean nothing to the Romans. So the religious
leaders had to accuse Jesus of crimes that would have concerned
the Roman government, such as encouraging the people not to
pay taxes, claiming to be a king, and causing riots. These accusations were not true, but the religious leaders were determined to kill
Jesus, and they broke several commandments in order to do so.

27:14 Jesus' silence fulfilled the words of the prophet (Isaiah
53:7). Pilate was amazed that Jesus didn't try to defend himself.
He recognized the obvious plot against Jesus and wanted to let
him go, but Pilate was already under pressure from Rome to keep
peace in his territory. The last thing he needed was a rebellion over
this quiet and seemingly insignificant man.

27:15, 16 Barabbas had taken part in a rebellion against the Roman government (Mark 15:7). Although an enemy to Rome, he may
have been a hero to the Jews. Ironically, Barabbas was guilty of
the crime for which Jesus was accused. Barabbas means "son of
the father," which was actually Jesus' position with God.

27:19 For a leader who was supposed to administer justice, Pilate proved to be more concerned about political expediency than
about doing what was right. He had several opportunities to make
the right decision. His conscience told him Jesus was innocent;
Roman law said an innocent man should not be put to death; and
his wife had a troubling dream. Pilate had no good excuse to condemn Jesus, but he was afraid of the crowd.

27:21 Crowds are fickle. They loved Jesus on Sunday because
they thought he was going to inaugurate his kingdom. Then they
hated him on Friday when his power appeared broken. In the face
of the mass uprising against Jesus, his friends were afraid to
speak up.

27:21 Faced with a clear choice, the people chose Barabbas, a
revolutionary and murderer, over the Son of God. Faced with the
same choice today, people are still choosing "Barabbas." They
would rather have the tangible force of human power than the salvation offered by the Son of God.

27:24 At first Pilate hesitated to give the religious leaders permission to crucify Jesus. He thought they were simply jealous of a
teacher who was more popular with the people than they were. But
when the Jews threatened to report Pilate to Caesar (John 19:12),
Pilate became afraid. Historical records indicate that the Jews had
already threatened to lodge a formal complaint against Pilate for
his stubborn flouting of their traditions — and such a complaint
would most likely have led to his recall by Rome. His job was in

starting, he took water and washed his hands in front of the crowd. "I am innocent
27:24
g Dt 21:6-8
of this man's blood,"*g* he said. "It is your responsibility!"

27:25
h Jos 2:19;
Ac 5:28
25All the people answered, "Let his blood be on us and on our children!"*h*

27:26
i Isa 53:5
26Then he released Barabbas to them. But he had Jesus flogged,*i* and handed
him over to be crucified.

Roman Soldiers Mock Jesus
(233/Mark 15:16–20)

27Then the governor's soldiers took Jesus into the Praetorium and gathered the
whole company of soldiers around him. 28They stripped him and put a scarlet robe
on him, 29and then twisted together a crown of thorns and set it on his head. They
put a staff in his right hand and knelt in front of him and mocked him. "Hail, king
27:29
j Isa 53:3
of the Jews!" they said.*j* 30They spit on him, and took the staff and struck him on
27:30
k Mt 16:21
the head again and again.*k* 31After they had mocked him, they took off the robe
27:31
l Isa 53:7
and put his own clothes on him. Then they led him away to crucify him.*l*

Jesus Is Led Away to Be Crucified
(234/Mark 15:21–24; Luke 23:26–31; John 19:17)
Jesus Is Placed on the Cross
27:32
m Heb 13:12
n Mk 15:21
(235/Mark 15:25–32; Luke 23:32–43; John 19:18–27)

27:33
o Jn 19:17
32As they were going out,*m* they met a man from Cyrene, named Simon, and
they forced him to carry the cross.*n* 33They came to a place called Golgotha (which
27:34
p Ps 69:21
means The Place of the Skull).*o* 34There they offered Jesus wine to drink, mixed
with gall;*p* but after tasting it, he refused to drink it. 35When they had crucified

---

jeopardy. The Roman government could not afford to put large
numbers of troops in all the regions under their control, so one of
Pilate's main duties was to do whatever was necessary to maintain
peace.

27:24 In making no decision, Pilate made the decision to let the
crowds crucify Jesus. Although he washed his hands, the guilt remained. Washing your hands of a tough situation doesn't cancel
your guilt. It merely gives you a false sense of peace. Don't make
excuses – take responsibility for the decisions you make.

27:27 A company of soldiers was a division of the Roman legion,
containing about 200 men.

27:29 People often make fun of Christians for their faith, but believers can take courage from the fact that Jesus himself was
mocked as greatly as anyone. Taunting may hurt our feelings, but
we should never let it change our faith (see 5:11, 12).

27:32 Condemned prisoners had to carry their own crosses to
the execution site. Jesus, weakened from the beatings he had received, was physically unable to carry his cross any farther. Thus a
bystander, Simon, was forced to do so. Simon was from Cyrene, in
northern Africa, and was probably one of the thousands of Jews
visiting Jerusalem for the Passover.

27:33 Some scholars say Golgotha ("skull") derives its name from
its appearance. Golgotha may have been a regular place of execution in a prominent public place outside the city. Executions held
there would serve as a deterrent to criminals.

27:34 Wine mixed with gall was offered to Jesus to help reduce
his pain, but Jesus refused to drink it. Gall is generally understood
to be a narcotic that was used to deaden pain. Jesus would suffer
fully conscious and with a clear mind.

27:35 The soldiers customarily took the clothing of those they
crucified. These soldiers cast lots and divided Jesus' clothing
among themselves, fulfilling the prophecy made by David. Much of
Psalm 22 parallels Jesus' crucifixion.

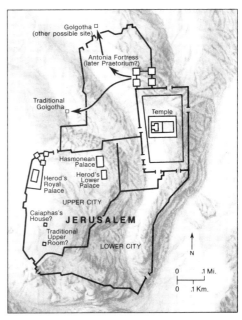

THE WAY OF THE CROSS The Roman soldiers took Jesus
into the Praetorium and mocked him, dressing him in a
scarlet robe and a crown of thorns. They then led him to the
crucifixion site outside the city. He was so weakened by his
beatings that he could not carry his cross, and a man from
Cyrene was forced to carry it to Golgotha.

him, they divided up his clothes by casting lots.ʲᵠ ³⁶And sitting down, they kept
watchʳ over him there. ³⁷Above his head they placed the written charge against
him: THIS IS JESUS, THE KING OF THE JEWS. ³⁸Two robbers were crucified with him,
one on his right and one on his left. ³⁹Those who passed by hurled insults at him,
shaking their headsˢ ⁴⁰and saying, "You who are going to destroy the temple and
build it in three days,ᵗ save yourself! Come down from the cross, if you are the
Son of God!"

⁴¹In the same way the chief priests, the teachers of the law and the elders mocked
him. ⁴²"He saved others," they said, "but he can't save himself! He's the King of
Israel!ᵘ Let him come down now from the cross, and we will believe in him. ⁴³He
trusts in God. Let God rescue himᵛ now if he wants him, for he said, 'I am the Son
of God.' " ⁴⁴In the same way the robbers who were crucified with him also heaped
insults on him.

27:35
ᵠPs 22:18
27:36
ʳver 54
27:39
ˢPs 22:7; 109:25
27:40
ᵗJn 2:19
27:42
ᵘJn 1:49
27:43
ᵛPs 22:8

Jesus Dies on the Cross
(236/Mark 15:33–41; Luke 23:44–49; John 19:28–37)

⁴⁵From the sixth hour until the ninth hour darkness came over all the land.
⁴⁶About the ninth hour Jesus cried out in a loud voice, *"Eloi, Eloi,*ᵏ *lama sabach-
thani?"* — which means, "My God, my God, why have you forsaken me?"ˡʷ

⁴⁷When some of those standing there heard this, they said, "He's calling Elijah."

⁴⁸Immediately one of them ran and got a sponge. He filled it with wine vine-
gar,ˣ put it on a stick, and offered it to Jesus to drink. ⁴⁹The rest said, "Now leave
him alone. Let's see if Elijah comes to save him."

⁵⁰And when Jesus had cried out again in a loud voice, he gave up his spirit.

⁵¹At that moment the curtain of the templeʸ was torn in two from top to bottom.
The earth shook and the rocks split. ⁵²The tombs broke open and the bodies of
many holy people who had died were raised to life. ⁵³They came out of the tombs,
and after Jesus' resurrection they went into the holy city and appeared to many
people.

⁵⁴When the centurion and those with him who were guardingᶻ Jesus saw the
earthquake and all that had happened, they were terrified, and exclaimed, "Surely
he was the Sonᵐ of God!"

⁵⁵Many women were there, watching from a distance. They had followed Jesus
from Galilee to care for his needs.ᵃ ⁵⁶Among them were Mary Magdalene, Mary
the mother of James and Joses, and the mother of Zebedee's sons.

27:46
ʷPs 22:1
27:48
ˣPs 69:21
27:51
ʸEx 26:31-33
27:54
ᶻver 36
27:55
ᵃLk 8:2, 3

ʲ 35 A few late manuscripts *lots that the word spoken by the prophet might be fulfilled: "They divided my garments
among themselves and cast lots for my clothing"* (Psalm 22:18)   ᵏ 46 Some manuscripts *Eli, Eli*   ˡ 46 Psalm 22:1
ᵐ 54 Or *a son*

27:40 This accusation was used against Jesus in his trial by the
Sanhedrin (26:61). It is ironic that Jesus was in the very process of
fulfilling his own prophecy. Because Jesus is the Son of God, who
always obeys the will of the Father, he did not come down from the
cross.

27:44 Later one of these robbers repented. Jesus promised that
the repentant robber would join him in paradise (Luke 23:39–43).

27:45 We do not know how this darkness occurred, but it is clear
that God caused it. Nature testified to the gravity of Jesus' death,
while Jesus' friends and enemies alike fell silent in the encircling
gloom. The darkness on that Friday afternoon was both physical
and spiritual.

27:46 Jesus was not questioning God; he was quoting the first
line of Psalm 22 — a deep expression of the anguish he felt when
he took on the sins of the world, which caused him to be separated
from his Father. *This* was what Jesus dreaded as he prayed to God
in the garden to take the cup from him (26:39). The physical agony
was horrible, but even worse was the period of spiritual separation
from God. Jesus suffered this double death so that we would never
have to experience eternal separation from God.

27:47 The bystanders misinterpreted Jesus' words and thought
he was calling for Elijah. Because Elijah ascended into heaven
without dying (2 Kings 2:11), they thought he would return again to
rescue them from great trouble (Malachi 4:5). At their annual Passover feast, each family set an extra place for Elijah in expectation
of his return.

● **27:51** The temple had three main parts — the courts, the Holy
Place (where only the priests could enter), and the Most Holy Place
(where only the high priest could enter, and only once a year, to
atone for the sins of the nation — Leviticus 16:1–35). The curtain
separating the Holy Place from the Most Holy Place was torn in two
at Christ's death, symbolizing that the barrier between God and
humanity was removed. Now all people are free to approach God
because of Christ's sacrifice for our sins (see Hebrews 9:1–14;
10:19–22).

● **27:52, 53** Christ's death was accompanied by at least four miraculous events: darkness, the tearing in two of the curtain in the
temple, an earthquake, and dead people rising from their tombs.
Jesus' death, therefore, could not have gone unnoticed. Everyone
knew something significant had happened.

Jesus Is Laid in the Tomb
(237/Mark 15:42–47; Luke 23:50–56; John 19:38–42)

27:60
b Mk 16:4

57As evening approached, there came a rich man from Arimathea, named Joseph, who had himself become a disciple of Jesus. 58Going to Pilate, he asked for Jesus' body, and Pilate ordered that it be given to him. 59Joseph took the body, wrapped it in a clean linen cloth, 60and placed it in his own new tomb*b* that he had cut out of the rock. He rolled a big stone in front of the entrance to the tomb and went away. 61Mary Magdalene and the other Mary were sitting there opposite the tomb.

Guards Are Posted at the Tomb
(238)

27:63
c Mt 16:21

62The next day, the one after Preparation Day, the chief priests and the Pharisees went to Pilate. 63"Sir," they said, "we remember that while he was still alive that deceiver said, 'After three days I will rise again.'*c* 64So give the order for the tomb to be made secure until the third day. Otherwise, his disciples may come and steal the body and tell the people that he has been raised from the dead. This last deception will be worse than the first."

27:66
d Da 6:17

65"Take a guard," Pilate answered. "Go, make the tomb as secure as you know how." 66So they went and made the tomb secure by putting a seal*d* on the stone and posting the guard.

Jesus Rises from the Dead
(239/Mark 16:1–8; Luke 24:1–12; John 20:1–9)

28:1
e Mt 27:56

28 After the Sabbath, at dawn on the first day of the week, Mary Magdalene and the other Mary*e* went to look at the tomb.

2There was a violent earthquake, for an angel of the Lord came down from

---

THE SEVEN LAST WORDS OF JESUS ON THE CROSS		
	"Father, forgive them, for they do not know what they are doing."	Luke 23:34
	"I tell you the truth, today you will be with me in paradise."	Luke 23:43
	Speaking to John and Mary, "Dear woman, here is your son. . . . Here is your mother."	John 19:26, 27
	"My God, my God, why have you forsaken me?"	Matthew 27:46; Mark 15:34
	"I am thirsty."	John 19:28
	"It is finished."	John 19:30
	"Father, into your hands I commit my spirit."	Luke 23:46

The statements that Jesus made from the cross have been treasured by all who have followed him as Lord. They demonstrate both his humanity and his divinity. They also capture the last moments of all that Jesus went through to gain our forgiveness.

27:57, 58 Joseph of Arimathea was a secret disciple of Jesus. He was a religious leader, an honored member of the Sanhedrin (Mark 15:43). In the past, Joseph had been afraid to speak against the religious leaders who opposed Jesus; now he was bold, courageously asking to take Jesus' body from the cross and to bury it. The disciples who publicly followed Jesus had fled, but this Jewish leader, who followed Jesus in secret, came forward and did what was right.

27:60 The tomb where Jesus was laid was probably a man-made cave cut out of one of the many limestone hills in the area. These caves were often large enough to walk into.

●**27:64** The religious leaders took Jesus' resurrection claims more seriously than the disciples did. The disciples didn't remember Jesus' teaching about his resurrection (20:17–19); but the religious leaders did. Because of his claims, they were almost as afraid of Jesus after his death as when he was alive. They tried to take every precaution that his body would remain in the tomb.

●**27:66** The Pharisees were so afraid of Jesus' predictions about his resurrection that they made sure the tomb was thoroughly sealed and guarded. Because the tomb was hewn out of rock in the side of a hill, there was only one entrance. The tomb was sealed by stringing a cord across the stone that was rolled over the entrance. The cord was sealed at each end with clay. But the religious leaders took a further precaution, asking that guards be placed at the tomb's entrance. With such precautions, the only way the tomb could be empty would be for Jesus to rise from the dead. The Pharisees failed to understand that no rock, seal, guard, or army could prevent the Son of God from rising again.

28:1 The other Mary was not Jesus' mother. She could have been the wife of Clopas (John 19:25). Or, if she was the mother of James and John (Matthew 27:56), she may have been Jesus' aunt.

●**28:2** The stone was not rolled back so Jesus could get out, but so others could get in and see that Jesus had indeed risen from the dead, just as he had promised.

heaven and, going to the tomb, rolled back the stone and sat on it. ³His appearance was like lightning, and his clothes were white as snow.ᶠ ⁴The guards were so afraid of him that they shook and became like dead men.

⁵The angel said to the women, "Do not be afraid, for I know that you are looking for Jesus, who was crucified. ⁶He is not here; he has risen, just as he said.ᵍ Come and see the place where he lay. ⁷Then go quickly and tell his disciples: 'He has risen from the dead and is going ahead of you into Galilee.ʰ There you will see him.' Now I have told you."

28:3
ᶠDa 10:6

28:6
ᵍMt 16:21

28:7
ʰMt 26:32

Jesus Appears to the Women
(241)

⁸So the women hurried away from the tomb, afraid yet filled with joy, and ran to tell his disciples. ⁹Suddenly Jesus met them. "Greetings," he said. They came to him, clasped his feet and worshiped him. ¹⁰Then Jesus said to them, "Do not be afraid. Go and tell my brothersⁱ to go to Galilee; there they will see me."

28:10
ⁱRo 8:29;
Heb 2:11-13, 17

Religious Leaders Bribe the Guards
(242)

¹¹While the women were on their way, some of the guards went into the city and reported to the chief priests everything that had happened. ¹²When the chief priests had met with the elders and devised a plan, they gave the soldiers a large sum of money, ¹³telling them, "You are to say, 'His disciples came during the night and stole him away while we were asleep.' ¹⁴If this report gets to the governor, we will

---

1. Even before the trial began, it had been determined that Jesus must die (John 11:50; Mark 14:1). There was no "innocent until proven guilty" approach.
2. False witnesses were sought to testify against Jesus (Matthew 26:59). Usually the religious leaders went through an elaborate system of screening witnesses to ensure justice.
3. No defense for Jesus was sought or allowed (Luke 22:67–71).
4. The trial was conducted at night (Mark 14:53–65; 15:1), which was illegal according to the religious leaders' own laws.
5. The high priest put Jesus under oath, but then incriminated him for what he said (Matthew 26:63–66).
6. Cases involving such serious charges were to be tried only in the Sanhedrin's regular meeting place, not in the high priest's palace (Mark 14:53–65).

HOW JESUS' TRIAL WAS ILLEGAL

The religious leaders were not interested in giving Jesus a fair trial. In their minds, Jesus had to die. This blind obsession led them to pervert the justice they were appointed to protect. Here are many examples of the actions taken by the religious leaders that were illegal according to their own laws.

●**28:5-7** The angel who announced the good news of the resurrection to the women gave them four messages: (1) *Do not be afraid.* The reality of the resurrection brings joy, not fear. When you are afraid, remember the empty tomb. (2) *He is not here.* Jesus is not dead and is not to be looked for among the dead. He is alive, with his people. (3) *Come and see.* The women could check the evidence themselves. The tomb was empty then, and it is empty today. The resurrection is a historical fact. (4) *Go quickly and tell.* They were to spread the joy of the resurrection. We too are to spread the great news about Jesus' resurrection.

●**28:6** Jesus' resurrection is the key to the Christian faith. Why? (1) Just as he promised, Jesus rose from the dead. We can be confident, therefore, that he will accomplish all he has promised. (2) Jesus' bodily resurrection shows us that the living Christ is ruler of God's eternal kingdom, not a false prophet or imposter. (3) We can be certain of our resurrection because he was resurrected. Death is not the end—there is future life. (4) The power that brought Jesus back to life is available to us to bring our spiritually dead selves back to life. (5) The resurrection is the basis for the church's witness to the world. Jesus is more than just a

human leader; he is the Son of God.

28:10 By "brothers," Jesus probably meant his disciples. This showed that he had forgiven them, even after they had disowned and deserted him. Their relationship would now be even stronger than before.

28:10 Jesus told the women to pass a message on to the disciples—that he would meet them in Galilee, as he had previously told them (Mark 14:28). But the disciples, afraid of the religious leaders, stayed hidden behind locked doors in Jerusalem (John 20:19). So Jesus met them first there (Luke 24:36) and then later in Galilee (John 21).

●**28:11-15** Jesus' resurrection was already causing a great stir in Jerusalem. A group of women was moving quickly through the streets, looking for the disciples to tell them the amazing news that Jesus was alive. At the same time, a group of religious leaders was plotting how to cover up the resurrection.

Today there is still a great stir over the resurrection, and there are still only two choices—to believe that Jesus rose from the dead, or to be closed to the truth—denying it, ignoring it, or trying to explain it away.

satisfy him and keep you out of trouble." 15So the soldiers took the money and did as they were instructed. And this story has been widely circulated among the Jews to this very day.

Jesus Gives the Great Commission
(248/Mark 16:15–18)

28:16
j ver 7, 10;
Mt 26:32

28:18
k Da 7:13, 14;
Php 2:9, 10

28:19
l Mk 16:15, 16

28:20
m Ac 2:42

16Then the eleven disciples went to Galilee, to the mountain where Jesus had told them to go.*j* 17When they saw him, they worshiped him; but some doubted. 18Then Jesus came to them and said, "All authority in heaven and on earth has been given to me.*k* 19Therefore go and make disciples of all nations,*l* baptizing them in*n* the name of the Father and of the Son and of the Holy Spirit, 20and teaching*m* them to obey everything I have commanded you. And surely I am with you always, to the very end of the age."

n *19* Or *into*; see Acts 8:16; 19:5; Romans 6:3; 1 Cor. 1:13; 10:2 and Gal. 3:27.

● **28:18** God gave Jesus authority over heaven and earth. On the basis of that authority, Jesus told his disciples to make more disciples as they preached, baptized, and taught. With this same authority, Jesus still commands us to tell others the Good News and make them disciples for the kingdom.

● **28:18–20** When someone is dying or leaving us, his or her last words are very important. Jesus left the disciples with these last words of instruction: they were under his authority; they were to make more disciples; they were to baptize and teach these new disciples to obey Christ; Christ would be with them always. Whereas in previous missions Jesus had sent his disciples only to the Jews (10:5, 6), their mission from now on would be worldwide. Jesus is Lord of the earth, and he died for the sins of people from all nations.

We are to go — whether it is next door or to another country — and make disciples. It is not an option, but a command to all who call Jesus "Lord." We are not all evangelists in the formal sense, but we have all received gifts that we can use to help fulfill the Great Commission. As we obey, we have comfort in the knowledge that Jesus is always with us.

28:19 Jesus' words affirm the reality of the Trinity. Some people accuse theologians of making up the concept of the Trinity and reading it into Scripture. As we see here, the concept comes di-

rectly from Jesus himself. He did not say baptize them into the *names*, but into the *name* of the Father, Son, and Holy Spirit. The word *Trinity* does not occur in Scripture, but it well describes the three-in-one nature of the Father, Son, and Holy Spirit.

28:19 The disciples were to baptize people because baptism unites a believer with Jesus Christ in his or her death to sin and resurrection to new life. Baptism symbolizes submission to Christ, a willingness to live God's way, and identification with God's covenant people.

● **28:20** How is Jesus *with* us? Jesus was with the disciples physically until he ascended into heaven, and then spiritually through the Holy Spirit (Acts 1:4). The Holy Spirit would be Jesus' presence that would never leave them (John 14:26). Jesus continues to be with us today through his Spirit.

● **28:20** The Old Testament prophecies and genealogies in the book of Matthew present Jesus' credentials for being King of the world — not a military or political leader, as the disciples had originally hoped, but a spiritual King who can overcome all evil and rule in the heart of every person. If we refuse to serve the King faithfully, we are disloyal subjects, fit only to be banished from the kingdom. We must make Jesus King of our lives and worship him as our Savior, King, and Lord.

STUDY QUESTIONS

Thirteen lessons for individual or group study

It's always exciting to get more than you expect. And that's what you'll find in this Bible study guide—much more than you expect. Our goal was to write thoughtful, practical, dependable, and application-oriented studies of God's Word.

This study guide contains the complete text of the selected Bible book. The commentary is accurate, complete, and loaded with unique charts, maps, and profiles of Bible people.

With the Bible text, extensive notes and helps, and questions to guide discussion, these Life Application Study Guides have everything you need in one place.

The lessons in this Bible study guide will work for large classes as well as small-group studies. To get everyone involved in your discussions, encourage participants to answer the questions before each meeting.

Each lesson is divided into five easy-to-lead sections. The section called "Reflect" introduces you and the members of your group to a specific area of life touched by the lesson. "Read" shows which chapters to read and which notes and other features to use. Additional questions help you understand the passage. "Realize" brings into focus the biblical principle to be learned with questions, a special insight, or both. "Respond" helps you make connections with your own situation and personal needs. The questions are designed to help you find areas in your life where you can apply the biblical truths. "Resolve" helps you map out action plans for that day.

Begin and end each lesson with prayer, asking for the Holy Spirit's guidance, direction, and wisdom.

Recommended time allotments for each section of a lesson:

Segment	60 minutes	90 minutes
Reflect on your life	5 minutes	10 minutes
Read the passage	10 minutes	15 minutes
Realize the principle	15 minutes	20 minutes
Respond to the message	20 minutes	30 minutes
Resolve to take action	10 minutes	15 minutes

All five sections work together to help a person learn the lessons, live out the principles, and obey the commands taught in the Bible.

Also, at the end of each lesson, there is a section entitled "More for studying other themes in this section." These questions will help you lead the group in studying other parts of each section not covered in depth by the main lesson.

Do not merely listen to the word, and so deceive yourselves. Do what it says. Anyone who listens to the word but does not do what it says is like a man who looks at his face in a mirror and, after looking at himself, goes away and immediately forgets what he looks like. But the man who looks intently into the perfect law that gives freedom, and continues to do this, not forgetting what he has heard, but doing it—he will be blessed in what he does. (James 1:22-25, NIV)

REFLECT
on your life

1 Briefly describe a time when you met someone you considered very important.

_____

_____

_____

_____

_____

2 How did this meeting affect you positively or negatively?

_____

_____

_____

_____

_____

READ
the passage

Read the introductory material to Matthew, Matthew 1:1-17, and the following notes:

❑ 1:1   ❑ 1:1-17   ❑ 1:16

3 What is the main purpose of the Gospel of Matthew?

_____

_____

_____

4 How far is it from Jerusalem to Caesarea Philippi? What town or city is about that far from where you live? (Use the map, "Key Places in Matthew," in the introductory material.)

_____

_____

_____

5 There are four women besides Mary mentioned in the genealogy of Jesus. Why might they have been included in a list of fathers?

_____

REALIZE
the principle

_____

_____

_____

6 Why was it important for Matthew to include a list of ancestors in his Gospel?

_____

_____

_____

_____

The purpose of the Gospels is to give us a clear picture of Jesus so we can get to know him better. They tell us who he was, what he came to do, and what he wants us to do. Matthew's unique snapshot gives us a picture of Jesus the King. By the time you reach the end of the Gospel of Matthew, your knowledge of Jesus should be deeper, your picture of Jesus should be clearer, and your understanding of what he wants you to be should be more mature. In the end, if you are willing, you will know him better, too.

7 Roughly how many times have you read the Gospel of Matthew all the way through? ❑ Never ❑ Once ❑ A couple of times ❑ Quite a few times
❑ Many times

RESPOND
to the message

8 Which of the five Megathemes (from the introductory material) are you most curious to understand better?

_____

_____

_____

9 Briefly describe how you would like your understanding of Jesus Christ to change.

_____

_____

_____

_____

_____

10 In what specific ways do you think you would be different if you knew Jesus better than you do right now?

_____

_____

_____

_____

_____

11 What can you do this week to get to know Jesus better?

_____

_____

_____

_____

RESOLVE
to take action

12 What question about Jesus do you hope to have answered through your study of Matthew?

_____

_____

_____

13 Throughout the coming week, pray that God will enable you to benefit from your study of Matthew by understanding yourself and Jesus better.

A Which of the Old Testament people in Jesus' family tree do you recognize? What do you know about them? Which people would you like to learn more about?

MORE
for studying
other themes
in this section

B Use the timeline at the top of the Matthew title page and the Blueprint outline to figure out what length of time is covered in each of the main sections in Matthew. How did Jesus spend most of his time during his ministry? What does this example say about our priorities? How might you adjust your priorities?

C Several titles and names for Jesus are used in the introductory material. Which one means the most to you? Why?

D What was the world political situation at the time Jesus was born? What longings did this create in God's people? How did God address those longings? What longings or desires does our present world create in you? Which of God's provisions helps you most with these desires?

REFLECT
on your life

1 What are some small decisions in life?

_____

_____

_____

_____

_____

2 What are some big decisions in life?

_____

_____

_____

_____

_____

READ
the passage

Read Matthew 1:18—4:25, Joseph's Profile, Herod's Profile, and the following notes:

❒1:18   ❒1:18-25   ❒1:19   ❒1:24   ❒2:3   ❒2:4   ❒2:8   ❒2:13   ❒2:16

❒4:1   ❒4:1ff   ❒4:1-10   ❒4:3, 4   ❒4:6   ❒4:8-10

3 What were Joseph's guidelines for making decisions (1:18-21, 24, 25; 2:13-15, 19-23)?

_____

_____

_____

_____

4 What were Herod's guidelines for making decisions (2:3-8)?

_____

_____

_____

_____

5 How did Jesus handle the tempting choices offered by Satan (4:1-11)?

_____

_____

_____

6 In what ways was God involved in the choices of the people in this passage?

_____

_____

_____

REALIZE
the principle

7 What was so tempting about the offers the devil made to Jesus?

_____

_____

_____

8 In what other ways do temptations hinder us from making good choices?

_____

_____

_____

Herod made many wrong choices. Though he built fortresses and palaces, he destroyed lives. And other people paid dearly for his bad choices. In contrast, Jesus made the right choices. Even though the devil tempted him directly and tried to lure Jesus with offers of fame, power, and authority, Jesus chose correctly in every decision. Likewise, Joseph had only one desire whenever he was faced with decisions: to do what God wanted. Whatever God desired was Joseph's desire. We learn from these examples that every opportunity to make a wrong choice is also an opportunity to make a right choice. The right choice will always honor God. How often do you consider God in your day-to-day choices?

9 Why should Christians include God in their decision making?

_____

_____

_____

RESPOND
to the message

10 In what kinds of choices should Christians actively seek God's guidance?

_____

_____

_____

11 Why do people leave God out of small decisions?

_____

_____

_____

12 Why do people leave God out of big decisions?

_____

_____

_____

13 How can you include God in more of your decisions?

_____

_____

_____

_____

14 With what day-to-day choices do you need to seek God's help more?

_____

_____

_____

_____

RESOLVE
to take action

15 For what big decision will you seek God's wisdom this week?

_____

_____

_____

_____

A What were some of Joseph's strengths or virtues (1:18—2:23)? How did he handle difficult or unexpected circumstances? What does this challenge you to do when you face difficult or challenging circumstances?

MORE
for studying
other themes
in this section

B Why is the Virgin Birth important to the Christian faith (1:18)? What makes it important to you personally?

C What was the role of angels in the birth and early life of Jesus (1:18-21; 2:12, 13, 19, 20, 22)? What is the role of angels today? How might this boost your confidence in God's ability and willingness to look out for you?

D Why did the Magi seek Jesus (2:1, 2)? How did they express their devotion (2:9-12)? How can we express devotion to Jesus?

E Why did John the Baptist call people to repent (3:2)? Of what do you need to repent?

F John the Baptist said harsh things to the Pharisees and Sadducees who came to see him (3:7-12). When is it good to use harsh language with people? How can you be sure to use harsh language only when it is necessary?

G In what way was the Trinity evident at Jesus' baptism (3:16, 17)? How does God make himself known today?

H Why do you think Peter and Andrew chose to leave their nets and follow Jesus when he asked them to (4:18-20)? What have you been challenged to leave in order to follow Jesus?

I What were the three main parts of Jesus' early ministry (4:23-25)? How are these same ministries carried on today? What is your part in God's work in your part of the world?

REFLECT
on your life

1 Complete this sentence in as many ways as you can: Happiness is . . .

_____

_____

_____

_____

2 To what do people typically turn for happiness today?

_____

_____

_____

READ
the passage

Read Matthew 5:1-48, the chart "Key Lessons from the Sermon on the Mount," and the following notes:

❏5:1ff ❏5:1, 2 ❏5:3-5 ❏5:3-12 ❏5:11, 12

3 Listed below are the Beatitudes, the qualities that make a person "blessed" (5:3-12). What do you think each means?

Poor in spirit _____

_____

Mournful _____

_____

Meek _____

_____

Hungry and thirsty for righteousness _____

_____

Merciful _____

_____

Pure in heart _____

_____

A peacemaker _____

_____

Persecuted because of righteousness _____

_____

4 How are the Beatitudes related to each other?

_____

_____

REALIZE
the principle

5 What response to this part of his sermon do you think would have pleased Jesus the most?

_____

_____

Though Jesus' disciples had left everything to follow him, they still had little idea of what he wanted them to do. With this list of Beatitudes, Jesus began their initiation. His description of the blessed person surely cut across the disciples' natural experience, as it does ours; we don't expect happiness to come from being poor, pure, or caught in the cross fire while making peace. Yet those who follow and obey Christ are more than merely happy—they are *blessed.* They are blessed because they have a hope and joy not based on feeling or circumstance. Following Jesus means living by standards entirely different from public opinion. Rather than making us eminently popular and famous, it often means facing opposition and misunderstanding. Yet all of this makes us blessed.

6 In what ways is a person who lives the Beatitudes blessed?

_____

_____

_____

7 How can a person exhibit the Beatitudes in his/her life?

_____

_____

_____

RESPOND
to the message

8 What natural tendencies go against the qualities that make a person blessed?

_____

_____

_____

9 Which of the qualities that Jesus mentioned in the Beatitudes are already a part of your life?

_____

_____

_____

10 Which of the Beatitudes are most lacking in your life?

_____

_____

_____

11 What changes in your life-style or priorities would help you conform more to Jesus' description of the blessed person?

_____

_____

_____

_____

12 Which Beatitude do you want to be more evident in your life?

_____

_____

_____

RESOLVE
to take action

13 In what ways can you live out this Beatitude?

_____

_____

_____

14 This week, pray that God will help you value what he values. Use the chart "Key Lessons from the Sermon on the Mount" to shape your prayer. Make each of the goals a specific request to God for his training of your mind to think more like Jesus.

MORE
for studying
other themes
in this section

A Describe what you imagine the scene was like when Jesus delivered the Sermon on the Mount. What characteristics of good teaching did Jesus demonstrate (5:1-48)? How do you think you would have reacted to the things Jesus said? What response do his words evoke in you now?

B Describe in one sentence what Jesus taught about the following subjects (5:1-48): The identity of believers in the world; God's law; anger; lust; divorce; the dependability of our words; revenge; relating to enemies. Which of these areas are you challenged to change? What change do you need to make?

C Why should Christ's disciples rejoice when they are persecuted (5:12)? When are you persecuted? In what way can you rejoice?

D To what was Jesus referring when he said that salt and light have a powerful effect on the world (5:13-16)? What can you do to have a significant effect on the world?

E What did Jesus mean by saying he wasn't abolishing the Law, but fulfilling it (5:17-20)? What are some steps we can take to avoid misusing or misapplying God's Word?

F What is your understanding of Jesus' statement, "Be perfect . . . as your heavenly Father is perfect" (5:48)? How is God helping us toward this goal? What should you be doing in the process?

G As Jesus moved from subject to subject in this sermon, what phrases did he keep repeating (5:21, 27, 31, 33, 38, 43)? What points did he emphasize with the repetition? Which of these points hits the area of greatest need in your life now? What can you do about this need?

REFLECT
on your life

1 What is a show-off . . .

in sports? _____

_____

at your place of work? _____

_____

at church? _____

_____

2 Why do people show off?

_____

_____

_____

3 In what ways do Christians sometimes show off?

_____

_____

_____

Read Matthew 6:1-34 and the following notes:

❐6:2   ❐6:3   ❐6:3, 4   ❐6:5, 6   ❐6:16   ❐6:17   ❐6:20   ❐6:22, 23   ❐6:33

READ
the passage

4 What kind of showy demonstrations did Jesus tell his disciples to avoid (6:1)?

_____

_____

_____

5 Summarize in a sentence what Jesus taught about showing off in each of the following areas:

Giving (6:2-4) _____

_____

_____

Prayer (6:5-8) _____

_____

_____

Fasting (6:16-18) _____

_____

_____

6 Why would Jesus express so many concerns about the public lives of his followers?

REALIZE
the principle

_____

_____

Tax deductions, appreciation by others, power, prestige, obedience to Christ, care for others—the reasons for doing good are frequently mixed. Identical actions can be done from any number of different motives. Actions tend to be public; motives are almost always hidden. Jesus expects his disciples to keep their motives focused on him. Christians cannot control who might notice what they are doing. The mistake Jesus wants us to avoid is doing good so that others will notice. Asking ourself one question will help keep our motives clear: Am I willing to obey Christ when no one else notices? Life will present us with many opportunities to test our answer.

7 Which of the three areas Jesus mentioned do you think a follower of Christ would find most difficult keeping private? Why?

_____

_____

_____

_____

8 In what situations would it be good to let your acts of devotion be seen by others in order to set an example or be a Christian witness?

_____

_____

_____

9 What role do motives play in where and how we choose to pray, fast, or give?

_____

_____

_____

RESPOND
to the message

10 If you were taking classes in giving, praying, and fasting, what grade would you give yourself for the last three months? (Give a separate grade for actions and motives.)

	Actions	Motives
Giving	_____	_____
Praying	_____	_____
Fasting	_____	_____

11 Which act of devotion do you find easiest to keep private?

_____

_____

12 Which act of devotion do you find the most difficult to keep private?

_____

_____

13 What are some concrete steps you could take this week to make sure you are doing your acts of devotion with proper motives?

Giving _____

_____

RESOLVE
to take action

Prayer _____

_____

Fasting _____

_____

14 As part of each day, ask God to help you have godly motives in all you do.

A What does Jesus' teaching about prayer have to say about praying in front of groups (6:5-13)? In what ways can public prayers be made appropriate or inappropriate? How can you be sure to follow Christ's guidelines when you pray in front of others?

MORE
for studying
other themes
in this section

B If the Lord's Prayer is meant to be a model for our praying, what specific areas ought we to keep in mind when we pray (6:9-13)?

C When will God withhold forgiveness from us (6:14, 15)? Whom have you not forgiven? How can you take a step toward forgiving this person?

D What is the difference between planning for tomorrow and worrying about tomorrow (6:25-34)? What do you need to plan? What aspects of the future do you need to entrust to God?

REFLECT
on your life

1 What's the worst storm you've ever been in?

_____

_____

_____

2 What is scary about storms?

_____

_____

_____

_____

READ
the passage

Read Matthew 7:1-29 and the following notes:

❐7:21   ❐7:21-23   ❐7:22   ❐7:24   ❐7:26   ❐7:29

3 Who will enter the kingdom of heaven (7:21-23)?

_____

_____

_____

4 What kind of person is like a builder who puts his house on solid rock (7:24, 25)?

_____

_____

_____

5 What kind of person is like a builder who puts his house on sand (7:26, 27)?

_____

_____

_____

_____

6 What is the main difference between the wise and foolish builders?

_____

_____

REALIZE
the principle

_____

_____

Jesus told his disciples that choosing whether or not to follow his instructions was much like choosing where to build a house. A life of submission to Christ and his teaching would be like a house built on a solid foundation, able to withstand the storms of life. A life built on our own ideas or public opinion would be like a house built on sand, completely unable to withstand trouble. In giving us his Word, Jesus offers us a solid foundation on which to build our life. What are you building your life on—Christ, or your own ideas?

7 What is the attraction of building a life on a foundation of sand?

_____

_____

_____

8 What are some of the hazards of ignoring God's instructions?

_____

_____

_____

9 What does it take to build a life on a rock?

_____

_____

_____

_____

10 Why do people ignore God's instructions?

_____

_____

_____

_____

11 How can we avoid the mistake of the foolish builder?

_____

_____

_____

_____

12 How does it feel to know that you are responsible to obey everything Jesus taught?

_____

_____

_____

13 If you could ask Jesus to clarify one expectation he has for your life, what would it be?

_____

_____

_____

_____

14 Skim through the Sermon on the Mount, beginning at Matthew 5:1. For what areas of your life do these instructions provide a solid foundation?

_____

_____

_____

_____

RESOLVE
to take action

15 What can you do this week to build your life on Christ?

_____

_____

_____

_____

_____

A What is the difference between judging and thinking critically (7:1-6)? How can we avoid judging without being naive or blind to the facts? About whom is it difficult for you to be objective? What can you do to be fair in your assessment of this person?

B What are the "pearls" we should not share with people who won't listen to God's message (7:6)? How can we practice discernment in what we say to others about God?

C Why is it good to do to others as you would have them do to you (7:12)? What is golden about the Golden Rule? Toward whom do you need to practice the Golden Rule more consistently?

D The crowds were amazed at Jesus' teachings (7:28, 29). What impresses you about Jesus' teachings? What difference does it make in your attitudes and actions that you feel this way?

MORE
for studying
other themes
in this section

REFLECT
on your life

1 What items do people commonly buy with coupons or try to get at a discount?

_____

_____

_____

_____

_____

2 When are people willing to pay full price?

_____

_____

_____

_____

_____

READ
the passage

Read Matthew 8:1—10:42, the chart "Counting the Cost of Following Christ," and the following notes:

❏8:19, 20 ❏8:21, 22 ❏10:17, 18 ❏10:19, 20 ❏10:22 ❏10:23 ❏10:25

❏10:29-31 ❏10:34 ❏10:34-39 ❏10:37 ❏10:38 ❏10:39

3 What costs might a person have to pay to follow Jesus (8:20, 22; 10:17-42)?

_____

_____

_____

_____

4 Why might these costs involve opposition or conflict (10:18-42)?

_____

_____

_____

_____

5 How was the disciples' understanding of Christ still quite naive?

_____

_____

_____

REALIZE
the principle

Many people wanted to follow Jesus, but many of them did not want to pay the price. That's why Jesus challenged those who wanted to follow him to count the cost, because following him would involve living with discomfort, self-sacrifice, and even rejection. Jesus meets each of us with the call, "Follow me." His request is simple and direct. But following Jesus is not like joining a wholesale club. What he's asking is for us to place him at the very center of our life, submitting all other values, people, and things to his authority. We must count these costs before saying we want to follow him.

6 What did it cost the disciples to follow Christ?

_____

_____

_____

7 What made it worth the price?

_____

_____

_____

8 What might it cost a person to follow Jesus today?

9 What costs keep people from following Christ?

10 What costs have you had to pay to follow Christ?

11 What costs have you been unwilling to pay in following Christ?

12 How might your plans for the future change if you became willing to pay any price to follow Christ?

13 What do you want to remember the next time you have to pay a price for doing what God wants?

_____

_____

_____

_____

RESOLVE
to take action

A Why did Jesus tell the paralyzed man that he was forgiven before he healed the man's condition (9:2-8)? What does Jesus most want to heal in every person? How can Christians reflect that concern in how they carry out God's work in the world?

MORE
for studying
other themes
in this section

B Where did Jesus go that caused the religious leaders to question his actions (9:10, 11)? Why did Jesus go there (9:12, 13)? Where and to whom can you go in copying Jesus' example?

C Why didn't Jesus' disciples fast (9:16, 17)? What are some good reasons for fasting? How could you use fasting as a spiritual discipline?

D What "impossible situation" did Jesus use his power to change (9:22)? Why did he step in to do something? With what impossible situation can you ask Jesus to help you?

E What is one need for which God specifically asks us to pray (9:36-38)? How can you fulfill this request in your own prayer habits?

F What special traveling instructions did Jesus give his disciples when he sent them out to perform miracles in his name (10:1-16)? What is timeless about these instructions? What areas of your life does this affect?

G How do you understand the meaning of Christ's words, "Whoever finds his life will lose it, and whoever loses his life for my sake will find it" (10:39)? When a person decides to follow Christ, what does he/she lose? What does he/she find? In what ways can you remember how the benefits of your faith outweigh the sacrifices?

REFLECT
on your life

1 What is the most successful gardening experience you've ever had?

2 What enabled your garden to do so well?

READ
the passage

Read Matthew 11:1—13:58 and the following notes:

❒13:2, 3 ❒13:8 ❒13:9 ❒13:10 ❒13:22 ❒13:23

3 In the parable of the sower, what happened to the seed the farmer planted (13:4-8)?

4 Why did only some of the seed grow (13:4-8)?

5 What four common responses do people have to God's Word (13:19-23)?

_____

_____

_____

_____

6 Why does God's Word make a lasting difference in the lives of some people and not others (13:19-23)?

_____

_____

_____

The people who heard Jesus speak responded to his message in many differ-ent ways. Some scoffed. Some followed him as long as it was easy. Some fol-lowed for a little while, but were lured away, like Judas, by other concerns. And some followed till the end. Those four basic actions cover the range of responses God's Word has always received and still gets. There are many forces working against a full response to God's Word. The devil, shallow convic-tion, worry, and money can each lure us away from God's truth. Our challenge is to understand God's Word and to practice what we hear.

REALIZE
the principle

7 Why do responses to the gospel differ from person to person?

_____

_____

_____

8 What steps can a person take to be like the good soil in receiving God's message?

_____

_____

_____

9 How could a person who is like one of the first three kinds of soil become like good soil?

_____

_____

_____

RESPOND
to the message

10 How can we stop the devil from snatching away God's message before it takes root in a person's heart?

11 What kinds of trouble or persecution test the strength of a Christian's conviction?

12 What worries of this life can choke out Christian faith?

13 What practical steps can you take to ensure that God's message takes root in your life?

RESOLVE
to take action

14 What troubles or worries have threatened your receptiveness to God recently?

15 What biblical truth or promise do you need to remember?

16 As you think of people who are close to you, visualize their lives as different kinds of soil. For whom will you pray? (Ask God to do whatever he needs to do to plow up their field into good soil.)

_____

_____

_____

A What was John the Baptist's relationship to Jesus (11:1-19)? What prompted him to send his disciples to ask Jesus a question? What is your relationship to Jesus? What would you like to ask him?

MORE for studying other themes in this section

B How did John prepare the way for others to hear about Jesus (11:2-19)? How can you prepare the way for your friends, coworkers, and neighbors to hear about Jesus?

C How did insensitivity to God's message hurt the people of Korazin, Bethsaida, and Capernaum (11:20-24)? How can you be sure to maintain your sensitivity to God's Word?

D In what way are little children wiser than educated people (11:25, 26)? In what way can you become wise like a child?

E What unique role does Jesus fill (11:27)? How does he fill this role in your life?

F From what burden or burdens does Jesus free us (11:28-30)? What makes Jesus' burden light by comparison? What burden do you carry that Jesus could lighten for you?

G What arguments did Jesus use to refute the accusation that his disciples were violating the Sabbath (12:1-8)? How can we make sure we don't put rules ahead of people?

H Whom did Jesus meet as he traveled (12:1-50)? How did Jesus respond to each one? Whom have you met over the last six months? How can you present Christ in a unique way to each one?

I How did Jesus anger the Pharisees (12:9-14)? What did they want to do to him? Why might people get angry at someone doing good? What does this help you keep in mind?

J What can people tell about us by the language we use (12:33-37)? What does your choice of words tell about you? What changes might this suggest for you?

K Who is Jesus' real family (12:46-50)? Whom does this include among the people you know? In what way does Christ draw you together?

L How did people's hardness of heart affect the way Jesus taught (13:13-15)? What can we do to avoid becoming hardened to God's Word?

M What hindered the people of Jesus' hometown from accepting Christ's identity (13:53-58)? What blocks people from accepting Christ today? What can we do to remove these barriers?

REFLECT
on your life

1 What kinds of power do you see?

_____

_____

_____

_____

_____

2 What kind of power do you need?

_____

_____

_____

_____

READ
the passage

Read Matthew 14:1—15:39, the maps, "Jesus Walks on the Sea" and "Ministry in Phoenicia," and the following notes:

❐14:14 ❐14:19-21 ❐14:21 ❐14:28 ❐14:30, 31 ❐14:35, 36 ❐14:36

❐15:23 ❐15:24 ❐15:29-31 ❐15:32ff ❐15:33

3 Fill in this chart about the five miracles recorded in Matthew 14—15:

	What was the miracle?	Over what did Jesus demonstrate power?
14:13-21	_____	_____
14:22-32	_____	_____
15:21-28	_____	_____
15:29-31	_____	_____
15:32-39	_____	_____

4 What often moved Jesus to perform miracles (14:14; 15:28, 32)?

_____

_____

_____

5 What did the people whom Jesus helped learn about Jesus?

_____

REALIZE
the principle

_____

6 What do these miracles show that Jesus can do for us?

_____

_____

_____

The disciples saw Jesus perform many miracles. In the events of this passage alone, they witnessed five. Among other things, they learned of Jesus' power through these miracles. He showed that he was ready and able to provide for them (14:13-21; 15:32-39), help them through difficult circumstances (14:22-32), free them from demonic forces (15:21-28), and heal them (15:29-31). Because Jesus lives and is God, his power is available to us today, too. God is able and willing to care for us with his mighty power!

7 Why might Jesus not use his power to heal or rescue us?

_____

_____

_____

RESPOND
to the message

8 What assurance do we have that God will:

provide for us? _____

_____

help us through difficult circumstances? _____

_____

protect us? _____

_____

heal us? _____

_____

9 Over what does Jesus have power today?

_____

_____

_____

10 Why do people often lack confidence in God's ability?

_____

_____

11 How can we have faith in God's ability to help us without having unrealistic expectations?

_____

_____

_____

12 If you had been with the disciples in the boat late that night when Jesus came walking on the water, might you have joined Peter going over the side, or would you most likely have waited in the boat with the others?

_____

_____

13 For what emergencies do you need to pray for help from Christ?

_____

_____

_____

14 How can you pray differently this week to show faith in God and his power?

_____

_____

_____

RESOLVE
to take action

15 What immediate worry or concern can you entrust to God's care?

_____

_____

_____

A Why did Jesus retreat to a solitary place (14:13)? When is it helpful for you to retreat for private prayer and reflection?

B What do you think the crowd talked about after Jesus miraculously fed them (14:19-21; 15:36-38)? How do people respond today when they are the recipients of God's goodness? What can you do to show that you are grateful?

C How did the people of Jesus' day avoid the responsibility of caring for their parents (15:3-6)? What are your responsibilities toward your parents and family? What often gets in the way of fulfilling your responsibilities to these people? How can you serve them better?

D What is important about a person's inner condition (15:16-20)? How can you nurture this part of your life?

E Why did Jesus first refuse to help the Canaanite woman (15:24-26)? Why did he then help her (15:27, 28)? What does this tell you about how you should pray?

MORE
for studying
other themes
in this section

L E S S O N   9
JUST DO IT
MATTHEW 16:1—18:35

REFLECT
on your life

1 Who are the two or three best teachers you ever had?

_____

_____

_____

2 What made each person a great teacher?

_____

_____

_____

_____

_____

_____

READ
the passage

Read Matthew 16:1—18:35 and the following notes:

❑16:13-17 ❑16:18 ❑16:20 ❑16:21 ❑16:22 ❑16:26 ❑17:5 ❑17:9

❑17:22, 23

3 Who is Jesus (16:13-20)?_____

_____

_____

4 What difficulties did the disciples have with Jesus' true identity (16:7, 21, 22; 17:4-8, 19; 18:21)?

_____

_____

_____

5 How was Jesus' transfiguration an important part of the disciples' training (17:1-13)?

_____

_____

_____

The disciples were first attracted to Jesus by his teaching. Even today, people who reject the idea that Jesus is God still find it hard not to admire him as a teacher. But there are two large problems with calling Jesus merely a great teacher. The first is that if we truly thought him to be a great teacher, we would follow his teachings. In reality, most people who call Jesus great do very little of what he said. The second problem is that Jesus claimed to be the Son of God. Could he qualify as a great teacher if he were not who he claimed to be? So to say he was a great man yet not the Son of God doesn't make sense. Who do you say Jesus is? As Jesus made clear to his disciples, admiring him but not submitting to him is the same as not recognizing his true identity at all.

REALIZE
the principle

6 What difference does a person's belief about Jesus' identity make in his/her life?

_____

_____

_____

7 Today, who do people often say Jesus was?

_____

_____

RESPOND
to the message

_____

8 Who do you say Jesus is?

_____

_____

_____

9 How has your understanding of Jesus changed over time?

_____

_____

_____

_____

10 At what times do you struggle with Jesus' authority over your life?

_____

_____

_____

11 In what areas and situations do you need to submit more to Christ's authority?

_____

_____

_____

_____

RESOLVE
to take action

12 What area of your life will you submit more to the authority of Christ this week?

_____

_____

_____

13 What does Christ want you to do in this area that you are not doing?

_____

_____

_____

_____

14 What will be your first step in submitting to Christ?

_____

_____

_____

_____

A Why wouldn't Jesus give some kind of sign to the people who were hounding him for evidence supporting his divine claims (16:4)? What kind of signs do people often demand from God today? What evidence do they already have? What can you say to people who want God to prove his existence with a sign?

MORE
for studying
other themes
in this section

B How is yeast like wrong ideas and teaching (16:6, 11, 12)? What false teaching do we need to beware of today?

C What does it mean to deny ourself and follow Christ (16:24-28)? What must we deny to follow Christ? What "cross" must we take up? What changes has following Christ brought to your life? What have you lost and gained?

D What did the disciples try to do in their own strength (17:14-22)? What do we often try to do in our own strength today? How can we exercise faith in these areas of our life?

E What kind of tax did Jesus and Peter pay (17:24-27)? In this instance, why did Jesus have them pay it? What did Jesus teach by example?

F Why is it important not to tempt others to sin (18:7-9)? What steps can you take to avoid tempting others?

G What does it mean to "welcome a little child" in Christ's name (18:5)? With what children do you come in contact on a regular basis? How could you welcome them in Christ's name?

H How do we know children are important to God (18:10-14)? In what ways do adults sometimes "look down on" children? How can we be sure to treat children as God values them?

I How are we to respond when someone sins against us (18:15-17)? Who has wronged you? What can you do or say to this person that would help you respond as God wants you to?

J In the parable of the unmerciful servant, why should the wicked servant have forgiven his borrower (18:21-35)? Of what debt has God forgiven you? How does this compare to the debts owed you? What change of attitude will help you forgive others who have offended you?

REFLECT
on your life

1 In running for office, what kind of image does a typical politician try to project?

_____

_____

_____

_____

2 In what ways have you found the image to be different from what the person was really like?

_____

_____

_____

_____

READ
the passage

Read Matthew 19:1—23:39, the chart "The Seven Woes," and the following notes:

❐21:30 ❐21:33ff ❐23:2, 3 ❐23:5 ❐23:5 ❐23:13, 14 ❐23:15

❐23:23, 24 ❐23:24 ❐23:25-28 ❐23:34-36

3 What was hypocritical about the religious leaders (21:23-27, 33-46; 22:15-22; 23:1-36)?

_____

_____

_____

4 Against what did Jesus warn people in his woes concerning the religious leaders (23:13-36)?

_____

_____

_____

5 Why did Jesus speak so harshly to the religious leaders (23:37-39)?

_____

_____

6 What hope did Jesus offer to those who were guilty of religious hypocrisy (19:20, 21, 25, 26; 20:25-28; 21:28-32; 22:29, 36-40)?

_____

_____

_____

_____

7 How did the Pharisees appear outwardly?

_____

REALIZE
the principle

_____

_____

8 What were the Pharisees like inwardly?

_____

_____

_____

The Pharisees and experts in the law were hypocrites. While they knew a lot, they did not do what they taught. Jesus did not criticize them for what they taught, but for how they lived. While believing in mercy, they did not practice it. While believing in devotion to God, they were actually devoted to fame and public praise. While believing in the law, they actually worked harder to keep their traditions, often at the expense of what God really wanted. Perhaps these areas were blind spots for them; perhaps they were deliberate inconsistencies. In any case, we must beware of the human tendency to say one thing and do another. It takes conscious thought and effort to make sure we are living according to the ideals we claim to uphold.

9 Why do people act hypocritically?

_____

_____

_____

10 What is the cure for hypocrisy?

_____

_____

_____

RESPOND
to the message

11 Which of the hypocrisies Jesus pointed out do you find to be an ongoing struggle in your own life (see the chart "The Seven Woes")?

_____

_____

_____

12 What inconsistencies are there between your faith and your life-style?

_____

_____

_____

13 How might Jesus challenge you to change?

_____

_____

_____

RESOLVE
to take action

14 In what area of your life do you need more consistency between what you project to people and what you are inside?

_____

_____

_____

_____

15 How can you become more genuine?

_____

_____

_____

_____

A What issues concerning marriage and divorce did Jesus clarify (19:3-12)? In what ways do Jesus' words clash with the value most people place on marriage? What can you do to preserve the integrity of marriage?

MORE
for studying
other themes
in this section

B In what way is it good to be like a child (19:13-15)? What areas of your life does this affect? What makes it difficult to be childlike toward God? How can you be more childlike in your faith?

C What basic human traits were the disciples displaying in rebuking the parents who brought their children to Jesus (19:13-15)? What conflicting priorities did this bring out? How did Jesus change his disciples' priorities? In what ways can we bring our attitude toward children more in line with Jesus' priorities for them?

D In what ways can money draw us away from God (19:23-30)? What can you do to keep money from becoming more important to you than God?

E What important spiritual principle about grace did Jesus illustrate with his parable of the workers in the vineyard (20:1-16)? How has God shown his grace to you? How might you show your gratitude?

F What interpersonal conflict arose when James and John's mother asked Jesus to give her sons special treatment (20:20-28)? Why do people expect special treatment? What is a better outlook to have?

G How did Jesus show his compassion toward the blind men on the way out of Jericho (20:29-34)? What means do you have for showing compassion?

H Who cheered Jesus at the Triumphal Entry (21:9-11)? What did many of those people say about him later (27:15-26)? Why did they change their mind? In what ways is our loyalty to Christ fickle? How can we make our devotion more consistent?

I What did Jesus show and teach about prayer (21:18-22)? How could you improve your prayer habits? When will you begin to make this change?

J In the parable of the wedding banquet (22:1-14), what response does the king seek from us? What holds people back from accepting his invitation? Why does this parable offer us hope?

K What important information about heaven did Jesus include in his answer to the Sadducees about the resurrection (22:23-33)? What do you look forward to about heaven?

REFLECT
on your life

1 Imagine losing your job and not being able to find another one, no matter how hard you try, for over two years. How might this affect you and your family?

_____

_____

_____

_____

_____

_____

2 How would you feel?

_____

_____

_____

_____

READ
the passage

Read Matthew 24:1—25:46 and the following notes:

❐24:3ff ❐25:1ff ❐25:29, 30 ❐25:31-46 ❐25:32 ❐25:34-40 ❐25:40

3 What do those who know God do for needy, weak, and helpless people (25:31-36)?

_____

_____

_____

_____

4 How will God reward his people (25:34, 46)?

_____

_____

_____

_____

5 In Matthew 24 and 25 Jesus used the word *watch* four times. In what different ways did he want his disciples to be watchful?

_____

_____

_____

_____

6 What will matter most when we stand before God in the Last Judgment?

_____

_____

_____

_____

REALIZE
the principle

Jesus' disciples knew they were following Israel's king. Though they didn't fully understand yet that Jesus would have to die and be raised to life, they expected him eventually to take his throne. How could they best serve their king? Through a parable, Jesus answered: by serving others. Of course, the weight of judgment will not rest on our acts of generosity to others, but the absence of generosity certainly shows a lack of understanding Jesus. The only way to be sure we are giving our king proper respect is to treat all people as if they were our king. Opportunities to serve hungry people, thirsty people, strangers, poor people, sick people, and prisoners are opportunities to serve Jesus, our king.

RESPOND
to the message

7 Who are the needy people in the world?

_____

_____

_____

_____

8 Who are the people with needs in your community?

_____

_____

_____

_____

9 Who are the needy people in your extended family?

_____

_____

_____

_____

10 What opportunities do you have to serve people with special needs?

_____

_____

_____

_____

RESOLVE
to take action

11 Which of the needy people you know about can you help this week?

_____

_____

_____

_____

12 When and how will you help them?

_____

_____

_____

_____

_____

MORE
for studying
other themes
in this section

A What will make people think Christ is returning (24:4, 5)? What makes people believe impostors' claims that they are Jesus returned? What is the best way to avoid being deceived by such impostors?

B What is one important milestone that must be passed before Christ returns (24:14)? What is your part in reaching this milestone?

C What three errors did the following people make: The wicked servant (24:48, 49); the five left-out bridesmaids (25:3, 13); the last servant (25:24-27)? What qualities mark the life of a pleasing servant?

D Why did the man in Jesus' parable of the talents give different amounts of money to each of his servants (25:14-30)? What are some of the talents God has entrusted to you? How can you invest them?

E What are we responsible to do with the talents God has given us (25:20-23)? If Christ came for the accounting today, how anxious would you be about meeting him? What changes would make you more ready for his return?

REFLECT
on your life

1 What objects of value do you see around you?

_____

_____

_____

_____

_____

2 What object has the least value?

_____

_____

_____

_____

3 How do people decide what is valuable to them and what isn't?

_____

_____

_____

_____

_____

Read Matthew 26:1—27:14, Lazarus's sister Mary's Profile, and the following notes:

☐26:6-13 ☐26:7 ☐26:8 ☐26:11 ☐26:14, 15 ☐26:15 ☐26:35 ☐26:48

☐26:56 ☐26:69ff ☐26:72-74 ☐27:5

4 What was important to Lazarus's sister Mary (26:6-13)?

_____

_____

_____

5 What was important to Judas (26:14-16, 20-25, 47-50)?

_____

_____

_____

_____

6 What was important to Peter (26:31-56, 69-75)?

_____

_____

_____

7 What difference do our values make in the way we live?

_____

_____

_____

Mary, Judas, and Peter were all disciples of Jesus. Yet from their actions, we can tell that each had different values. Mary valued Jesus above all else, so she thought nothing of using expensive perfume to honor him. Judas loved money, so he thought nothing of betraying the Son of God to a band of murderers. And Peter, otherwise loyal, cared very much about his reputation, causing him to deny his association with Jesus when pressed at an embarrassing moment to identify with him. Their experience is just like ours; from time to time we will be forced to choose between God and things, or God and our reputation. We will hold on to the one we value most and sacrifice the other. Mary's example is the one we should follow.

8 Why is it difficult to let go of our possessions and reputation to serve God?

_____

_____

_____

_____

9 Why does God deserve to be valued above all else?

_____

_____

_____

_____

RESPOND
to the message

10 What objects of value do people commonly hold on to?

_____

_____

_____

_____

11 In what ways do you place a higher value on things and reputation than on God:

at home? _____

_____

at work? _____

_____

at church? _____

_____

in your private life? _____

_____

12 What stands between you and true devotion to Christ?

_____

_____

_____

_____

13 What can you do this week to demonstrate your devotion to God?

_____

_____

_____

_____

RESOLVE
to take action

14 What will help you remember to cling to God above all else each day?

_____

_____

_____

_____

A What motivated Judas to betray Jesus (26:14-16)? What weakness tends to drag you down? What can you do to compensate for this weakness?

B Where does the practice of celebrating Communion come from (26:26-29)? What should a Christian do to prepare for Communion? How can you celebrate Communion so that it affects your daily life?

C What failure did Peter think he would avoid (26:31-35)? What does this tell us about our own weaknesses? How can we lean on God's grace in times of weakness?

D How does the experience of prayer in the garden between Jesus and the disciples compare to your own practice of prayer (26:36-45)?

E Why did Jesus not defend himself at his various trials (26:62, 63; 27:14)? In what way did his deeds speak for him? In what situations should you let your deeds speak for you?

MORE
for studying
other themes
in this section

REFLECT
on your life

1 What is one of your favorite Easter traditions?

_____

_____

_____

2 What is one unusual Easter custom that you celebrate with your family?

_____

_____

_____

_____

_____

_____

READ
the passage

Read Matthew 27:15—28:20 and the following notes:

❐27:51   ❐27:52, 53   ❐27:64   ❐27:66   ❐28:2   ❐28:5-7   ❐28:6   ❐28:11-15

❐28:18   ❐28:18-20   ❐28:20

3 Where were Jesus' disciples during his resurrection (26:56)?

_____

_____

_____

4 What difference did it make to Jesus' followers when they realized that he was raised from the dead (28:8, 9, 16, 17)?

_____

_____

_____

5 Why did the chief priests and elders make up a story to explain the resurrection (28:11-15)?

_____

_____

_____

6 How did the resurrection change the disciples' lives (28:18-20)?

_____

_____

_____

7 Note below the three parts of Jesus' final words to his disciples in Matthew 28:18-20. What is the importance of each section?

REALIZE
the principle

Statement _____

_____

Command _____

_____

Promise _____

_____

When Jesus was arrested, his disciples fled. They didn't show their faces in public again until after Jesus had been raised and shown himself to Mary, Mary Magdalene, and others. Once these cowardly men fully realized who Jesus was and what he had done, they were changed forever. The resurrection of Jesus did not merely intrigue them or become a footnote in history; it was the turning point for the disciples and for us. With the resurrection, Jesus sealed our forgiveness, brought us power for living, and gave us a new commission. Now it's our turn to give back to him all we can.

8 Why is the resurrection of Christ important?

_____

_____

_____

RESPOND
to the message

9 How does the fact that Jesus is alive affect your life?

_____

_____

_____

10 What would be an appropriate way to thank Jesus for taking away your sins?

_____

_____

_____

11 What are the implications of Jesus' being alive today for:

the way you pray? _____

_____

_____

your confidence in God? _____

_____

_____

your worries? _____

_____

_____

your purpose in life? _____

_____

_____

12 This week, make it your goal to talk to the living Jesus each day. For what will you thank him?

_____

_____

_____

RESOLVE
to take action

13 For what will you ask his forgiveness?

_____

_____

_____

14 What requests will you bring to him?

_____

_____

_____

15 For what will you praise him?

_____

_____

_____

A Why did Jesus stir up controversy (27:11-26)? Why is religion such an emotional topic? What can we do to minimize people's defensiveness about their religious views? With whom can you take these steps in talking about Jesus?

B What were Jesus' last words on the cross (27:45-50)? Why were those words significant? What do those words reveal about what Christ accomplished for you on the cross? How can you say thank you?

C Throughout these last events of Christ's life, which of the people would you like to have been beside (Judas, Peter, James, John, other disciples, Mary, Mary Magdalene, chief priests, Pharisees, Sadducees, elders, Pilate, Simon from Cyrene, Roman soldiers, thieves on the cross)? Why?

D What Christian hymn about the crucifixion is most meaningful to you? Why?

E What Christian hymn about the resurrection is most meaningful to you? Why?

MORE
for studying
other themes
in this section